1991

Hidden Anxieties

Family Life Series

Edited by Martin Richards, Ann Oakley, Christina Hardyment and the late Jacqueline Burgoyne

Published

Forthcoming

Hidden Anxieties

Male Sexuality, 1900–1950

Lesley A. Hall

Polity Press

Copyright © Lesley A. Hall 1991

First published 1991 by Polity Press in association with Basil Blackwell

Editorial office:
Polity Press, 65 Bridge Street,
Cambridge CB2 1UR, UK

Marketing and production:
Basil Blackwell Ltd
108 Cowley Road, Oxford OX4 1JF, UK

Basil Blackwell Inc.
3 Cambridge Center
Cambridge, MA 02142, USA

ISBN 0 7456 0741 1   ISBN 0 7456 0933 3 (pbk)

British Library Cataloguing in Publication Data
A CIP catalogue record for this book is available from the British Library.

Library of Congress Cataloging in Publication Data
Hall, Lesley A.
  Hidden anxieties: male sexuality, 1900–1950 / Lesley A. Hall.
    p. cm.—(Family life series)
  Includes bibliographical references and index.
  ISBN 0-7456-0741-1   ISBN 0-7456-0933-3 (pbk)
  1. Men—Sexual behavior—History—20th century. I. Title.
II. Series
HQ28.H35 1991
306.77'081—dc20
                                                90-25304
                                                    CIP

Typeset in 10 on 12 pt Palatino
by Graphicraft Typesetters Ltd., Hong Kong
Printed in Great Britain by
T.J. Press (Padstow) Ltd, Padstow, Cornwall.

Contents

Acknowledgements

The thesis upon which this work is based was undertaken during full-time employment as an archivist at the Wellcome Institute for the History of Medicine. I should therefore like to express my gratitude to the Wellcome Trustees for their provisions for their employees to undertake study for higher degrees. I have been indeed fortunate in the stimulating intellectual environment of the Wellcome Institute. I am indebted to Dr W. F. Bynum of the Academic Unit at the Wellcome Institute, my supervisor, for his help and encouragement. I am also extremely grateful to my colleagues of the Wellcome Institute Library whose support and cooperation made it possible to pursue my research, in particular Julia Sheppard of the Contemporary Medical Archives Centre for her patience with a preoccupied colleague. Jeanette Lake was most helpful in making available to me relevant printed material from a cataloguing limbo. I should also like to express my thanks to the Library Desk, stack and photocopying staff (especially Andy Foley) and to all my colleagues for their interest and support.

While I was able to pursue much of my research within the Wellcome Institute Library I should also like to thank the following individuals and institutions: Dorothy Sheridan and the Tom Harrisson-Mass Observation Archive at the University of Sussex; David Doughan and the Fawcett Library at the City of London Polytechnic; the British Library, in particular the Department of Manuscripts, and especial gratitude to Dr Anne Summers; the

Eugenics Society; the Church House Record Centre, Westminster; the Scout Association Archives.

To Roy Porter and Jeffrey Weeks my gratitude is immense, not only for the hugely stimulating viva of my thesis and for less formal discussions of the various issues, but for reading earlier versions of this work and providing me with very helpful suggestions for converting thesis into book. Martin Richards pointed out a number of places where my contentions could be clarified. Dorothy Porter's enthusiasm has been perhaps even more valuable than her contributions on venereal disease control and public health. Heather Creaton of the Institute of Historical Research has been involved with this project from my first considerations to the final manuscript and I am most grateful for her friendship and support, as well as for many references I might otherwise have missed.

Over the years in which I have been engaged in this project I have been sustained by the companionship of Ray McNamee. He may not have done my typing or made me cups of coffee, but his support extended to waiting in second-hand bookshops while I scoured the shelves for copies of obsolete sex-manuals, carrying these home and building bookshelves to hold them. He also provided me with a non-specialist's perspective on the manuscript.

Earlier versions of some parts of this book were published in the form of articles in the *Journal of Contemporary History*, 20 (1985), and the *Bulletin of the Society for the Social History of Medicine*, 39 (December 1986), to the editors of which I am grateful for permission to reproduce this material.

Material from the Contemporary Medical Archives Centre at the Wellcome Institute for the History of Medicine is cited courtesy of the Wellcome Trustees. Published and unpublished writings of Marie Stopes are quoted by kind permission of the Royal Society of Literature, material from the Eugenics Society Archives by permission of the Galton Institute, and material from published and unpublished works by E. F. Griffith with the kind permission of Mrs J. E. Griffith. Material from the Mass Observation 'Sex Survey', copyright the Tom Harrisson-Mass Observation Archive, is reproduced by permission of Curtis Brown Ltd. I am also grateful to the following for permission to quote from published works in copyright: Sigmund Freud Copyrights, The Institute of Psychoanalysis and The Hogarth Press, and Basic Books, Inc., Publishers, New York, for passages from the *Standard Edition of the Complete Works of Sigmund Freud* translated and edited by James Strachey; Dr H. Beric

Wright for Helena Wright's *The Sex Factor in Marriage*; William Heinemann Ltd for extracts from Dr Isabel Hutton's *Memories of a Doctor in War and Peace*; Professor James McCormick of Trinity College Dublin for passages from his book *The Doctor: Father Figure or Plumber*; and the editor of *The Lancet* and Mr Phillip Day for an extract from 'Point of View: The Samaritans and the Medical Profession' by the late Dr George H. Day.

Every effort has been made to trace all copyright holders, but if any has been inadvertently overlooked, the publisher will be pleased to make the necessary arrangement at the first opportunity.

This book is dedicated
to my parents,
Frederick and Marjorie Hall.

Introduction: deconstructing the monolithic phallus

In the past two decades there has been an upsurge in historical writing about sex in history. Much of this has sprung from the interests of feminist and gay historians, although work by historians of demography and the family has also shed light on sexual conduct. Most of this work has looked at women or at 'deviant minorities' or at the rise of the birth control movement. Foucault, in *The History of Sexuality. Volume I: An Introduction*, claimed that the rise of sexology in the later nineteenth century explicitly defined and categorized (for purposes of control) the hysterical woman, the onanistic child, the deviant and the Malthusian couple as the objects of this new, medicalized (as opposed to religious) discourse around sexual behaviour.[1]

It is certainly to these groups that most historiographical attention has been paid. Unexamined by this trend, and often assumed to be monolithic, unchanging, unproblematic, stands the 'normal' male. The implication tends to be that sexual discourses operated exclusively for his benefit and that there was no ambiguity or ambivalence in his position, no possible constraint upon him. He and his sexuality have not been accorded the attention given to attitudes to female sexuality and the construction of deviant identities, or to examining changing reproductive behaviour within families.

This study examines this apparently unitary and transhistorical figure. The particular historical period under consideration was one of enormous social change during which marriage and the relationships of the sexes were profoundly affected. The ways in which 'normal male sexuality' was perceived, from the later nineteenth century up to the middle of the twentieth century, will be discussed and changes pointed out. Evidence will be adduced indicating that there were considerable tensions between the ideals set up and the lived experience of men as they perceived it, and that the 'normal' male and male sexuality were more problematic than they are usually assumed to be.

'Predominantly open and aggressive'

The essentialist argument thinks of sex itself as a 'natural urge' or an instinct, and with regard to the two sexes promulgates a view of the natures of male and female as essentially different and unchanging throughout history and in all different societies. Under this schema (to be simplistic) males are forceful, aggressive, promiscuous, 'instrumental', while females are nurturing, maternal, monogamous, 'expressive'. At its most reductive, men have innate sexual desires and women have the innate capacity to arouse them. Any attempt to change this order of things given by either God or Nature is doomed to failure. Nature tends, in arguments of this kind, to mean either 'the way things are' or 'the way I think they ought to be'.

This notion of a constant natural and transcendent difference between the sexes is often merely an un-thought-out popular assumption, although it still has its academic defenders. There have been great variations throughout history and in different societies of what masculinity and femininity are expected to be and how they have been experienced.[2] Even motherhood, often assumed to be the ultimate 'natural', has varied according to historical circumstance, as Fildes has shown in her study of infant feeding, and Hardyment in her account of changing ideas on child-rearing.[3] The biological capacity of the human organism exists within symbolic environments which both act upon and can be manipulated by the individual, leading to a vast potential for variations. The experience of individuals does not necessarily match precisely with the roles prescribed for them at any particular point in time, as can be seen by contrasting the ideology of manhood with actual problems experienced by men. In most societies above a certain level of complexity any individual is likely to be receiving mixed and contradictory messages about the meanings of sex and appropriate gender-role behaviour. While eschewing, therefore, the more deterministic arguments of the 'socialization' theory of sex-roles, this study is located within a conceptualization of sex-roles as being constructed and experienced within particular historical and social contexts.

For the purposes of argument it is necessary to define the 'normal male'. Too often he has been simply assumed to be someone who is not a woman, someone who is (at least consciously) not homosexual, someone who by his nature is privileged within society as women and homosexuals are not. In this study, the 'normal male' is a man who would define himself as heterosexual, wants to marry and lead a conventional conjugal life, and has no 'deviations of object' in his sex-life, beyond, perhaps, the odd mild fetishism. In fact, he is a man who would think of himself as 'normal', and for that reason perhaps not puzzle himself much about the wilder intricacies of sexual desire. The pioneer sexologist Havelock Ellis (1858–1939) remarked of the male sexual impulse

> To deal with it broadly as a whole seems unnecessary, if only because it is predominantly open and aggressive. Moreover, since the constitution of society has largely been in the hands of man, the nature of the sexual impulse in men has largely been expressed in the written and unwritten codes of social law.[4]

This idea of the simplicity and straightforwardness of male desire is part of the constructed package.

'Normality' does not exclude sexual anxiety. Because of these assumptions about male sexuality, its problems have often been ignored. The one problem that may be voiced is over the control of this potentially dangerous insurgent force. Control of women was, still is, often presented under rhetoric of the dangers of arousing masculine lusts by inappropriate dress or behaviour, with the prostitute seen as a temptress beguiling men into sin by playing on their vulnerability. In the later nineteenth and the early twentieth centuries, however, this fear of unbridled male sexuality led to the rise of anti-masturbation literature and other propaganda in favour of male purity. It might be supposed that only women had any vested interest in controlling male lusts, but men were also engaged by the problem of male purity. There was a certain class dimension to this question of control over male desire. Mastery over baser lusts was seen as appropriate and desirable behaviour (a form of internalized moral policing) for the middle classes or would-be respectable, but hardly to be expected of the lowest classes. The concept of the rampant nature of male sexuality, and the need for it to be controlled by women for the good of both sexes, is still to be found in writers on sociobiology and is at the heart of most essentialist arguments. It sometimes figures as a plea in mitigation in rape cases.

Male desire is not necessarily so rampageous as such fears would suggest. Men suffer from considerable anxieties around their sexuality. In adolescence they may be perturbed or even terrified by spontaneous nocturnal emissions, and worried about the consequences of masturbation, since folk 'wisdom' still carries all sorts of warnings about this practice even if sex-manuals have gone from condemnation to reassurance to advocacy. Men may be excessively concerned by what they perceive to be some abnormality of the external genitalia: smallness or largeness or lack of symmetry. The statistical frequency of impotence and premature ejaculation still seems to be a well-kept secret: to judge from the tenor of recent books written for general practitioners dealing with sexual problems,[5] men with these difficulties continue to feel themselves to be uniquely cursed: 'among the most miserable of all patients that the doctor is called upon to treat', as 'the young man with a disorder of sex' was described in 1930.[6] And not just young men, either. The sexual problems arising in middle-aged men are equally shrouded in silence, and cause despair. Doctors are often reluctant to discuss the implications for sexual life of certain common conditions or operations such as prostatectomy, or the effects on libido of some commonly prescribed drugs.

Apart from these perhaps solipsistic worries, men worry about sexual difficulties within relationships. During the period of this study, birth control was a major anxiety: this was a matter of concern to husbands as well as wives. Far from leaving the whole business up to the woman, many men were so concerned that it was the condom which was the most widely used form of artificial marital contraception, while in spite of the dire warnings about the effects of coitus interruptus, this continued to be a common practice. Men were not, either, indifferent to their wives' sexual pleasure. It could be argued that this was an essentially egotistical worry; mutually enjoyable intercourse being more pleasurable, women who enjoy sex will let their husbands have it more often, and satisfying his partner enhances a man's self-esteem. There is, however, evidence that men did care for their wives' wellbeing and health over and above any relation to their own gratification.

While this study considers mainly the functional sexual disorders, attitudes to venereal disease, its causes and prevention, will be examined as a nexus of attitudes having a much wider bearing on perceptions of sexuality and gender roles. Men contract venereal diseases to a far greater extent than women: once statistics became available following the Public Health Regulations instituted under the recommendations of the Royal Commission on Venereal Diseases, 1916, the figures for patients attending the clinics and receiving treatment disclosed that men made up the vast majority in both categories, male patients constituting approximately three-quarters of the total during the early 1920s.[7] This sex differential, though not as great, was still noticeable in the 1970s, in spite of the effect on the figures of the inclusion of certain non-venereal genital tract conditions more prevalent in the female. All other conditions were seen far more often in the male. The numbers of male patients who attended the clinics but required no treatment far exceeded those for women in similar case, an interesting statistic in view of the fact that women are generally considered to seek medical consultations far more frequently than men.[8]

In a witty essay, 'If Men Could Menstruate', the American feminist Gloria Steinem has advanced the conceit that if men rather than women had periods enormous attention and financial resources would be given to problems such as dysmenorrhea.[9] The operation of power within society is not quite so clear-cut as this, as can be seen from a consideration of the interaction between (male) patient and (male) doctor over a crisis to do with the operation of sexual functioning. Such encounters raise fruitful questions about the construction of male sexuality within society as well as about the medical profession itself. This particular interaction provides a point where male power and medical power (in itself predominantly male) impinge upon one another, rather than intersecting in any simple graphic way. Foucault described sexuality as 'an especially dense transfer point for relations of power', although rather surprisingly did not cite the doctor–patient relationship in his list of the relationships in which sexuality particularly manifests this characteristic.[10]

A majority of the medical profession is still male, and it was male-dominated to an even greater extent earlier in this century. There has been a great deal of discussion, both sociological and historical, about the attitudes and behaviour of male doctors to female patients, particularly in the fields of gynaecology and obstetrics and of psychiatry. Doctors have been accused of reducing all female disorders to the sexual/reproductive, of unnecessary interventions, of colonizing and controlling the female sex in the bodies and minds of their patients.[11] Some doctors did keep their female patients in ignorance: married women with syphilis contracted from their husbands were not told of the nature of their disease.[12] It has been suggested that doctors were far more forthright with men: for example, in discussing birth control.[13] However, at least up to the 1930s, most doctors might tell husbands that their wives should have no more children but would be unlikely to suggest how, apart from abstinence, this might be accomplished, and would tend to evade any specific enquiries on birth control methods.

There is a general assumption that men were better served in medical encounters, that doctors were more at ease with them, treated them more like equals. However, the doctor–patient relationship involves a considerable imbalance of power, and medical sociologists have pointed out that the doctors' ideal patient has many 'feminine' characteristics, such as passivity and compliance.[14] Given the dominance/submission dynamic within the relationship, doctors may be happier with situations where this is quite explicit in terms of general social relations. There are problems here to do with the nature of the doctor–patient relationship in general. It should not be presupposed that there was necessarily any alliance or sympathy between male doctor and male patient on grounds of shared gender. The very similarity of sex seems to have been a reason why in certain matters, such as dealing with sexual problems, doctors failed to meet their male patients' needs. Also, men had profound reservations about exposing sexual difficulties to other males, particularly those, such as doctors, who appeared to be in a position of authority.

Doctors were supposed, as a result of their medical training, to be privy to a whole body of sexual knowledge from which the lay person was excluded, a myth promulgated by lay and medical writers alike. Formal medical education was in fact remarkably lacking in even the most basic information about normal sexual activity. In spite of the prevalence of syphilis and gonorrhoea, venereology was not taught at the undergraduate level. Doctors shared with their patients preconceptions, indeed misconceptions and anxieties, about sex which seriously affected their professional efficacy in this field. Modern writing on the treatment of sexual problems continues to reiterate that the usual distant authoritative manner has to be discarded. The doctor protagonist of a 1976 novel by William Cooper has made a successful Harley Street career out of reiterating the simple formula 'You're not alone: it happens to us all' to the sexually troubled, a benign reassurance it is implicit that his patients have not found elsewhere.[15]

Doctors have been particularly reluctant to discuss the reproductive disorders of the male. Although it has been known since late in the nineteenth century that an examination of the semen would disclose whether a man was producing viable spermatozoa, during the earlier part of the twentieth century and even today doctors have proved reluctant to perform investigations into male fertility. Although this is a simple and non-invasive technique, requiring only a microscope and a fresh semen sample, doctors went on treating the female half of infertile couples without ever determining if the failure to conceive were in fact her 'fault', or that of her husband.[16] This reluctance of doctors to contemplate sexual disorder in the male can have fatal consequences: although testicular cancer is the most common malignant tumour in men between the ages of 24 and 30, and on the increase, doctors do not routinely examine men's testicles in the way they do female breasts or cervixes, even though the disease is usually curable if diagnosed in time.[17]

The medical refusal to contemplate male sexual and reproductive disorder with anything like the fervour it brings to gynaecological and obstetric problems is an outstanding example of the general reluctance in society to make explicit the difficulties of the male, in particular when the problem is that of malfunction of specifically masculine attributes. If men menstruated, it seems entirely probable that common wisdom and that of the massed ranks of the medical profession would concur that Real Men don't have period pains or PMT.

'An avalanche of demand, enquiry and appeal'

At the centre of this study lies a unique collection of letters pertaining to sexual problems, written to Marie Stopes, author of *Married Love: A New Contribution to the Solution of Sex Difficulties*, which was first published early in 1918 at her own expense (or, rather, at that of her soon-to-be fiancé Humphrey Verdon Roe) with prefaces by Jessie Murray, one of the first British psychoanalysts, Professor E. H. Starling, the physiologist, and Father Stanislaus St John, a Catholic priest (this last withdrawn from later editions as Stopes became notorious for her advocacy of birth control).

The story which is generally accepted about the origins of this work, and which was promoted by Stopes herself, was that, as she stated in the preface,

> In my first marriage I paid such a terrible price for sex-ignorance that I
> feel that knowledge gained at such a cost should be placed at the
> service of humanity.[18]

In 1911 she had married Reginald Ruggles Gates, a fellow-botanist.
Some years later, concerned that she had not yet become pregnant,
she embarked on a course of investigation among the works held in
the 'Private Cupboard' at the British Museum, to which, as a scien-
tist and university lecturer, she had access. This led her to conclude
that her marriage had never been consummated. Stopes proceeded
to seek a decree of annulment, which was granted in 1916. According to Stopes this debacle led to the writing of *Married Love*,
although since 1913 at least she had entertained hopes of performing
some work of great service to humanity. She was a supporter of the
suffrage movement, retained her maiden name subsequent to marriage at a time when this was extremely uncommon, and agitated for
reforms in the tax laws relating to married women, but hoped to
benefit the whole of humanity, not just one sex, by her work.

She had been involved with contemporary movements for sexual
reform, and in 1915 had met the American birth control agitator
Margaret Sanger in the company of Havelock Ellis. Her response to
reading Ellis's own *Studies in the Psychology of Sex* was to remark that
it was 'like breathing a bag of soot: it made me feel choked and dirty
for months.'[19] The emphasis in her own works was on the normal,
the natural, the healthy, the clean: as she stated in the preface to
Married Love,

> In this book average, healthy, mating creatures will find the key to
> happiness which should be the portion of each...I hope it may save
> some others years of heartache and blind questioning in the dark.[20]

Although her publishers had had so little confidence in the book's
success that she had had to pay for it to be printed, and although
the first editions, due partly to this attitude and partly to war
restrictions, were very small, *Married Love* went through five editions and sold 17,000 copies in the first year alone (it far outsold
bestselling fiction of the era).[21] It was received with some enthusiasm by the medical press: *The Lancet* described it as 'an extremely
sensible little book' which 'is really needed as a public adviser'[22] and
the *British Medical Journal* paid tribute to Stopes's 'literary skill, sympathetic insight, idealism, and more than common courage'.[23] By
1925 sales of *Married Love* had passed the half-million mark, and

they achieved the million in the early 1950s. These figures do not include English language editions for the USA, Australia, Canada and India, or translations into fourteen foreign languages and Braille. Copies were circulated among friends and relatives, so the total number of readers must have been much higher.

Married Love was the most successful of Stopes's works but the others also sold well. *Wise Parenthood: A Sequel to Married Love. A Book for Married People*, with an introduction by the novelist Arnold Bennett, had sold over half a million copies by 1930, had gone into twenty-five editions by 1951 and was translated into twelve languages. Stopes geared her approach to different groups. She has often been jeered at for the recommendation in *Wise Parenthood* that the contraceptive cap be inserted 'when dressing in the evening',[24] but this book was addressed to the middle-class readership which had already devoured *Married Love*. Stopes was careful to slant her shorter work on birth control, the pamphlet *A Letter to Working Mothers: On How to have Healthy Children and Avoid Weakening Pregnancies* (subsequently entitled *Practical Birth Control*), towards the pockets, circumstances and reading abilities of working-class women. She had a considerable awareness of differing audiences, proved by the phenomenal response to her articles in *John Bull*, which produced a deluge of letters from poor women, many of which were later published under the title *Mother England*. Other successful works by Stopes were *Radiant Motherhood: A Book for Those Who are Creating the Future* (1920) and *Enduring Passion: Further New Contributions to the Solution of Sex Difficulties, being the continuation of Married Love* (1928).

Stopes's ideas had wide currency and her very name became a by-word for sex-advice and birth control. This was helped rather than hindered by her 1923 libel suit. A book by the Catholic doctor Halliday Sutherland attacking birth control in general accused her of opening the Mother's Clinic in Holloway in order to experiment on poor women. In spite of the work's very limited circulation, Stopes took Sutherland to court, gaining herself and her teachings even more publicity. A considerable increase in her correspondence and in the sales of her work resulted.[25]

The enthusiastic and personal response of her readers (who represented a wide social mix) was attested to not merely by the sales of her works but by the fact that her readers wrote to her in great numbers, immediately following the first publication of *Married Love*. If her correspondents from the poorest classes were mostly interested in the prevention or termination of pregnancy, her ideals of marriage found a ready response among members of the respectable working classes, the expected middle-class readers, officers of the armed forces, members of the Indian and other colonial services, and even the aristocracy (but although she sent a copy of *Married Love* to the Princess Elizabeth in 1947 on the occasion of her marriage to Prince Philip, there is no record that it was read). Letters of praise and admiration massively outnumbered those of condemnation and criticism, which tended to be anonymous: those who supported Stopes signed their names. She remarked herself in *Enduring Passion* (1928) that

> Ten years have passed with such amazing rapidity that it seems in some ways but a few weeks since, by publishing that book [*Married Love*], I let loose upon my shoulders an avalanche of demand, enquiry and appeal from humanity for just that deeper probing of marriage which I postulated.[26]

This correspondence continued until her death in 1958, although it tailed off considerably from the mid-1940s.

The letters to her survive in quantity, alongside, in many cases, carbon copies of her replies or at least notes for her secretaries, which demonstrate her own continued interest in helping couples to attain her ideals of married love. This mass of correspondence forms a rich and unique source for the study of sexual ideas and attitudes in the 1920s and 1930s in particular (the period during which her popularity was at its height).[27] It demonstrates the immense impact her works had on those who read them, and the questions raised in their minds to which they sought further answers.

Her work did not only appeal to women suffering from too many pregnancies or neglected sexual desires. In spite of Stopes's reputation as an apostle of birth control and bearer of a mission to a suffering womankind overburdened with pregnancies and by male lack of consideration, *Married Love* was in fact dedicated to 'Young husbands, and all those who are betrothed in love', and well over 40 per cent of her correspondents were male. Nearly all the correspondence indicated a positive response to her works; very little of it was condemnatory or even mildly critical. (It does not seem as though she destroyed the unfavourable letters. Some of these survive, and her habit of preserving just about everything suggests she would be unlikely to have thrown anything away.) Most of her male readers, at least the ones who were sufficiently impressed one way or another to put pen to paper on the subject, regarded her work as a welcome revelation, a shaft of light into an area of murky darkness.

This is not to imply that the letters she received from women are of no interest. However, female reactions to Stopes have already been studied, beginning with Stopes's own *Mother England: A Contemporary History Self-written by Those who have no Historian* (1929), in which she published letters she had received from working-class women. Furthermore, the women's letters, though fascinating, are not the surprising revelation that the letters from men are, although they contradict any theory that birth control was a eugenic and authoritarian measure being imposed upon the lower classes, or that Stopes was attempting to force upon innocent individuals her own ideology of heterosexual matrimony. A further argument against yet another study of women, valuable though one based on these letters would be, is that yet again this would be the gaze directed to the female. To turn the gaze onto the male, when this is not a matter of staring at a clothed and triumphant hero, is a subversive project. Stopes's correspondents were heroes of a very different kind; many of them had been through the war and numbers of them were still serving in the armed forces or colonial services. It is quite apparent that they found speaking of sexual vulnerability far more terrifying than any more conventionally frightening experiences.

Although this correspondence was international in its spread, the letters used as evidence for this study have been selected from among those received from British citizens resident in the United Kingdom, serving in various parts of the Empire or working overseas. Letters from the Dominions and Eire have been cited because of the cultural similarities. Letters from the USA, continental Europe and the non-European citizens of the Empire have been excluded. Letters from women pertaining to the problems of their husbands or male friends have in some cases been drawn upon. No names or identifying details have been disclosed for reasons of preservation of individual privacy, and all references are to covering file number only.

This collection appears to be unique at least in terms of size (sixty archive boxes containing over 300 files held in the Contemporary Medical Archives Centre, Wellcome Institute for the History of Medicine: also a small sample kept with the Stopes papers at the British Library, amounting to several thousand actual letters). Other writers on the subject received similar pleas for help: Dr Isabel Hutton received numbers of letters in connection with her work *The Hygiene of Marriage*, a popular sex-manual of the 1920s and 1930s, which no longer survive.[28] Such letters were often destroyed by their recipients. Stopes, however, was a great hoarder, three tons of her papers arriving at the British Library for sorting after her death in 1958.

Given the construction of the male in so much of the literature of the period as insensitive, egotistical, clumsy, selfish, the letters constitute a remarkable revelation about the attitudes of men themselves to sexuality and its problems. There can be no doubt of the authenticity of most of the letters: their sincerity is surely guaranteed by the candour with which the writers wrote of sexual failings and anxieties and about behaviour which they as much as respectable society deplored, such as recourse to prostitutes, premarital sexual relations and masturbation. Authenticity is also underwritten by the frequency with which the same problems recur and the similarity of the wording (often echoing Stopes's own phraseology) employed. These letters were not written as self-conscious texts but as acts in order to obtain something of which the writers felt in sometimes desperate need: reassurance, advice, help. These men were prepared to reveal to Stopes things about themselves which they had never before communicated to another being, things which in many cases, prior to reading her works, they had believed were unique to themselves alone.

While some of the letters do display a certain eccentricity, most of them are articulate and coherent epistles on a difficult subject, varying from the very laconic to extended narratives. There are variations in the type of paper and ink and styles of handwriting, usually to do with class or economic conditions. Some men wrote to Stopes more than once, sometimes over considerable intervals.

A study of these letters undermines any simplistic assumptions about men as sexual beings and about the relationship of the sexes within marriage during the period in which Stopes's writings were most influential. The stories they tell open up an undiscovered world of suffering and emotion. It might perhaps be argued that the men who wrote to Stopes were a small and atypical minority of their sex, and that these letters, interesting though they may be, were hardly representative of male feelings. It could, however, equally well and perhaps even more plausibly be argued that they represent the tip of an iceberg. No-one would seriously contend that the women who wrote to Stopes were the only members of their sex desperate for birth control and anxious to achieve a better sex-life. Those who organized themselves to write, requesting further help beyond that received in her publications, or who had merely registered her name as that of an expert in these matters, were surely a tiny minority of all those who might have wanted help or been vaguely conscious of something not right.

It may not have been all men to whom Stopes's works would have appealed. There was doubtless a particular type peculiarly responsive to the appeal of her writings, but given the wide circulation of her books it is possible that this type of man was perhaps more commonly to be found than one might suppose. Given the enormous diversity of class, occupation and locality from which her correspondents were drawn (quite exclusive of questions of nationality and race), this seems to be a reasonable assumption.

In order to establish the background of sexual 'knowledge' against which these letters were written, the next three chapters consider various messages about sexuality that the men who wrote them might have received. Attitudes towards sexuality which were prevalent in the earlier twentieth century did not spring into being fully fledged in 1900, and the ideas of the Victorians continued to be important for a very long while. The notions of sexuality promoted by Victorian writers were held as received ideas, the way things were, 'natural', well into the twentieth century, long after one might have supposed them outdated and obsolete. Such ideas were also important because so much twentieth-century sexual rhetoric deliberately set out to counteract 'Victorianism'. Therefore the first two, and part of the third, chapters are to a considerable extent concerned with the Victorian and immediately post-Victorian era. The first deals with the respectable or orthodox ideas about sex to be found in the writings of the medical profession, including the new and evolving discipline of sexology, and put forward by other makers of public opinion such as proponents of social purity and educationalists. The notions of male sexuality encoded in provisions for the treatment of venereal disease will also be discussed. The following chapter will examine the evidence of less orthodox sexual discourses: the writings and other activities of quacks and alternative practitioners, information communicated as part of a male subculture and implicit in the existence of prostitution. The third chapter looks at the evolution of the marriage manual and at the changing concepts of marriage which were embodied in the very existence of this genre. Stopes's own works will be considered in the context of contemporary writers in the genre and of changing perceptions of marriage. This is followed by an analysis of the attitudes towards married life and the role of the male in marriage depicted by her correspondents, which precedes an examination of the actual disorders and anxieties about functioning presented by them. Attitudes of the medical profession to male sexual dysfunction and the attitudes of men with sexual dysfunction to the medical profession will then be elaborated. In the conclusion changes in attitudes towards sexual mores taking place by 1950 will be commented upon and evidence brought forward to indicate that male sexual function and dysfunction are still unmentionable subjects.

1

'A very delicate and difficult subject': orthodox and respectable views on sex to 1920

In this chapter orthodox discourses on sexuality are considered. Attitudes of the medical profession to male sexual functioning are delineated. The rise of sexology as a separate study is discussed, with what it said about the 'normal' male as opposed to the 'deviant', and also how far it was influential within more general medical thinking. The didactic literature produced by the social purity movement to warn the young of the dangers of indulging the 'baser instincts' is described. Venereal disease meant that sex had a public health aspect as well as a more narrowly clinical one: the provisions for the venereally infected make certain statements about the acceptability or otherwise of promiscuous intercourse. The changes wrought by therapeutic improvements and the social upheaval of the First World War are analysed.

'Wrote decently on subjects not usually decent'[1]

The figure usually taken to epitomize Victorian attitudes to sexuality is William Acton, MRCS. Following the theories adumbrated by Steven Marcus in *The Other Victorians* (1966),[2] there has been considerable debate about this controversial figure, and how typical his views about sexuality were, particularly as embodied in *The Functions and Disorders of the Reproductive Organs in Youth, Adult Age and Advanced Life, considered in their Physiological, Social and Psychological Relations* (first published 1857).[3] Acton cannot be readily dismissed: he was a far more significant and typical figure than revisionists such as Peter Gay or Barry Smith would like to believe.[4] Certainly not all Victorian marriages were characterized by wives who closed their eyes, opened their legs and thought of England, and by husbands who informed their wives that ladies did not move. However, while eroding ancient polemical stereotypes, recent work risks setting up new and equally misleading generalizations about the Victorians, minimizing the very real sexual anxieties and inhibitions that existed, quite probably even in the happiest marriages. It is symptomatic that Acton was singled out by the later sexologist Havelock Ellis as the epitome of what was both typical of and wrong with Victorian attitudes to sex.[5]

Acton's influence and significance have been mostly either promoted or dismissed on the basis of his statements about decent women seldom desiring sexual gratification on their own behalf, and submitting only from the desire of maternity and to please their husbands; a view in accord with received ideas about the sexless passivity of the Victorian female. This concentration upon women, while largely ignoring the ideology around male sexuality – apart from the occasional nod to the 'double standard' and its presumed prevalence – suggests that the male, as sexual being, has not been regarded as problematic. His sexuality is taken as a given and supposed to be less plastic than that of the female to the changing tides of ideology and social pressure. Acton, however, problematized the male: it was the male's control over his own sexuality which Acton perceived as the crucial problem and not, or only incidentally, keeping all but an excluded pariah class of women chaste for motherhood.

The main subject of Acton's *Functions and Disorders* was not women at all. Two passages, a very small proportion of the whole, dealt with the female sexual response, or lack of it. The rest was entirely concerned with the male sexual organs, their functions and disorders (mainly disorders). One of the reasons Acton discussed the female response at all was to reassure anxious males that they would not be expected to perform superhuman sexual feats within marriage. He regarded female frigidity as a great assisting factor in the avoidance of marital excesses (which according to Acton could be just as deleterious as solitary excesses) because he admitted that there was nothing very exciting or stimulating about making love to an unresponsive partner.

For Acton, sex was a dangerous force which had to be held in check; any indulgence might, probably would, lead to enslavement in sensual habits which were not only morally bad but physiologically dangerous. Although he also wrote on prostitution and was an advocate of the Contagious Diseases Acts, in *Functions and Disorders* he was not principally concerned with the dangers of fornication with potentially diseased prostitutes. He warned against the waste of the vital spermatic fluid by whatever means. Overindulgence (even in legitimate marriage) could lead to the wasting disease of spermatorrhoea. (Spermatorrhoea was a factitious ailment, the symptoms of which were involuntary seminal emissions waking and sleeping, causing debility and worse.) Acton's arguments against indulgence invoked moral discipline, for a man who had been wont to gratify his urges by self-abuse was undermining his self-discipline to resist other temptations. But his arguments' main force depended on the belief, by no means unique to him, in the physiologically deleterious effect of seminal losses. He also feared sexual pleasure was too debilitatingly intense to be experienced safely with any frequency.

If sexlessness was the ideal for Victorian womanhood, it was also the most desirable state for the man. The very occasional relief in the celibate by nocturnal emissions was often depicted as excusable; analogous, as a discharge of bodily waste products, to menstruation in the woman, and occurring, ideally, cyclically on a similar time-scale. Male sexual desires should be so subdued that they were expressed, consciously, only under man's will in legitimate wedlock for the purposes of reproduction. Acton did, however, grant the seal of approval to some limited indulgence of the sexual impulse within marriage, believing this to be actually conducive to health (in the male at least) and beneficial to the individual beyond its reproductive aspect.

How typical of opinion in the medical profession and generally was he? Acton's project was seen by contemporaries as a daring – 'Mr Acton has never feared to touch pitch', said *The Lancet*[6] – but important contribution to knowledge. Victorian doctors, if one can generalize at all, if they did not necessarily subscribe completely to Acton's shock-horror warnings, were convinced of the physical as well as the moral evils of self-abuse, the dangers of excessive losses through any kind of indulgence. Dr James Copland's *Dictionary of Practical Medicine*, a more general guide than Action's specialist work, was equally vehement about the dangers of 'pollutions', in particular those produced by 'manustupration' [sic]. To this cause he attributed the lesser life-expectancy and greater morbidity of those who remained unmarried.[7] His views had considerable and enduring circulation.[8]

Sir James Paget's clinical lecture on 'Sexual Hypochondriasis', published in 1875 and presumably given earlier, is sometimes cited as a counter to the Actonian thesis. Paget insisted on the necessity for continence, and the doctor's duty to refuse to prescribe fornication, but was emphatic that masturbation did no harm, at least no more than any other indulgence carried to excess, and certainly did not lead inevitably to the lunatic asylum. Paget held this belief even though he described self-abuse as 'so nasty a practice; an uncleanliness, a filthiness forbidden by God, an unmanliness despised by men'.[9] Paget's *Clinical Lectures*, however, of which 'Sexual Hypochondriasis' was only one, went into only two editions. *Functions and Disorders* was a great deal more successful as a publication, going on being reprinted well after Acton's death.

Dr George Drysdale, the Malthusian writer of *Elements of Social Science* (first published 1854), was sufficiently anxious about his professional status to publish the earlier editions of this work anonymously. Constantly reissued up until the time of the First World War, *Elements of Social Science* is remembered for its advocacy of 'preventive intercourse', its recommendation of early marriage with the use of contraceptive measures. Drysdale's view of sexuality was antithetical to the Actonian belief that sex was a dangerous force requiring constant vigilance to keep it in check. For Drysdale, sexual problems were the results of the unnatural restraints society placed on the indulgence of natural urges. In his scheme of things, it was celibacy which led to those ailments which other authorities attributed to indulgence.[10]

Because it was necessary for the generative organs to have 'due exercise from the time of their maturity, which takes place at puberty, till that of their decline', prolonged continence during the years of youthful vitality led relentlessly to 'injurious habits of self-pollution',[11] which Drysdale, like Acton and unlike Sir James Paget, regarded as essentially pernicious, laying in puberty the foundations of lingering disease.[12] Abstinence he believed far more harmful than the evils of excess, since there existed natural checks upon unbridled excesses.

Elements of Social Science had a considerable circulation among the lay public, in fact probably more so than among Drysdale's own profession. It alarmed the youthful Havelock Ellis by its predictions of spermatorrhoea as the dire sequel to nocturnal emissions,[13] but nevetheless Ellis considered that if 'by no means in every respect a scientific or sound work' it was one which 'came into the hands of many who never saw any other work on sexual topics'.[14] As a work of philosophical, medical and political justification for the limitation of families by artificial means rather than a practical birth control tract, it escaped the legal action which befell Knowlton's *Fruits of Philosophy*, reprinted by Drysdale's fellow-Malthusians Charles Bradlaugh and Annie Besant in 1877 with his own editorial emendations,[15] and H. A. Allbutt's *Wife's Handbook* of 1886.[16]

Allbutt was struck off the medical register for publishing *The Wife's Handbook* at a price which made it available to the poor. The *British Medical Journal* remarked that he 'might have ventilated his views without let or hindrance from professional authority had he been contented to address them to medical men instead of to the public'.[17] It is not clear that his reception would have been any more favourable had he done so. General feeling within the medical profession probably supported C. H. F. Routh rather than the Malthusians. In Routh's 'On the Moral and Physical Evils Likely to Follow if Practices Intended to Act as Checks to Population be not Strongly Discouraged and Condemned' (1878), he carefully pointed out that he had only been induced to discuss the subject at all by 'some distinguished members of the profession'. He felt 'the responsibility of having one's notions misconstrued', but was nevertheless 'ready to fulfil a manly and generous part'. It was 'almost defilement even thus cursorily to allude to these vile practices', such as 'sexual fraudulency, conjugal onanism'. The medical man had to point out the dangers, but the very mention of the subject, even in outright condemnation, was regarded with suspicion.[18]

'It does not become members of the medical profession to object to dealing with filth'[19]

By the 1890s sex was becoming more widely recognized as a legitimate subject for scientific study. Some years before the first volume of his own *Studies in the Psychology of Sex* appeared, Havelock Ellis edited the Contemporary Science Series, intended to present aspects of contemporary scientific advance in a way accessible to the average intelligent reader.[20] The first volume was *The Evolution of Sex* by Patrick Geddes and J. Arthur Thomson. The polymathic Geddes was described in the *Dictionary of National Biography* as 'biologist, sociologist, educationist and town-planner', while Thomson was a zoologist. The biological and post-Darwinian approach of this work

looked at human sexuality in terms of 'the fundamental unity underlying the Protean phenomena of sex and reproduction'. In spite of
the authors' claim in the preface that they took up 'an altered and
unconventional view upon the general questions of biology',[21] their
attitudes towards the two sexes and their differences, and the implications of their work on ideas pertaining to sexual conduct, would
seem to place them on a far less radical section of the spectrum than
Ellis himself. Their work, being a cheap and deliberately accessible
volume, doubtless had a far wider circulation than Ellis's massive
Studies, and moreover probably accorded far more closely with prevalent ideas.

Underlying all their arguments was the belief in 'the divergent
evolution of the sexes', which they expressed in terms of 'anabolic'
or constructive and conservative energies, assigned by them to
the female, and 'katabolic' or disruptive and destructive energies,
assigned by them to the male. To illustrate this thesis they drew
examples from all of organic creation, in order to prove that 'what
was decided among the prehistoric protozoa cannot be annulled
by Act of Parliament'[22] (therefore women should not have the
parliamentary suffrage). It seemed to them that the 'average truth
throughout the world of animals' consisted of 'the preponderating
passivity of the females, the predominant activity of the males'.[23]
This conclusion was drawn from the cochineal insect, and further
illustrated by a description of the threadworm. Drawing upon
observations of insects and arachnids they further generalized that:

> as we should expect from the katabolic temperament, it is the males
> which are especially liable to exhaustion...the temporarily exhausting
> effect of even moderate sexual indulgence is well known, as well as
> the increased liability to all forms of disease while the individual
> energies are thus lowered.[24]

After a detailed ascent of the evolutionary ladder, Geddes and
Thomson concluded, in their final chapter on 'Psychological and
Ethical Aspects', that

> It is generally true that the males are more active, energetic, eager,
> passionate and variable...The more active males, with a consequently
> wider range of experience, may have bigger brains and more
> intelligence...being usually stronger, have greater independence and
> courage...The stronger lust and passion of males is likewise the
> obverse of predominant katabolism...greater cerebral variability and
> therefore more originality...Man thinks more, woman feels more.[25]

Although these two authors invoked 'all scientific relativity instead of a dogmatic authority', their interpretation of 'the biological factors of the case'[26] did not take them very far from the teachings of 'dogmatic authority'.

The new sexology of the 1890s, however, is far more often associated with the development of discourses around the pathological and the deviant rather than the 'normal'. Opinions on this development differed. The *British Medical Journal* reviewer in 1893 said of Krafft-Ebing's *Psychopathia Sexualis* that although there were 'many morally disgusting subjects which have to be studied by the doctor and by the jurist...the less such subjects are brought before the public, the better', and concluded that 'the book may be valuable as a book of reference, but it is altogether one not to be left about for general reading'.[27] In 1898 *The Lancet* commented upon the seizure and prosecution of Havelock Ellis's *Sexual Inversion* that the subject 'has its proper claims for discussion' but that this should be limited to 'persons of particular attainments'. The matter was not one for discussion by 'the man in the the street, not to mention the boy and girl in the street'.[28] The *British Medical Journal* was more sympathetic, conceding that while 'the subject is extremely disagreeable' it was 'one of those unpleasant matters with which members of the medical profession should have some acquaintance'.[29] Most medical discussion about sex in the nineteenth and early twentieth centuries was prefaced with similar rhetoric: it was necessary to talk about this horrible subject in order to be aware of its dangers, but discussion was to be confined to the profession.

Havelock Ellis (1859–1939),[30] a man of considerable eccentricity and polymathic learning, had received what seemed to him a revelation of his life's work, to elucidate the mysteries of sex, while employed as a schoolteacher in a remote area of Australia. He regarded gaining a medical qualification as the necessary first step, a wise tactical move, and therefore returned to England to study medicine. After much trial he obtained the minimum qualification necessary for legitimate medical practice, the Licentiate of the Society of Apothecaries, in 1889, and abandoned practice after a very short time in order to devote himself to his life's work. He must be one of the few Licentiates of the Society of Apothecaries ever to have become a Fellow of the Royal College of Physicians, which honour he was awarded in 1938 shortly before his death.[31] This was doubtless partly due to the changing climate of sexual discussion by the 1930s, by which decade the medical press was recommending Ellis's short compendium, *Psychology of Sex*, for use as a textbook in medical schools.[32]

Ellis was a retiring man who found the adverse publicity associated with the confiscation of *Sexual Inversion* a devastating blow. While he had wide and international contacts of friendship and common interest, this early setback led him to withdraw from engagement in public controversies and to devote himself to the work of scholarship. His own sex-life seems to have been somewhat unorthodox: he was a urolagnist (particularly stimulated by women urinating) and his own sexual powers seem to have been dubious. He had numerous amorous friendships with women, besides being married twice (the first time to the predominantly lesbian Edith Lees), but none were fully consummated before, at the age of 59, a time of life when most men tend to find their sexual powers fading, he achieved full congress with his second (common-law) wife (though some biographers doubt that this occurred). Hormonal deficiency has been suggested in the light of Ellis's reportedly high, squeaky voice: however, he managed to grow the long beard so prominent in his portraits. Whatever his phallic defects, he seems to have exercised a charismatic effect over the women who associated with him, many of them intellectuals and social reformers in their own right.[33]

Besides his monumental *Studies in the Psychology of Sex*, Ellis produced volumes of essays and travel writings and literary work; he was the editor of the Mermaid Series of texts of Elizabethan and Jacobean dramatists. His *Studies*[34] were a vast compilation of material drawn from an enormous variety of sources, from medical writings, the researches of anthropologists, the work of biologists, literature from many countries and the self-disclosures of individuals about their own sexual experiences. If this work could be said to have one underlying theory it was that all sexual behaviour lay somewhere upon a continuum, that the 'perverse' was often the exaggeration of normal tendencies, and that one of the highest virtues was liberal toleration for difference. Thus in spite of Ellis's sympathies towards such contemporary movements as eugenics he was very chary of anything in the nature of compulsory measures.

Ellis explicitly associated himself with a 'progressive' sexual programme, and was a founder member of the British Society for the Study of Sex Psychology. This movement was more concerned about the sexual rights and wrongs of women and the amelioration of the harsh legal system *vis-à-vis* persons of 'deviant' desires than it was about the normal male, whose sexual impulse had been described by Ellis as 'predominantly open and aggressive', its nature and needs inscribed 'in the written and unwritten codes of social law'.[35] To a great extent the normal male was perceived as being part of the problem, depicted as insensitive and clumsy, his sexual technique compared to an ape endeavouring to play the violin.

Ellis's thoughts on *The Sexual Impulse* (Volume III) mainly concerned that of the female: two other volumes of the *Studies* bore on matters affecting most men. In *Auto-Erotism*, part of Volume I of *Studies in the Psychology of Sex*, first published in 1899 (as Volume II), Havelock Ellis turned a radically critical gaze on the received wisdom concerning masturbation, and commented

> It seems to me that this field has rarely been viewed in a scientifically sound and morally sane light, simply because it has not been viewed as a whole...The nature and evils of masturbation are not seen in their true light and proportions until we realize that masturbation is but a specialized form of a tendency which in some form or in some degree affects not only man but all the higher animals.[36]

Ellis went on to explode many of the contemporary myths surrounding auto-erotic practice: that it was inevitably physically, mentally or morally debilitating, that it was a uniquely human trait and that it was a sad side-effect of civilization.

He was by no means altogether in favour of deliberate masturbatory practices, considering that they might produce 'a divorce... between the physical sensuous impulse and the ideal emotions',[37] a possible outcome which Sigmund Freud also suggested might eventuate since 'in the phantasies that accompany satisfaction the sexual object is raised to a degree of excellence which is not easily found in real life'.[38] Ellis also echoed numerous writers on the subject by attributing, at least to the persistent and habitual masturbator, the traditional 'morbid heightening of self-consciousness without any co-ordinated heightening of self-esteem'.[39] He suggested that boys might well be more inclined than girls to internalize very negative attitudes towards masturbation, through encountering prevalent attitudes that it was an 'unmanly' practice and by coming across terrifying quack literature (or indeed, religious warnings) on the subject.

Reading *Auto-Erotism* would have been more likely to alleviate than create anxiety. Although Ellis certainly did not ignore the possibility of undesirable results in certain categories of masturbator – prolonged, habitual or combined with a morbid constitution – the very fact that he saw masturbation as inevitably deleterious only in specified circumstances must have put many minds at rest. His writings on the subject certainly foreshadowed, and probably even influenced, changing attitudes towards masturbation. Their direct effect, however, given the limited circulation of *Studies in the Psychology of Sex*, must have been somewhat circumscribed.

Volume VI of the *Studies, Sex in Relation to Society* (1910), was the one in which Ellis, as much as he ever did, summed up his own views on the problems of sexuality, within the context of society as it existed at the time. It was in this work that Ellis delineated English (middle-class) males' attitude to erotic matters:

> They have been taught to be strenuous and manly and cleanminded, to seek by all means to put out of their minds the thought of women or the longing for sensuous indulgence. They have been told on all sides that only in marriage is it right or even safe to approach women. They have acquired the notion that sexual indulgence and all that appertains to it is something low and degrading, at the worst a mere natural necessity, at the best a duty to be accepted in a direct, honourable and straightforward manner. No-one seems to have told them that love is an art.[40]

Reading this, it is no surprise that Marie Stopes discovered premature ejaculation distressingly prevalent among middle-class British men, quite apart from the 'ordinary haste and carelessness' of which so many were guilty.[41]

Ellis's concern about the relationship is notable, contrasting with Victorian writers who tended to regard the male as a creature whose prime aim was to preserve himself from unduly wasting vital bodily fluids, a kind of self-contained and isolated mechanism. Ellis was a little before his time: *The Lancet*'s reviewer had reservations about Ellis's recommendations to contemporary British bridegrooms:

> Even though ardent young husbands are apt to be too hasty and too clumsy in the introduction of their wives to the mysteries of the marriage bed, it is doubtful if the refinements in the *ars amandi* detailed in this chapter are desirable for general adoption.

Nevertheless, he recommended *Sex in Relation to Society* 'to the medical world and to serious students of social problems', adding that Ellis had 'given the dignity of scholarship to a very delicate and difficult subject'.[42] Ellis, like Acton before him, had become the acceptable medical man who had taken on the unlovely task of dealing with sexual matters, to be held up against quacks, and foreigners like Krafft-Ebing. *Studies in the Psychology of Sex* were clearly the result of serious scholarly labours, and were produced in limited, expensive and hard-to-obtain editions.

The most radical thinker on sexual matters at this period was undoubtedly Sigmund Freud. His *Three Lectures on the Theory of Sexuality*, first published in German in 1905, were an epoch-making contribution to the study of the subject. It is by no means clear how influential they were in Britain. The *Three Lectures* do not seem to have been reviewed in the *British Medical Journal* or *The Lancet* either on their first appearance in German or later in English translations. In the first lecture Freud described popular received ideas of the sexual instinct, as

> absent in childhood, to set in at the time of puberty in connection with the process of coming to maturity and to be revealed in the manifestations of an irresistible attraction exercised by one sex upon the other; while its aim is presumed to be sexual union.

His own conclusion, however, was 'that these views give a very false picture of the true situation'.[43] Further on, in a footnote, he went so far as to maintain that

> From the point of view of psychoanalysis the exclusive sexual interest felt by men for women is also a problem that needs elucidating and is not a self-evident fact based upon an attraction that is ultimately of a chemical nature.[44]

This was so extremely contrary to received ideas and attitudes that later writers, while making a token obeisance to Freud's great work in elucidating the mysteries of the psyche, far from wrestling with the implications of this notion of sexuality, applied 'Freud' like icing to the same old cake. His name was a guarantee of a writer's commitment to modernity, but this did not mean any engagement with such subversive notions as 'the sexual instinct and the sexual object are merely soldered together'.[45]

Freud's teachings were regarded with a good deal of suspicion by the British medical establishment. Even W. H. R. Rivers, in his ground-breaking article in *The Lancet* in 1917 on the uses of psychoanalysis and Freud's concepts in the abreactive treatment of shellshock, deplored the overemphasis on sex and its role in the aetiology of neurosis.[46] Freud's ideas continued to come in for a certain amount of derision. At the 79th Annual Meeting of the Medico-Psychological Association in August 1920, at which a number of speakers paid tribute to the work of Freud and the therapeutic value of psychoanalysis, Sir Robert Armstrong-Jones suggested that 'Freudism' might be 'applicable to life on the Austrian and German frontiers, but not to virile, sport-loving open-air people like the British'. Speakers who praised Freud nevertheless denied to 'sex tendencies...anything like the universality claimed by Freud's disciples'.[47]

As far as Freud's influence went, his writings were of course copiously cited by Ellis. In their 1914 Home University Library volume on *Sex*, Geddes and Thomson displayed an acquaintance with his ideas, and Arthur Cooper, author of *The Sexual Disabilities of Man and their Treatment* (1908), in later editions referred to works by Freud.[48] By the 1920s, watered-down Freudianism made its appearance in popular manuals of sex-education and advice, in combination with the old elements found in such works, which sat uneasily with the new jargon of 'repressions'. A certain lip-service was paid to Freud's doctrines without consideration of their profounder implications.

By about 1920, new ideas about sexuality which had been known and discussed in certain limited circles from the 1890s were gaining wider currency, although 'Victorianism' was very far from being dead. The ideas conveniently epitomized by the name of William Acton still had their adherents. Writers such as Ellis and Freud were known to a few, probably more among certain sections of the lay public than the medical profession.[49]

'What a young man ought to know'

The members of the medical profession believed that they were required to inform themselves about matters of sex, a study believed best confined to their own and other, equally learned, callings. However, well before the end of the nineteenth century a strong current of opinion favoured breaking the 'conspiracy of silence' respecting the dangers of unlicensed sexual conduct. (These comprehended both the venereal diseases spread through fornication and the debility and worse believed to be the outcome of self-abuse.) The young ought to be made aware of these perils in order to avoid them; ignorance could lead to unwitting sin. Girls, to a certain extent, were sheltered; but boys were exposed to temptation. And boys and young men had desires which could be carelessly aroused and unthinkingly indulged, to the detriment of the individual and of society as a whole.

Support for a single moral standard was not confined to groups which may, somewhat ahistorically, be defined as 'feminist'. Arguments in favour of male purity were advanced by a wide spectrum of interests, and not always in ways particularly favourable to women. Medical views on the dangers of sexual indulgence in the male have already been cited, and the need to encourage male continence could, for example, be used to support greater policing of street prostitution and the control of women.

The age of marriage in the later nineteenth century was high, for the middle-class man in particular. Many men at the peak of their virility were thus compelled to lead a celibate life, their sexual energies uncontained by marriage. It was an age when increasing numbers of single men were living on their own, or at least away from their families. In more traditional societies such men might be controlled by community custom; at times of less social mobility family pressures would have borne more heavily upon them. These men, while escaping from traditional modes of moral policing, lacked certain concomitants of affection and support.[50]

A movement for some kind of sex-education, at least warning against dangers, was catalysed around about the 1880s, out of the movement to repeal the Contagious Diseases Acts and the furore caused by W. T. Stead's articles in the *Pall Mall Gazette*, 'The Maiden Tribute of Modern Babylon', which culminated in the passing of the Criminal Law Amendment Act of 1885, with its raising of the age of consent and its criminalization of male homosexual activities. Various social purity organizations emerged, believing that a higher standard would never be achieved by a continuation of the 'conspiracy of silence'. Religiously affiliated bodies such as the White Cross League and the Alliance of Honour produced numerous pamphlets specifically aimed at the inculcation in men of a high and single standard of chastity. 'True Manliness' by 'JEH' (the purity worker Jane Ellice Hopkins) reached a large audience: over one million copies had been sold by 1909,[51] a figure not including its circulation in *The Blanco Book*, a compilation of White Cross League pamphlets produced for issue to troops.

'True Manliness', as its title suggests, aimed to inculcate an ideal of the true male as pure and chivalrous. This was partly done by vivid metaphoric depiction of the dangers men faced, with a description of the crossing of a mountain glacier by a narrow path, and partly by emphasizing the heroic struggle which the maintenance of continence required. Man was 'an intelligent being mounted on a spirited horse' which he had to master. The dangers of ignorantly abusing the developing sexual function were threefold: such abuse would damage the maturing organism; the sexual faculties were designed for occasional, not continuous use and did not need to be called into action until this was legitimate; and they were not for selfish enjoyment but intimately connected with the good of future wife and family. Knowing this, would the young man

> run the risk of tainting your blood and making it a fountain of corruption, till you have to loathe your body, the temple you have made into a charnel-house, reeking with the very breath of the grave?

Or would he 'play the man, and fight against everything low and beastly, determined that your life shall have no shameful secrets in it?' The reader was exhorted, 'you know what is right, what is manly, what is noble, what is true to your nature.'

Adhering to a high moral standard of conduct would accrue benefits, moreover, beyond the mere spiritual self-satisfaction of self-discipline, for 'stored-up passion' would create 'splendid energy'. The religious and moral messages were blended with the medical, including exhortations to stay away from quacks but to seek the help of reputable medical men if necessary. Occasional nocturnal emissions were reassuringly described as 'Nature's method of relief'. This work, though couched in religious rhetoric, was notable for its directness and its getting straight to the problems at issue, even if it was sometimes hard to detect whether fornication or masturbation was being subsumed under the description 'dirty, shameful, secrets in your life': perhaps they were simply differing aspects of the general problem of impurity.

'True Manliness' suggested that, in spite of 'the devil's lie, "that...no man is really pure"', in fact

> every pure man knows that he is only one of a great multitude in England and America wearing 'the white flower of a blameless life'. There are scores and scores of men all around you who are just as pure as any woman.[52]

This was not a position often taken by the purity lobby. Reverend E. Lyttelton, in his *The Causes and Prevention of Immorality in Schools* (1887), was appalled by the prevalence of the solitary vice and impurity generally:

> Of all the sins to which a boy is tempted at school the most prevalent, the most alluring, and the most enduring and deadly in its effects is

impurity – and it is the only one not warned against as a matter of course.

The 'two great causes', he believed, were 'curiosity and dirty talk', and the only effective preventive measure was warning against this uniquely awful sin.[53]

Increasing numbers of publications were produced during the 1890s and early 1900s, directed either at parents and guardians or at young people themselves, warning against the dangers of sexual sin. The actual demand for these is hard to estimate since so many were privately printed by purity or youth organizations and purchased in bulk by similar bodies, and the constraints of commercial publishing did not apply. The success of works such as the Self and Sex Series published by Dr Sylvanus Stall, an American divine, which had wide sales in Britain, suggests that a demand did exist beyond any mere imaginings about a rising tide of impurity threatening the nation.

Stall's works were typical examples of the literature coming to be produced on this subject. Their very titles became a kind of general description of it: 'What a Young Boy/Young Man/Young Husband/Man of Forty-Five Ought to Know'. The gradation by phase of life was also typical; it was assumed that certain kinds and levels of knowledge were appropriate to certain ages. The age at which warnings should be given was moving backwards to an earlier stage, as, presumably, purity workers discovered that 'bad habits' were often acquired prior to the surges of puberty.

Warnings aimed towards younger boys had to be couched rather less directly than had been regarded as appropriate in 'True Manliness' or in Lyttelton's pleas against impurity in schools. It was at this era that the slow ascent of the evolutionary ladder, as pioneered by Geddes and Thomson, came to be employed in sex-education literature and thus associated it with 'the birds and bees'. The beauties of nature and the natural reappeared with clichéd regularity in these works. The spirochaete and the gonococcus, in this context, did not count as part of 'nature', always described as beautiful and benign, if not abused or perverted.

Stall, in *What a Young Boy Ought to Know*, written in the formula of chats to a young boy called Harry, began with nearly fifty pages on 'God's purpose in endowing plants, animals and Man with reproductive organs'.[54] After that he moved straight on to the danger of abusing the reproductive organs: this was the outcome of the existence of that organ which differentiated man from the animals – his hand:

Man is possibly the only animal which persistently pollutes and de-grades his own body, and this would not have easily been possible if God had not given him hands, which He designed should prove useful and a means of great help and blessing to him in his life upon the earth.[55]

Boys endangered their 'moral intellectual and physical powers' by

polluting their bodies, by handling and toying with their sexual mem-ber in such a way as to produce a sensation, or feeling, which may give a momentary pleasure, but results in the most serious injuries.[56]

There was not much room for doubt about what vice Stall was at-tacking, threatening 'idiocy...early decline and death...consump-tion...total mental and physical self-destruction'. If a boy lived to manhood and managed to become a father, the 'inferior quality' of his sexual secretion' would manifest itself in his offspring.[57] Stall's prescriptions for the avoidance of falling into this pernicious habit, and for recouping strength if it had been succumbed to, involved life-style rather than patent remedies: wholesome light diet, healthy exercise, early rising, hard beds, the pursuit of mental improvement, cold baths, etc. Similar warnings were to be found in *What a Young Man Ought to Know*, which dealt also with the risk of venereal diseases and the problems of the courtship period.[58]

Many of these widely circulated books emanated from the USA, while British productions became more common after the turn of the century. Purity also concerned writers whose works were not exclu-sively dedicated to the purpose of sex education. The works of Lord Baden-Powell, *Scouting for Boys* and *Rovering to Success*, probably reached a far wider audience than any more narrowly directed works. Self-abuse, according to 'BP', 'brings with it weakness of head and heart, and, if persisted in, idiocy and lunacy'.[59] He advised scouts that 'there is one temptation that is pretty sure to come to you at one time or another and I want just to warn you against it'.[60]

In *Rovering to Success*, addressed to an older age group, 'Women' were among the 'Rocks you are likely to bump on', but the problems dealt with under this heading dealt more with masturbation and the problems of continence during the 'rutting season' of growing into manhood.[61] Readers were reminded that 'the Germ is a Sacred Trust for carrying on the race', and recommended to keep 'the organ clean and bathed in cold water every day' as the best precaution against excessive nocturnal emissions or the temptation to self-abuse.[62] Baden-Powell also warned against venereal diseases, which were 'sure, sooner or later, to overtake those who indulge their sex desires unwisely', but also 'very easily caught – even from a kiss or from drinking out of a cup used by an infected person'.[63] Such warnings about the ease of catching sexually transmitted diseases by apparently innocent means were common. Baden-Powell was not influenced, over the years during which his works continued to be republished, by any consideration of changes in debates upon sexuality. His breezy, common-sense tone stayed the same, as did his ideas of the deleteriousness of masturbation, though he was clearly convinced of the possibility of recuperation by leading a healthy scouting life.

More sophisticated writers in the field of sex-education were, by the time of the First World War, uneasily aware of theoretical developments tending to undermine many of the beliefs embodied in their work. A certain lip-service to Freud could be found, for example, in the fourth edition of *Towards Racial Health: A Handbook for Parents, Teachers, and Social Workers on the Training of Boys and Girls*, published in 1920 (with an introduction from J. A. Thomson). Norah March, B.Sc., Member of the Royal Sanitary Institute, declared, in a footnote, 'we are indebted to the work of Professor Freud of Vienna for great illumination of this field of sex psychology'.[64] Nevertheless her work was imbued with the belief in an inborn 'racial instinct' which did not readily blend with the libidinal theory of sexual development. Her views on the distinct and separate natures of the two sexes rested more on the work of Geddes and Thomson than on a reading of the *Three Lectures on Sexuality* (which did not appear in her list for further reading), as she argued in terms of the differing role of the father and the mother in reproduction resulting in the male instinct being direct and the female diffused, as a natural outcome of evolution. There was a detailed chapter on the use of nature study 'towards inducing a reverent and responsible attitude towards questions of sex and parenthood'.[65] (An advanced knowledge of botany had proved of singularly little practical help to Marie Stopes and her first husband.)

March's prescriptions for discouraging 'sexual laxity and distress' in the growing boy had a familiar ring:

[He] should absolutely free himself from the dominion of eroticism...
the male mental attitude should be pure and cool enough to refrain
from susceptibility...the more frequently he exerts his will-power to

triumph, the more easily will it act for him in the day of sudden emergency.

March did not ignore the usual physical prescriptions prophylactic against incontinence, reiterating the usual exhortations about early rising, hard beds, wholesome diet, cold baths, etc.[66]

The paramount sexual sin inveighed against by sex-educators was masturbation, perhaps naturally in view of the fact that they were addressing themselves to an age-group for which it was far more likely a temptation than actual fornication. Self-abuse was not merely regarded as a disgusting and sinful habit, but believed dangerously depleting to health. It could be the first step in a course of impurity leading to fornication, disease and death, by eroding self-discipline and self-control: as Lyttelton put it in *The Causes and Prevention of Immorality in Schools*, 'the least defilement by hand enormously increases the difficulties of continence in manhood'.[67] Opinions differed. In the White Cross League pamphlet 'The Testimony of Medical Men', some echoed Lyttelton in considering that 'the precocious indulgence of boyhood' might 'ripen into the ungovernable passion of manhood and become responsible for the support of prostitution'.[68] Others believed that 'the habit of solitary sin, learned and contracted at school, and not discontinued even in later and more mature years' would eventually become 'the one absorbing and uncontrollable passion of life'.[69]

'A justified penalty for sexual immorality'[70]

While masturbation was regarded with a horror which perhaps owed something to hysterical displacement of more general sexual anxieties, there were serious grounds for sexual fear in the nineteenth century. Venereal diseases were extremely prevalent, syphilis was incurable and lethal, and while the long-term effects of gonorrhoea were not realized it was even more widespread.

The Contagious Diseases Acts (1864, 1866, 1869) and the agitation against them have been extensively discussed by historians.[71] They were regarded at the time as giving the sexual double standard the force of law by setting up a system which endeavoured to provide clean prostitutes for members of the armed forces by the compulsory inspection of women alleged to be prostitutes in certain designated garrison and naval towns. This provision was not universal, but aimed specifically at maintaining in fighting health a stigmatized group of the population consisting almost entirely of unmarried men from the lower social classes. Even the legitimate wives of soldiers were despised.[72] Fears of what might happen if the 'brutal and licentious soldiery' did not have its sexual needs provided for focused on unbridled anarchy and the dangers to respectable women if suitable outlets were not supplied. The Acts attempted to deal with the problems of venereal disease by endeavouring to control the source, as prostitutes were perceived. The measures were inspired by the regulationist systems which existed in continental Europe, but were only, even at their height, in force in certain designated towns, and bore almost exclusively upon women of the working classes.

Historians of Victorian sexuality have often cited the statement of the 1871 Royal Commission on the Contagious Diseases Acts that

We may at once dispose of [any recommendation] founded on the principle of putting both parties to the sin of fornication on the same footing by the obvious but no less conclusive reply that there is no comparison to be made between prostitutes and the men who consort with them. With the one sex the offence is committed as a matter of gain; with the other it is an irregular indulgence of a natural impulse.

The double standard was enshrined in law not only by the Contagious Diseases Acts but in the Divorce Law of 1857, under which a husband could divorce his wife for a single act of adultery whereas a woman had to prove adultery plus bigamy, cruelty, desertion, incest, rape or unnatural offences to obtain a decree. A much higher premium was placed upon female than upon male chastity.[73]

Such opinions were neither monolithic nor uncontested. The emphasis placed by many writers on the importance of male continence has been indicated. Many men in their own lives specifically rejected the assumptions of the double standard. Opposition to the Acts did not come from one sex alone. Men, not only the middle and educated classes but working men, objected to this state regulation of immorality, on grounds of moral outrage, of protest against the violation of 'their women' and of the protection of civil liberties. There was far from unanimous support in Victorian Britain for the idea of a double standard of sexual morality and the notion that prostitution was a necessary social evil to be granted official legal recognition.

The Acts' medical efficacy was not unqueried. Syphilis is characterized by long asymptomatic stages and a patient whose gonorrhoea has passed the stage of acute symptoms can continue infectious, creating problems of diagnosis and how to determine whether a case is infectious. Whether the treatment available had any therapeutic benefits at all was somewhat dubious. Doubts were expressed as to the medical soundness of providing for only one of the partners in the sexual transaction.

There is little ground for believing that contracting venereal disease was a venial matter for a man in Victorian Britain. The venereal diseases were stigmatized complaints. Many voluntary hospitals would not admit patients suffering from them.[74] There was an unwillingness among subscribers to hospitals to contribute for what were perceived as 'undeserving' cases, although the 'innocently' infected might be admitted as in-patients for treatment. Friendly Societies usually refused to pay sickness benefits to subscribers with venereal disease.[75] The stigma associated with these diseases affected male sufferers and the provisions for their treatment. While fornication might not exile a man from decent society, venereal diseases in the male were not regarded as any less of a stigma or less shameful than they were in women.

Venereal diseases were extremely widespread. In 1916 the Royal Commission on Venereal Diseases suggested that as many as 10 per cent of the urban population had syphilis and an even greater proportion gonorrhoea. These diseases appeared to be proportionately much more common among the male than the female population, though accurate statistics on venereal diseases were, because of the misrecording consequent upon the stigma, very hard to come by. They were also more immediately obvious in the male, at least to the sufferer himself. Women may be unknowingly infected, the sores or lesions being hidden inside in the vagina or obscured in the vulval folds. Men could not ignore sores and chancres on their penises or oozing discharges from the urethra. The effect of such very apparent wages of sin must have been considerable.

The subject of venereology was not taught as part of the undergraduate medical syllabus,[76] but could be acquired only by postgraduate study. These diseases were sufficiently prevalent among the better-off classes for 'the financial rewards of private practice in venereology [to be] large indeed', and one surgeon founded a London teaching hospital out of 'the large fortune he acquired from his VD patients'.[77] However, most medical practitioners tended to shrink from the stigma that hung about the 'pox-doctor'. The standard treatments were not pleasant:

Local treatment of [gonorrhoea] held the field during this period with irrigations using a multitude of chemicals, instillations of concentrated dye-stuffs, and vigorous instrumentations of the poor long-suffering urogenital mucous membrane...the cure was long, laborious and painful and a sensitive patient after having gone through the whole gamut of therapeutic procedures would never think of contracting the infection again.[78]

L. W. Harrison, one of the founders of the modern approach to venereal disease treatment, commented on the prevalence of urethral stricture consequent upon this heroic practice which he had seen in his early years as an army doctor.[79] The mercurial treatment which was the most common therapy for syphilis was less locally painful but exceedingly unpleasant.

Many cases went untreated or were attended to by unlicensed practitioners of various kinds. The Local Government Board's *Report as to the Practice of Medicine and Surgery by Unqualified Persons in the United Kingdom* (1910) discovered that 'in many of the great towns the treatment of venereal diseases is largely in the hands of unqualified persons'.[80] This was not only because herbal or homeopathic remedies might be less brutal. The Royal Commission on Venereal Diseases in its Report of 1916 suggested that

The fear of disgrace and the consequent desire for concealment necessarily render the sufferer from venereal disease specially liable to attempt self-treatment, or to entrust his treatment to persons who are in no way qualified to deal with the disease.

This was not solely a question of financial capacity: 'the upper classes resort to quacks as readily as the poor'[81] out of 'shame or because they are misguided by advertisement or misleading recommendations'.[82]

For twenty years prior to the issue of the Royal Commission's Final Report there had been attempts to inspire the government to take action on the venereal disease problem. Of those who sought an enquiry into the subject, most, if not all, were opposed to the reintroduction of the Contagious Diseases Acts. They looked to the inclusion of men in any scheme, on grounds of both justice and efficacy, while making no suggestions as to the registration or licensing of vice. Emphasis was laid, as it frequently was at this period, on formulating a scheme 'to protect the innocent from contagion' and check the spread of these diseases. 'The innocent' in this context meant the wives and children of ('guilty') infected men (infection in children, when not congenital, was usually attributed to the spread of infection through the use of common towels and household implements, not sexual abuse). Innocent also were those who had acquired the disease through sharing a cup or an innocent social kiss with a sufferer, and medical and nursing personnel who had contracted the diseases in the course of treating the diseased. The 'guilty' sufferer by the turn of the century was far more often perceived as male, conveying disease to the innocent women and children of his family, as opposed to a contaminated prostitute infecting healthy young male bodies. The fact that this question of guilt and innocence was a central issue demonstrates how little impunity was granted venereally diseased men.

Finally appointed in 1913, and gaining a great deal of media attention for a previously taboo subject, the Royal Commission, chaired by Lord Sydenham, spent several years in hearing copious evidence on the current state of the prevalence of venereal disease and the provisions for its diagnosis and treatment, as well as recommendations as to what should be done to combat the 'terrible peril to our Imperial race'.[83] The new therapeutic hope given in 1909 by the discovery of an effective treatment in Salvarsan contributed to the perception that action was needed. In 1916 the Commission produced its final report. It was concluded that such was the national importance of these diseases that only state action could adequately deal with them. Above all, it was essential to get away from the old stigmatizing and punitive attitudes to sufferers. In the interests of public health rather than human rights, the Report advocated no distinction between the sexes, between 'good' and 'bad' women or between the classes in making its recommendations for tackling the problem.[84]

'In favour of a high venereal rate'

It is ironic that shortly after the appointment of a Royal Commission had been achieved, the First World War broke out, and brought the problem of venereal diseases forcibly to the fore as national preoccupation changed to a war mentality. The prevalence of these diseases was easier to detect in the armed forces, and treatment, once indicated, compulsory. This treatment might not have been particularly efficacious or in line with current advances but facilities for early diagnosis and administration of treatment were better developed.

The existing system was placed under considerable stress by the outbreak of war. 'The rates for the whole British Army, including Dominion forces, compare[d] favourably with the rates for the three previous peace years 1911–1913', the rates of admission per 1000 per annum of all troops actually declining from 60.5 in 1911 to 36.7 in 1916, with a slight rise in the following two years.[85] This relative decline did not reflect the absolutely larger numbers of men involved. Even prior to the introduction of conscription, the numbers in the forces had vastly increased, while conscription made the risks of venereal infection a particularly sensitive subject. In the course of the war, 4 August 1914 to 11 November 1918, 400,000 cases were treated, gonorrhoea comprising 66 per cent of the total, greatly outnumbering syphilis and other afflictions. Syphilis represented only about a quarter of the cases.[86] There were enormous variations by theatre of war and whether the troops were in the front line or not. Venereal diseases were regarded by the authorities, understandably, as wholly a bad thing, but some of the men themselves seem to have taken a different view, deliberately courting infection to avoid the trenches.[87]

The problem for the medical corps was that 'in all other infectious diseases the medical services endeavour to prevent infection reaching the personnel of an army': with venereal diseases the situation was different; 'the causes are well known, and officers and men, knowing how infection is contracted, individually take the risk.'[88] Their control was important not only because of the enormous amount of wastage of manpower they caused at a time of national emergency, but because they 'incurred the likelihood of permanent damage to the individual, infection to others, and an heritage which might stain an innocent life'.[89]

It was recognised, or assumed, that 'social conditions operated strongly during the war in favour of a high venereal rate'.[90] It was not necessarily war as such which was the problem but the dislocation of individuals. There was a considerable difference between the number of cases among British troops and those from the Dominions: the Tommy on leave would tend to go home, and if he had any kind of sexual activity this would be with a girlfriend; certainly a 'careful enquiry in some thousands of cases' amongst British troops revealed that 'over 60 per cent of the infections resulted from intercourse with women who were not prostitutes in the ordinary sense of the word'.[91] The Dominion soldier, however, far from home and family, would seek the bright lights of the wicked city and succumb to the wiles of prostitutes. The highest rate of all was found, for some reason, among Canadian troops,[92] and about 60 per cent of infections in Australian soldiers were due to professional prostitutes, attributed to 'the higher pay of the soldiers'.[93]

Means of reducing the prevalence of venereal diseases among the troops varied. Exhortations to sexual continence, most famously Lord Kitchener's address to the British Expeditionary Force, were sometimes employed. With the inception of the National Council of Combatting Venereal Diseases and the training of special lecturers, these exhortations, given a medical rather than a purely moral basis, may have had some effect. Such measures did not succeed in giving every member of the forces at least the knowledge of the existence of these diseases: one man wrote to Marie Stopes in 1921

> I was in the Navy during the War and knew nothing of the horrors of this scourge. I was caught by bad company and contracted gonorrhoea in August 1918.[94]

What might seem from other writings on the subject to have been an unprecedented torrent of information about the sexually transmitted diseases had clearly passed this man by. Another of Stopes's correspondents admitted to encountering some form of instruction but 'many of the lectures etc one ever hears in the service on "dangers" etc rather pass over my head'.[95]

Particularly in France, where such a system already existed, reliance was placed on the provision of '*maisons tolerées*', licensed brothels in which the women were regularly inspected. Bridget Towers has suggested in her article on 'Health Education Policy, 1916–1926: Venereal Disease and the Prophylaxis Dilemma' that a British class leadership believed 'army morale was contingent on sexual activity.' This was not necessarily regarded by the Medical Corps as the most effective course of action, since by that time many Medical Officers were committed to a medical approach instead of social control.[96]

There was considerable dissension over what actually constituted the most effective medical preventive approach to venereal diseases in the fighting forces, complicated by the pressures of influential groups on the Home Front. Public opinion, for example, forced the closing of licensed brothels for the troops, but only as late as 1918. Early treatment of the potentially infected was one recommendation: this involved setting up an ablution area where treatment could be given as soon as possible after exposure. American and Dominion forces placed reliance upon the issue of prophylactic packs, containing preventives and equipment for self-disinfection. This was allied to far stronger punitive measures against those who did become infected. But when more stringent controls were called for in this wartime ambience, they were tending to focus more and more on the man himself, even if control of prostitution also formed part of the package.

During the war, and in the attention given in the press to the findings of the Royal Commission on Venereal Diseases, knowledge of the existence of these diseases, how they were transmitted and their long-term effects, was widely disseminated. This growing awareness of the dangers of sexual promiscuity may have contributed to the rise of the new monogamic ideal of the 1920s, in which eroticism was incorporated into marriage rather than being something pursued outside it.

2
Evil companions, scarlet women and pernicious quacks: the subcultures of sex

It was extremely hard for young men to retain that untouched innocence about sexual matters which was assumed to be innate in their sisters. While there were men whose sexual ignorance was such that they had failed to consummate their marriages or even realize what this entailed,[1] on the whole it was unlikely that a boy in growing up would avoid all mention of sex (a different matter from acquiring practical competence in the act). He might come by information about male sexuality and functioning from a variety of different sources. Those emanating from respectable and orthodox interest groups and embodied in certain public health provisions have already been discussed in the previous chapter. Other messages from less worthy and well-meaning (if also less morally authoritarian) sources also shaped concepts of male normality and sexual functioning.

'Undesirable and debased characters'

Some boys learnt of sex directly in a context which might be defined as abusive. Texts on the upbringing of children often mentioned the dangers of sexual corruption by servants:

Boys are abused by ignorant and libidinous nurses, who play with their organs, both to gratify their own sensuality, and to keep the children quiet.[2]

The motivation for this behaviour was not always perceived as sexual: it was sometimes explained as a pernicious but ignorant means of soothing a fractious child:

Even nurses, sometimes, in ignorance of the terrible evil and sad consequences of their act, practice this destructive habit upon very young children for the purpose of diverting their thoughts, so that they will not cry, or in order that they may be quieted and fall asleep.[3]

Paranoid myth-making about the lower classes? A few of Marie Stopes's correspondents recounted experiences of sexual behaviour by servants. Given the youthful age at which most of these incidents were described as occurring, seduction does not seem to be an appropriate term, suggesting as it does a kind of *droit de seigneur* initiation, a rite of passage. There was nothing romantic in the following accounts. In some cases the assault had taken place when the child was very young:

When very young I was taught the exquisite but pernicious soul and body destroying sin of masturbation by a servant girl who used to play with my sexual organs.

From the age of 4 owing to a nursemaid I got into the solitary vice habit.[4]

Others wrote of sexual connections taking place at a somewhat older age, though still in prepubescence:

When about 12 years of age a maid of ours, then about 20 years of age, caused me to have intercourse with her before I knew anything about such things.

I attribute my weakness to having connections with a servant maid two and three times daily over a long period before I reached puberty.[5]

It was not only servants who were the perpetrators, nor was it an exclusively middle-class trauma:

> As a young child of six I was often looked after by a young neighbour
> aged about 16. One day she exposed herself to me with a great display
> of detail.[6]

None of the victims of these assaults appear to have perceived these assaults as a means of placating and soothing them.

Such assaults and abuse were not unique to the male child. Sons of the privileged classes, however, sent away to school at a very early age, faced perils to which their sisters were not exposed. Much of the rhetoric of the sex-education movement was predicated on the assumption that public and boarding schools could be hotbeds of vice. A few of Stopes's correspondents described school-day incidents involving force and reluctance (not mutual explorations in adolescence): one had been 'degraded at the age of six at a high-class boarding-school', while another at a public school had found 'self-abuse was more or less thrust on me in my sleep by a master!'[7]

Apart from this direct and brutal contact with sex, a major source of the transmission of sexual information or misinformation was talk between young males. In the rhetoric of self-conscious proponents of the need for sex-education about the importance of providing 'clean and healthy' sex instruction for young men, this presumably mutual exchange of bits and scraps of knowledge or speculation was transformed into 'corrupt companions' tainting the innocent child: boys 'imbibed their ideas from the coarser of their companions' and thus failed to escape the 'acquisition of degraded ideas on the subject of sex'.[8]

This corruption of the innocent was sometimes attributed to older boys or even men: in the White Cross League pamphlet 'The Testimony of Medical Men', A. M. Edge, Physician to the Salford Lock Hospital, referred to the 'poisonous advice which he too often receives from others a little older than himself'.[9] Drs Schofield and Vaughan-Jackson, in *What A Boy Should Know* (1913), warned of the danger of

> men who take an evil delight in telling young boys about themselves,
> and telling them in such a manner as to encourage them to commence
> or continue this injurious habit. They will say 'It will do you no harm,'
> or 'It will make a man of you', or make some such untrue remark.

They went on warn that these men 'will lead you further, and towards more injurious and disgusting practices', which appears to be a covert warning against homosexual advances: it is not clear if their warning was based on observation or paranoia. (They recommended that if anyone made such suggestions the reader ought to be prepared to 'punch his head'.)[10] Accounts by one or two of Stopes's correspondents seem to bear out such cautions when they said of masturbation: 'I was told by grown-up men that it was good for me and that kind of thing made a man of one'; 'I then learnt from elder boys that pernicious and shameful habit.'[11]

The outbreak of war in 1914 and the subsequent introduction of conscription exposed numbers of men to discussions on sexual topics they would not necessarily have previously encountered and might even have avoided. The general coarseness of male talk in the army was impossible to avoid, so that 'decent kindly men [were] taken and crushed and stamped into the Army mould', as Stephen Graham put it in *A Private in the Guards* (1919). He deplored

> learning to be impure. It is only a strong character that can resist the infection of impurity. Inevitably you do or think things which are obscene and brutal, and many go and do the sort of things they say and think.

An inquiry into *The Army and Religion* similarly mentioned the 'constant flow of filthy language, the drunkenness, and, more especially, the immorality'.[12] One of Stopes's correspondents confirmed these accounts: 'what I had heard from the usual talk one had to get accustomed to in the Army'.[13] The extreme and habitual crudity of male speech in the forces was such that works such as T. E. Lawrence's ('Aircraftman Shaw') *The Mint* and Frederic Manning's *Her Privates We*, which aimed at a realistic depiction of forces life during and just after the First World War, were not published until well after the Second World War, having previously been regarded as unacceptable.[14]

Apart from fleeting references it is very hard to discover of what these communications from this male subculture actually consisted. In letters received by Marie Stopes her correspondents occasionally mentioned that they had picked up such sexual information as they had had prior to reading her book from such suspect sources, which they described in terms which suggested the unpleasant aura of the furtive or coarse which hung about talk of this kind:

> I married 8 years ago with only a very limited knowledge of sexual matters – mostly gathered from smutty tales, or talks with men one meets on the daily path.

I have certain knowledge which is more or less common property but the sources from which I acquired it are such that I have grave doubts as to the advisability of making use of it.[15]

They were not specific about its content.

A folk myth which persisted well into the twentieth century (although not mentioned by any of Stopes's correspondents), presumably circulated by this male subculture, was the noxious belief that venereal disease could be cured by intercourse with a virgin. A case was reported in 1884 of a man with primary and secondary syphilis, with an indurated ulcer on his penis, raping a girl of fourteen 'with the object of being cured of his disease'.[16] This superstition was still prevalent thirty years later, being mentioned in evidence to the Royal Commission of Venereal Diseases in 1913:

A certain superstition exists that if a man has contracted venereal disease and he can have connexion with a virgin he will transmit that disease to her and himself escape free; the idea has existed for a very long time, I am afraid.[17]

Another myth about venereal disease, that it was contracted through intercourse with a menstruating woman, was voiced by one of Stopes's correspondents.[18] These beliefs and others may have lingered on, perhaps longer than equivalent beliefs relating to other diseases, because of the secrecy and shame in which venereal diseases and sexual matters generally were shrouded. In the absence of any other mode of gaining information on the subject, the male peer group was often the only resource many men had.

Men who wrote to Stopes mentioning learning self-abuse in adolescence were not always explicit as to the role of their peers in the matter. A few did mention advice or example from others as a factor: 'acting on the advice of other young boys I began to relieve myself in this artificial manner'.[19] A number of Stopes's correspondents described habits of masturbation pejoratively as picked up from 'bad company', 'undesirable and debased characters', 'a rotten set':[20] the role of older men has already been mentioned. This miasma of corruption and degradation may not have been universal: one correspondent reported that at one time he had been much troubled by strong desires but hated the idea of 'buying relief' and had been told by his brother that he 'could obtain release by applying friction to the penis with the hand and this I did every now and then', a practice which as he had 'always understood it is quite harmless'.[21]

This male subculture continued to be (and presumably still is) one of the chief sources by which men acquire some form of sexual 'knowledge'. In spite of an apparent flood of literature being published aiming at enlightenment in sexual matters, many individuals still gained much if not most of their information on sex from 'school, college, or workshop companions'.[22] During the 1930s men continued to write to Marie Stopes with comments such as:

> naturally I had an idea, but it was obtained from the crude and unreliable source of workshop and barrack-room talk, both of which were and are so indecent that I left sex alone. [Soldier serving in Egypt, 1937]

> What sexual knowledge I did gain was just 'picked up' from bad sources, was very fragmentary and largely quite wrong. [1935]

> Living as I do in the Navy I have naturally heard these subjects discussed freely, perhaps too freely, but never by persons with a technical knowledge. [1935][23]

Such random observations were borne out by the researches of Mass Observation in the later 1940s in their 'Sex Survey'.[24] In the finished Report, the chapter on 'Discovering Sex' noted the 'haphazard, surreptitious passing on of information'. The conclusion was that

> Most of the people who are grown up today 'picked up' their sex knowledge – off the street-corner, from workmates, from other children, from whatever literature, 'respectable' or otherwise, they could lay their hands on, or just by keeping their eyes and ears open.

In a statistical breakdown of sources reported (some respondents gave more than one), 25 per cent said they had 'picked it up', 13 per cent that they had learned from other children and 12 per cent that it 'came naturally' or by experience; 11 per cent (probably mostly girls) had been instructed by their mothers, 8 per cent had found out through reading, 6 per cent (most likely boys) had been told by their fathers and 6 per cent by a teacher; 6 per cent learnt from workmates, 5 per cent by getting married, 4 per cent in the armed forces and 10 per cent from other sources. The older respondents were more likely to have claimed knowledge of 'natural' origin.[25]

Respondents describing information haphazardly picked up were as pejorative in their remarks as Stopes's correspondents: 'I never at any time heard anything about sex but what was smutty and sordid.'[26] Misinformation started in the early years: 'as small boy, had entirely wrong information imparted by schoolfriend',[27] and was characteristic of the youthful peer group, according to men who found out 'the nastier things from youths around my own age' and from 'schoolmates' dirty stories'.[28] During army service some men

> discovered how beastly some men are. Their conversation and bragging of their exploits made unpleasant something which should between two people in love be the fulfilment of their love and passion.[29]

Others, though not specific about context, said that they had learnt

> From smutty stories.

> From all sorts of people in a most repulsive and incorrect manner. The damage was done before I found the right literature.

> Through smutty jokes and conversation. Rather pleasant but also rather dangerous.[30]

The value of information gained from this subculture was thus extremely dubious, being both misleading and, as many men described it, repulsive and smutty.

'These harpies'

A certain amount of surreptitious word-of-mouth communication about sex was surely common to adolescents of both sexes. But there were forms of information to which young men were far more likely to be exposed. The streets themselves were regarded as a potent source of danger for young men. Respectable men were believed to be in far greater peril from temptations and solicitations than women of the same class. Innocence in women was assumed to be its own best protection and of course men were often obliged to go into 'social spaces' where women of their own class would never have intruded. Night-time streets, for example, had a sufficient reputation to condemn any young woman who might be found out upon them unchaperoned. The existence of prostitution is in itself a statement about assumed male sexual needs. There were, however, considerable arguments during and after the Victorian era that streets needed to be kept free of prostitutes for the sake of the young male. It has been suggested that nobody thought the worse of men resorting to prostitutes, but this fear of laying temptation in the way of young men suggests that this was not altogether the case.

In England prostitution was not illegal and there was no police of morals such as existed in the regulationist states on the continent. Many lower-class women drifted in and out of prostitution for economic reasons. One of the horrors of the Contagious Diseases Acts for poor women was that under them they risked being permanently labelled as prostitutes.[31] Except in the towns designated under the Acts and for their duration, women who came into contact with the law for offences to do with prostitution were in fact arrested under laws relating to disorderly conduct and the causing of nuisance which were theoretically of universal application. The prostitute conducting her trade with discretion was far more likely to be arrested than a man blatantly making himself offensive to female passers-by. Scarcely more than a hundred or so men were charged with accosting women to their annoyance in the course of two or three years, but '6000 unfortunate women are arrested every year for alleged annoyance of men.'[32] It is far harder to reconstruct the historical existence of the prostitute in British society than in continental regulationist societies.

Even harder is the attempt to reconstruct the prostitute's customer. Commentators have suggested that during the nineteenth century it was regarded as acceptable and inevitable for all men to patronize prostitutes, and that this was so trivial an occurrence that it was strongly believed that it should not be penalized. Perhaps too much reliance has been placed upon the pronouncements of upper-class legislators and high-court judges, where class bias combined with gender prejudice to designate fourteen-year-old working-class girls as 'harpies' preying on the naive Oxbridge sons of privilege. During Parliamentary debates on the Criminal Law Amendment Act of 1885 concerning the raising of the age of consent, most MPs did not think that it should be criminal to have intercourse with a girl of fourteen. While the public were concerned about this issue, their legislators were not, fearing rather that the Bill would 'jeopardise masculine liberties for the sake of protecting slum girls who were already corrupted by their environment'.[33] During debates on the Criminal Law Amendment (White Slave Traffic) Bill of 1912, great horror was expressed at the notion of making male importuning a criminal offence. The young prostitute was described as a temptress leading young men into mischief.[34] There was a great outcry in favour of instituting flogging as a punishment for 'bullies' living off prostitutes' earnings. Receiving money from a prostitute was a far worse offence than purchasing her sexual favours. Similar attitudes recurred yet again in House of Lords Debates on the Criminal Law Amendment Bill of 1920. Lord Dawson expressed the opinion that young men up to the age of twenty-five were powerless against the 'allurements' of girls under seventeen.[35]

There were fears that these dreadful designing harpies would 'trump up' stories in order to blackmail young men and boys. If fornication was assumed to be a physiological necessity one would have imagined that no grounds for fears of blackmail would have existed (unless the fear was of that other great male paranoid anxiety, the spurious accusation of rape?). Sufficient stigma attached to the activity for men who had been robbed in the course of a transaction with a prostitute to be sometimes reluctant to press charges.

Literature describing continental attitudes indicated that the first dose of gonorrhoea was regarded as a young man's rite of passage.[36] British medical literature did not reflect any such insouciant acceptance of the need to 'sow wild oats'. Indeed, the rhetoric about lower-class female temptresses might be taken to imply that their 'victims' were innocent young men devoted to the pursuit of chastity until irresistibly solicited. However, although it was rarely explicitly stated that men required sexual outlets and that prostitutes were necessary for this purpose, the 'wild oats' doctrine was 'tacitly given and accepted...winked at or jestingly repudiated':[37] something which it is very hard to calibrate from published sources.

Differences between British and continental practices were recorded by an American, Abraham Flexner, in his survey of *Prostitution in Europe* during the early years of the twentieth century. While they may indicate nothing more than a greater furtiveness and subterfuge indicative of traditional British hypocrisy in matters sexual, it would certainly seem that by the early 1900s prostitution in Britain was less blatant than in the European cities, where, although regulated, it was also exceedingly prevalent in clandestine forms. Flexner was inclined to believe that the state of London had greatly improved as a result of the trend of public opinion against overt manifestations of prostitution. He quoted the social purity reformer W. A. Coote, who described London at the time of writing as 'an open-air cathedral' compared with forty years previously. Flexner, while finding London by no means perfect from the moral point of view, contrasted it favourably with continental cities where regulation was in force.[38]

The prevalent assumption was that if men committed fornication, they indulged with prostitutes and not with nice girls of their own class – so prevalent that in the works of sex-education emerging in the early years of the twentieth century, girls were warned about provocative dress and behaviour not because of the danger these presented to the preservation of their own virtue, but because they might so inflame their men friends that the latter would be driven into the arms of prostitutes.[39]

The place of prostitution in a young man's education in sex and as a preparation for marriage was deplored by writers on sex quite separately from the issue of disease. Havelock Ellis wrote in *Sex in Relation to Society* (1910):

> The training and experience which a man receives from a prostitute, even under fairly favourable conditions, scarcely form the right preparation for approaching a woman of his own class who has no intimate erotic experiences.

He suggested that there were two opposite extremes of behaviour which might result; the man might treat his bride as a prostitute herself, or else with exaggerated respect.[40] Marie Stopes expressed similar opinions in *Married Love*, quoting August Forel's remark that men looking among prostitutes for a key to the sexual psychology of women found 'only their own mirror'.[41] The differentiation many men perceived between wives and prostitutes was summed up by one man, of middle years and not lacking in premarital experience, writing to Stopes:

> But for your advice I should not have hazarded preliminaries for fear of shocking my wife and giving her the feeling that I was treating her as a mistress.[42]

The question of the prostitute and her public visibility was thrown into glaring prominence by the advent of the First World War. Some authorities regarded the prostitute as a necessary comcomitant of combat. In some theatres of war, licensed brothels in which the women were regularly inspected were set up to provide for this military necessity. *The Shield* suggested that men soon came to find the atmosphere in these establishments 'too sordid, and the transaction too mechanical and degrading for men to tolerate long'. In the brothel near the convalescent camp near Cayeux-sur-mer, Somme, fifteen women were visited by 360 men per day. This figure gives credence to *The Shield*'s view, and it is not surprising that the women in these establishments were 'horribly brutalised in manner and appearance'. Rather than the degradation of the circumstances leading the men to eschew sexual indulgence altogether, however, the implicit permission conceded by these provisions encouraged the men to seek the same indulgence in more aesthetic circumstances, with prostitutes who were not subject to any form of regular medical examination and licensing.[43]

Such expedients took place, if not at the Front itself, in areas dominated by the military, in foreign countries. Far greater anxiety was generated well beyond the pages of social hygiene journals by the efflorescence of visible prostitution in Britain itself. The Dominions troops passing through London and other cities had never, it was said, encountered such open vice in their lives. Anxiety was expressed about the impact this would have on the families at home who learnt of the moral danger into which their boys had been plunged. Young men, the pick of colonial manhood and prepared to fight in the war to end wars, were apparently wholly impotent in the face of female blandishments. Alison Neilans of the Association for Social and Moral Hygiene inferred that 'most of the men who have come from far and wide to protect the Empire are totally incapable of protecting themselves from the solicitations of women and girls.' They were exculpated from any blame for these mercenary encounters by the continuing assumption that 'when a woman solicits a man it is depravity, but when a man yields to the solicitation it is merely human nature.'[44]

A new problem emerging during the First World War was that of the 'amateur', the young woman who was free with sexual favours not necessarily for financial reward but in repayment for being taken out and given presents, or simply for fun. This undermined arguments about the control of venereal disease by controlling overt prostitution. The preference for women who at least appeared not of the prostitute class was even attributed to the campaign against venereal disease, with its emphasis on the dangers of consorting with prostitutes.[45] Men were apparently reluctant to employ prophylaxis against venereal disease, when indulging with a casual but non-professional partner, 'as conveying a doubt as to the ladies' chastity or at least immaculateness'. It became 'almost a point of honour not to use the preventive appliance'.[46]

However deplorable, these often transient sexual relationships of a non-pecuniary nature were, many felt, on a higher moral level than the resort to prostitutes, though some decried this development as involving a lowering of women to the moral standard of men, rather than the raising of the latter to the former. There was a feeling abroad that the fastidious man would prefer not to indulge in a crude financial transaction, which indeed would tend to reflect badly on his ability to obtain gratuitous female companionship. This significant social change, which had begun taking place by the end of the First World War, may have existed rather less as an actual phenomenon than as a myth, but would point to a growing public sense of the lack of acceptability of male resort to prostitutes, irrespective of any legal changes. Sir Arthur Newsholme, considering the declining rate of syphilis, thought it probable that 'prostitution is decreasing, while more stable irregular unions are partially taking their place', or at least that it was not 'improbable that there has been actual decrease in sexual irregularities, in some measure at least'.[47]

There is some evidence about male attitudes towards prostitution, presumably formed during the early years of the century, among the correspondence received by Marie Stopes. Her correspondents manifested considerable honesty in writing to her about the less acceptable facets of sexual behaviour, in spite of the ideal of chaste monogamy expressed in her works. Some men actually described premarital sexual relations with prostitutes:

> When I was at the University at home I used occasionally to go with prostitutes.

> I first had sexual intercourse when I was not quite 22, a harlot, but the amount of 'life' it put into me I cannot explain.

> I had union with several prostitutes in Montreal about 3 years ago.[48]

Other men, though not explicit about the status of their partners in sin, described having had a 'wild life' or leading a 'bachelor life'[49] or having led a promiscuous life. Others again told of having had liaisons with 'girlfriends', even '[?married] women of intelligence and imagination'.[50] Some of them seemed to have regarded a certain amount of sexual activity as a normal course for the male: 'I have had the usual sexual history of men'; 'I am 31 and have led a fairly normal and I suppose promiscuous bachelor existence.'[51]

Others remarked that they had not 'indulged in "bought love" as you term it' or ever 'been with a prostitute'. Some were explicit in their revulsion from prostitution as an acceptable outlet for male passions:

The idea of going to prostitutes was always repugnant to my ideas because I could not bring myself to the idea of sleeping with a girl whom I did not love and who did not love me.

I have never had any physical connection with any female I would never think of such a thing outside marriage.

This was so even when they knew this was a commonly accepted expedient: 'of course the usual advice is to seek the prostitute but I do not want to do that.'[52] Reasons for refraining were not necessarily idealistic, given the increasing awareness of the dangers to health involved: 'I most sincerely hope to enter the married state clean and free from all the usual diseases.' One man admitted that he had 'never had union with a woman, being always somewhat afraid of the experience'.[53] Among the men who wrote these letters there was neither clear and outright support for the double standard nor a universal shrinking from the ideology of manhood which it represented.

The decline in professional prostitution and the rise of the 'amateur' continued. With the rise of new, commercialized recreational activities such as the cinema and dance-halls, there were far greater opportunities for young people in particular to meet one another in a casual and unsupervised way. Pubs were becoming less of an exclusively masculine purlieu and the development of roadhouses and cocktail bars were part of the emergence of leisure spaces into which women could enter without automatic stigma. With increasing employment of women, and fewer of them employed as living-in domestic help with the restrictions that entailed, they had the money and the opportunity to attend places of entertainment, and less economic motivation to take up prostitution as a career.[54] They might trade off their favours for pleasures they could not afford themselves, but they did not need to use them to earn a living.

'Prostitution...becomes promiscuity' was certainly the perception of venereologists, from their experiences in the clinics set up as a result of the Royal Commission's recommendations. Some of their evidence for this would appear to be anecdotal. One considered, in 1928, that chancroid, which he considered particularly closely connected to professional prostitution, was dying out, while gonorrhoea and syphilis were taking its place.[55] Another, in suggesting that men were very seldom truthful concerning the status of their partners, declared that 'young men tend to deny having had anything to do with a prostitute, regarding it as a slight on their attractions that it be thought that they had to pay for what they wanted', while older men who had been 'brought up to regard prostitutes as the only "fair game"' would state that their partner had been one, 'though in fact she may turn out later to have been his housekeeper or an old acquaintance'.[56] There was a perception that male pride had become invested in not having to pay for sexual favours, and that to do this was a disgrace. During the Second World War 'many men who for ethical, aesthetic, or other reasons, would not approach a prostitute' would 'willingly expose themselves to risk with a "girl-friend"'. Soldiers who had 'walked out' with a casually met girl for a few weeks would have unprotected intercourse in the belief that 'she must have withstood indefinitely the overtures of all their predecessors.'[57]

The double standard still lingered. *The Shield* continued to point out the weight of inequitable responsibility laid on young girls in court cases involving intercourse with under-age girls (since 1922 'reasonable cause' to believe the girl over 16 had been accepted as a sufficient defence).[58] Regulations for the control of venereal diseases apparently applying to both sexes fell more heavily on women: habitual infectors were usually perceived as either professional prostitutes or the 'vicious female amateur'.[59] Men were certainly not innocent victims in sexual transactions; Tyneside almoners and social workers pointed out the disproportionate numbers of referrals to contacts which involved certain pubs known to be 'picking-up' places. Not all of the men involved were as discriminating about casual partners as some of the rhetoric might suggest; a considerable proportion seen in one Tyneside clinic had been too drunk on the occasion of infection to remember anything at all about their partner.[60] While there might have been some truth in *The Shield*'s 1938 contention that 'men's morals are better; they are more responsible and their relations with women are less sordid than in the old days',[61] and that 'crude prostitution is falling into disuse in the better walks of life',[62] prostitution was still rife.

There was a developing interest in the type of person who contracted venereal disease: by the later 1940s this was seen, at least in professional journals, as someone who was neurotic or inadequate rather than sinful or unfortunate.[63] The venereal disease rate in a military unit, it was alleged, was an accurate register of its morale, high morale being correlated with few cases of VD.[64] Not all experts agreed, however: in a discussion on 'The Psychological Aspects of Venereal Disease' a number of venereologists argued in old-fashioned style that 'fighting soldiers of the finest type', 'fine physical specimens', 'magnificent specimen[s]' contracted these diseases, either because promiscuity was 'an entirely natural reaction, especially under conditions of soldiering' or because these splendid creatures were 'subjected to more temptations than the ordinary soldier'.[65]

This new psychological approach still failed to answer certain questions to do with the male market for prostitutes. It continues to be unclear to what extent resort to commercial sex was habitual or occasional or even a one-off event, or how many potential clients were unmarried, married or in some occupation involving travel, and how these factors varied in different eras.

It is also hard to determine how much of the anxiety about the 'amateur' was really to do with premarital sex between young men and girls whom they intended, ultimately, to marry, in a changing social climate in which family and community controls over courting couples were no longer so powerful. 'Promiscuity' may have been the perception of an older generation or a different social class of what the participants themselves would have deemed courtship. Restrictions upon access to the Registrar-General's records make it impossible to determine the numbers of premarital conceptions in couples who got married prior to the birth of the child, which would provide some clue to the frequency of premarital intercourse.

Promiscuity rather than the prostitute was perceived as the danger by the 1950s. Sex-education literature warned against 'careless sexual relations' and the 'rather fast girl' who let herself be picked up, while prostitution might not even be mentioned.[66] This hussy was, however, still regarded as a danger and a temptation to (?innocent) young men.

'Advertising imposters who publish books full of *secrets*'[67]

It was not only the activity of the direct market for sex in public areas which was perceived as a menace to the young man. The streets held other perils. *The Lancet* and the *British Medical Journal* fulminated at recurrent intervals during the later nineteenth century against the purveyors of quack pamphlets and remedies, who were preying on prevalent fears about sexual weakness and anxieties about sexual functioning.[68] The ever greater role of advertisement and the growing protests against it reflected an increasingly literate society; literacy was becoming widespread in Britain even before the 1870 Education Act made school attendance compulsory.[69]

Professional rivalry was involved in the medical diatribes, as can be seen in the tone of the praise which accrued to Acton. For example, in 1857 *The Lancet* averred in a review of the first edition of *Functions and Disorders of the Reproductive Organs* that

> The only way by which some of the most important functional ailments affecting humanity can be rescued from the grasp of the most disgusting and villainous quackery, and treated with benefit to the patient, is by the scientific and conscientious practitioner *openly* taking them under his own charge.[70]

The theme was reiterated in the 1862 review of the third edition: 'That the entire practice relating to what are called "secret diseases" should be wrested from the hands of quacks is most desirable.'[71]

A great deal of paper was being devoted to profitable works stirring up this anxiety; fears of sexual debility were a steady source of income. The quacks were well aware of the existence of the anxieties on which they preyed, and had a more realistic perception, perhaps, than the profession had of the sexual problems, real or imagined, of the man in the street. They knew what would sell and were prepared to drum up trade. Even when the medical profession was exhorted to give counsel to the sexually distressed,[72] there was of course no suggestion that they should make this service widely known. Lacking belief that such problems would be sympathetically dealt with by a regular doctor, patients continued to turn to quacks.

The category of 'quack' was a very loose one and had more to do with marketing than content. It was presumably this which led to the downfall of Samuel La'mert, author of *Self-Preservation: A Medical Treatise on Nervous and Physical Debility, Spermatorrhœa, Impotence and Sterility, with Practical Observations on the Use of the Microscope in the Treatment of Diseases of the Generative System*, which went into numerous editions during the 1850s and 1860s. This work, which bears all the stigmata of a work of quackery, was in fact the production of someone entitled to refer to himself quite legitimately as a doctor,[73] until being struck off the register for, among other things, publishing *Self-Preservation*, described in court as 'an indecent and unprofessional treatise' during a test-case of the power of the General Medical Council to police the profession.[74]

But what La'mert actually said differed very little from Acton's message. La'mert emphasized the dangers of sexual indulgence. He made the following appeal:

> Let moderation in the enjoyment of the highest physical pleasure be
> the motto of the married as well as of the single. The most powerful
> and healthy body with which man was ever blessed, could not sustain
> without permanent damage, more than a very prudent and well-
> regulated amount of intercourse,[75]

warning, just like Acton, of the perils of overindulgence in these
heady pleasures in the intoxicating days of early wedlock. These
were just as dangerous, he alleged, as the accepted perils of self-
abuse and spermatorrhoea, against which he also cautioned.

What made *Self-Preservation* obscene, one must conclude, was that
it was on sale at a low price to the general public, rather than being
a learned treatise intended for consumption by the profession alone.
It was self-published, and at the end La'mert printed numerous
testimonials from those who had undergone treatment at his Bed-
ford Square consulting room, with advertisements for it (he preferred that patients visited him in person but was prepared to advise
by post). La'mert was quite overtly trying to make money out of his
project; while it is probable that Acton's reputation in the field
gained him patients, he was not blatantly commercial about it and
proceeded in such a way as to gain the support rather than the
vilification of his colleagues.

Besides doctors who were insufficiently discreet about their professional interest in sexual difficulties, there were also those who
were not, perhaps, predominantly, or at least solely, motivated by
commercialism. The proponents of alternative systems of health
care, often of what would now be described as a holistic nature, also
took an interest in sexual disorders, their cause and their cure.
Phrenologists, homeopaths, hydropathists, herbalists: all of these
had remedies to promote, and were concerned about the same
things as the medical profession and outrightly commercially motivated quack writers. It was a rare voice that proclaimed masturbation innocuous or spermatorrhoea a factitious ailment. The writers
were more likely to suggest that the latter could be an unsuspected
cause of ill-health even in the absence of symptoms (uncontrollable
involuntary seminal emissions) apparent to the sufferer.

The prolific American phrenological writer O. S. Fowler, while
promoting the importance of mutual conjugal delight, was as fero-
cious as any on the problem of self-abuse: 'masturbation outrages
Nature's ordinances more than any or all the other forms of sexual
sin man can perpetuate.' It was a positive plague and 'millions' were
'ruined by it before they enter their teens'.[76] T. L. Nichols, an

American hydropathic practitioner latterly settled in the UK, was one of the most stringent of writers on sex, in spite of his 'free-love' associations. In his popular work *Esoteric Anthropology*, conjugal sex was declared to be permissible only for reproductive purposes, although it was also to be mutually pleasurable to both parties. From the 'abuse of amativeness' (masturbation)

> the skin becomes dry and withered; the eye dull; the mind weak and disordered; all noble feelings lose their force; the whole system falls into weakness and disorder; and then comes spinal disease, palsy, or some form of consumption.[77]

Remedies prescribed by the Victorian medical profession for self-abuse and spermatorrhoea are supposed to have been brutal in the extreme, and perhaps encouraging sufferers to seek out alternative cures. *The Lancet*, in 1870, recommended in cases of sexual debilitation that

> it is necessary to guard the penis for a time against improper manipulation. This is best done by keeping up slight soreness of the body of the organ, either by blistering liquid or tissue, tartar-emetic ointment, nitrate of silver, or any other suitable application. The soreness should be sufficient to render erection painful.[78]

Cauterization might be generally recommended for 'over-sensitivity' of the organ. Treatments to render erection uncomfortable were not solely the province of the orthodox profession. The 'American Remedy', attacked in *The Lancet* in 1857 under the heading 'The Spermatorrhœa Imposture', 'consisted of a ring of common metal, with a screw passing through one of its sides, and projecting into the centre, where it had a button extremity. This was to be applied to the "part affected" at bed-time.' It was purchased and applied by a patient who 'stated that he had been suffering from some time past from spermatorrhœa' and 'that he had been undergoing the treatment of various advertisers', of which this device was the 'last expedient', which 'had been recommended to him as an infallible cure'. From his account of these recommendations it was 'probable that it has been extensively used'.[79] Anti-masturbatory devices were not always imposed, as sensational discussions suggest, by doctors upon victimized patients. The horror was widespread in popular belief, applying not merely to deliberate self-abuse but to involuntary seminal emissions as well. Such stringent remedies, savouring of the punitive, may even have been particularly acceptable to sufferers racked by guilt and shame.

A major objection by the medical profession was the accessibility of 'quack' works to anyone who had sixpence or so to spend on them. Sometimes even the few pence were not required. Quacks displayed considerable persistence in drumming up custom, and their pamphlets, intended to convince the reader that he was suffering from the ailment the advertiser purported to cure, were not merely free but hard to avoid. It was said in 1929 that 'any youth walking in a London street some thirty years ago ran the risk of having thrust into his hand a pamphlet describing the terrible results of "solitary vice" and urging him to seek treatment from some pernicious quack.'[80] In 1885 it had been remarked that there were 'few capitals where more temptation and more indecency of literature are permitted in the streets than in this metropolis.'[81]

'Handbills, pamphlets and advertisements' would have been hard to escape, given this aggressive marketing technique. Their dissemination often met curiosity and a desire for enlightenment. The *British Medical Journal* in 1885 answered the question 'why do the young so often regard an obscene work or print with such fearful but such irresistible curiosity?' with a suggestion that it was 'not from mere depravity' but in an unconscious search for 'information which they have a right to possess'. It was a 'most unfortunate effect' of 'mistaken methods of secrecy'.[82] Quacks played upon the understandable curiosity of the young in order to encourage their own trade.

A device used by quacks, and playing upon this curiosity as much as upon more prurient interest, was the 'anatomical museum'. These displayed such exhibits as 'models of genitalia and other parts of the body alleged to show the signs of Venereal Disease' of a 'grossly exaggerated and inaccurate' nature alongside depictions of the dangers of self-abuse. For example, 'face of an old bachelor; a confirmed onanist. He became idiotic and rapidly sank into second childhood' was juxtaposed with 'face of a man shewing the evil effects of secondary symptoms of syphilis' and 'twenty models of the human face...showing secondary symptoms of syphilis and gonorrhoea' with 'onanism in man, showing its dreadful effect on the organ of generation'. These images were mingled with representations of operations, horrifying examples of childbirth and monstrosities, and must have created very gruesome associations with sex.[83] Peter Sutcliffe, the 'Yorkshire Ripper', is reported to have returned obsessively to a surviving specimen of such a museum in Morecambe.[84]

Such museums were run as a 'come-on' and a front by publishers of quack pamphlets and purveyors of spurious remedies for factitious ailments. In 1879, during a trial subsequent to the confiscation of certain obscene quack pamphlets at the instigation of the Society for the Suppression of Vice, the defendants were 'only hired servants of the principal offender, the proprietor of a notorious museum'. This museum was described as 'for twenty-five years a disgrace and scandal to the metropolis' before being closed down by the efforts of the aforementioned society. 'A similar so-called museum, kept by an individual who called himself "Dr Hunter", in one of our largest provincial towns' had also been the target of the society's activities.[85]

Besides the street devices of the quacks, there were other means by which they intruded even into homes: they advertised widely in newspapers. These were not only the lower sort of periodicals but included 'religious newspapers, daily evening papers of high class and aim, cheap and highly popular social journals' that accepted advertising material of which 'the mischievous pretences are transparent or very thinly veiled.'[86] In contradistinction to plaints about quacks and corruption in the streets, which would seem to continue a long tradition of seeing the city as a haven for corruption and vice, newspaper advertisements were seen as being particularly pernicious in the provinces and in rural areas. A letter to the editor of *The Lancet* in 1870 enclosed a country newspaper containing specimens of advertisements of 'a most objectionable character' and propounded the theory that 'it is from the remote country districts that the advertising quack draws his best hauls', suggesting that 'Londoners as a rule know to whom and where to go.' An editorial comment would seem to substantiate this claim about the greater sophistication of city slickers: 'in London their game is wellnigh played out.'[87] 'Country newspapers' were indicted once more over thirty years later by T. S. Clouston in *Clinical Lectures on Mental Diseases*, in the chapter on 'The Insanity of Masturbation'. Of these, Clouston wrote

> those shameful quack advertisements put into the country news-
> papers...aggravate the miseries of those who are suffering from the
> minor effects of this vice by keeping them constantly before their
> minds; they suggest evil thoughts to those who might be free from
> them, and they fatten the vilest of mankind.

He believed these scaremongering advertisements to be as potent a cause of insanity as (though no greater than) masturbation itself.[88]

These advertisements made their pitch to 'the weak, nervous and debilitated', sufferers from 'nervous weakness, loss of strength and energy'. They offered 'health, strength and vigour restored in four weeks', 'a simple means of self-cure', 'strong men made from weaklings', 'weak men made strong'. They spoke of 'Strength: How lost, how regained' (with a picture of a lion). In almost all cases they offered as a come-on a pamphlet free for the sending: 'write for the book today, it is free'; 'an interesting book for young men...sent free on application'; 'drop us a line and we will forward our treasure-book'; 'Free Book! send us the following coupon and let us post our Illustrated Book to you...It contains 96 pages of good reading and sound advice.'[89] Such promises were to be found in the Australian press around 1907, and similar inducements and enticements were held out by British advertisers, with invitations to 'write for book on lack of vigour variocele and all urinary complaints', as well as 'Treatment that cures. Exhaustion, lost energy, variocele and premature decay', and advice on

How to preserve strength and retain the powers
To the inexperienced. The married or those contemplating marriage.
No other work contains so much helpful or sensible advice.[90]

A typical example of one of these pamphlets identified

with diabolical ingenuity the ordinary and frequent symptoms of 'lassitude', 'debility', 'loss of memory', 'low spirits' etc, especially common in adolescents and nervous dyspeptic or hypochondriac young men, with serious maladies and personal faults of conduct or habit. They fill the minds of such readers with dire despondency and erroneous fears, and by describing what are often physiological phenomena incidental to adolescence as evidences of deep-seated mischief, fraught with peril to mind and body, they thus make confirmed invalids and hopeless patients of those who only need a little sound lecturing or gentle remonstrance, or cheery reassurance.

This 1892 diatribe in the *British Medical Journal* was inspired by the suicide of a 21-year old butcher of Westminster, who had had a 'varied selection' of pamphlets of which it was said at the inquest that 'a young man reading them might think he was suffering from every disease imaginable.' It was suggested that 'no doubt the deceased had worried himself by reading the pamphlets.' Besides suicides, the *British Medical Journal* also blamed such publications for countless cases of protracted misery, alarm and depression from mental anxiety amongst young men of less educated and wealthy classes at a time of life and under circumstances when such suffering greatly prejudices their careers.[91]

In the absence of more openly circulated and less commercially motivated information about sex, young men might be readily persuaded to send for the gratuitous pamphlets so generously offered by advertisers, even without these being thrust into their hands in the streets.

Quack literature had a ready-made market in the growing numbers of single men living on their own in cities and towns apart from their families or traditional communities, tending to marry late for economic reasons but with enough disposable income to be worth exploiting. They doubtless had pre-existing anxieties about sex and the associated dangers of ill-health, but these businessmen had a vested interest in defining normal physiological phenomena as pathological and in diffusing a miasma of fear, shame and anxiety around sexual functioning. However dreadful, punitive, judgemental and horror-mongering much social purity and medical literature were in the later nineteenth and earlier twentieth centuries, were they anything like as formative of pernicious attitudes as this widely disseminated commercial literature?

Quack literature and the anxieties around male sexuality upon which it battened did not disappear during the twentieth century in spite of changing social and economic conditions. The Mass Observation 'Sex Survey' of the late 1940s commented upon

the advertisements in sex interest periodicals...aimed at a market anxious about their loss of 'youthful vigour'...a glance through almost any of the current sex interest magazines shows offers of literature on birth control, proferred cures for sexual difficulties and fears...and finally, the glandular advertisements.[92]

A quantity of material relating to proprietary medicine and tonics was accumulated during the course of the survey. Fears of loss of male vigour and the development of sexual debility had not vanished over a period of fifty or so years, although the means for treating it seem to have changed with changing fashions and ideas; by the 1940s 'glands' and 'hormones' were being touted as the remedy.[93]

The average man of the later nineteenth and earlier twentieth centuries, therefore, might well have picked up various kinds of sexual information and myth. He would not have needed to put himself to any great effort to obtain it; in fact he might have found it hard to avoid unless leading an exceptionally sheltered life. It would not have been easy for him to be totally unaware of notions to do with 'sexual debility and male weakness' and their apparent prevalence, or to be completely ignorant of the existence of prostitution. Double standard or not, sexual activity was prevalently constructed as a hazardous pursuit for the British male. If sometimes perceived as a necessity, it was seen as one which involved considerable risks.

3

'Most men act in ignorance': the marriage manual and changing concepts of marriage

'Not perceptibly injurious'

The Victorian public had no lack of works advising them on the conduct of their marital relations. There was always the perennial *Aristotle's Masterpiece*. If this strange little volume had more to say about generation and birth than actual copulation, it also spoke of the 'happy state of matrimony' and warned about 'errors in marriage', although the editions in circulation during the nineteenth century seem to have been expurgated of details found in versions of an earlier era.[1] Drysdale and the other Malthusians, in cheap works for the general public, wrote more about the prevention of the usual outcome of copulation than how it should be conducted.[2] The implication in these very different works was, however, that sex was an enjoyable and natural activity in which most couples would happily indulge as much as they could, if not for fear of innumerable offspring.

Writers of popular works on health often included chapters on the right conduct of sex. In *Creative and Sexual Science*, first published in 1870 and much reprinted, the prolific American phrenological writer O. S. Fowler promoted the importance of mutual conjugal delight, claiming that 'normal fulfilment' of the conjugal act carried with it 'a feeling of moral elevation, consecration and sanctity unequalled'. He informed readers that 'mutual participancy is Nature's Law.'[3] T. L. Nichols, an American hydropathic practitioner latterly settled in the UK, author of the popular work *Esoteric Anthropology*, was tainted with a 'free love' stigma,[4] although this work took an extremely stringent attitude towards conjugal sexual indulgence. The 1873 and subsequent British editions of *Esoteric Anthropology* omitted the condemnations of marriage and its abuse, and the free love rhetoric, of earlier American editions, but free love in Nichols's formulation had always had little or nothing of the carnal in it. For Nichols any sexual union without reciprocal love, inside or outside marriage, was prostitution.

According to Havelock Ellis, 'considered a respectable source of information on these secret subjects',[5] *Esoteric Anthropology* conceded that sexual intercourse should be a mutually pleasurable act. However, Nichols believed that many women in the corrupt state of modern life were incapable of sexual enjoyment, and were 'sometimes deeply injured in their nervous systems by the efforts of their husbands to make them participate in, and so heighten, their enjoyments'.[6] 'After fifty', men would find, 'sexual pleasures are very exhausting. They often bring on paralysis or apoplexy.'[7] Ideally, intercourse was to be indulged in solely for procreation. Nichols was more concerned to give hints for the maintenance of continence than the achievement of erotic pleasure, and he taught that 'every mode of prevention, other than living in chastity, is an evident violation of nature.'[8]

In works such as *Esoteric Anthropology* or *Creative and Sexual Science*, matters of sex and conjugality were discussed among other more general problems relating to health, in the context of a hydropathic or phrenological approach to human wellbeing. During the later nineteenth century, works appeared specifically and exclusively discussing problems of sex and marriage. Two examples of these were *Sexual Physiology and Hygiene* by R. T. Trall, MD, and *Confidential Talks with Husband and Wife* by L. B. Sperry, AM, MD, both of which originated, like Nichols's work, in the USA, were published in the UK and went into numerous editions well into the twentieth century. In their emphasis on the marriage relationship and its right conduct they could be regarded as the precursors of the marriage manual as it evolved during the 1920s.

Some themes could already be perceived emerging, such as the importance of the wedding night and the dangers that lay in wait there. Sperry warned

Many men also have found it one of the most delicate and important events in their own lives...Now is the time for the husband to show himself *a man*, instead of a selfish sensualist or a careless and ungovernable brute.[9]

Another theme was that sexual intercourse was an important part of the married relationship separate from any generative function, because 'an occasional sexual connection...unquestionably cultivates affectionate mutual regard and unselfish devotion', according to Sperry.[10] Trall agreed that 'normally exercised, no act of an intelligent being is more holy, more humanising, more ennobling.'[11]

The very Victorian problem of how much of this could be permitted taxed these writers: Sperry conceded that 'a moderate amount of sexual indulgence' was not 'perceptibly injurious to the normal husband or wife' but feared that it was 'difficult to determine the exact limits of moderation'.[12] Trall regretted that

Between love and lust it may not always be easy to draw the line of demarcation...With the great masses of the people the only rule of conduct is appetite, and this is to a great extent morbid.[13]

It was the husband who stood in greater need of restraint, for it was 'seldom that sexuality should be nursed or cultivated in a man', according to Sperry.[14] While Trall argued that 'married men are not always as sensual in character, nor as cruel in disposition, as they seem', he deprecated the fact that 'with many, sexual intercourse becomes a habit' which they indulged 'reckless and thoughtless of its consequences to themselves or to their wives'.[15]

While intercourse 'should be as agreeable as possible to both parties', it was not necessary 'to describe in detail the proper position for copulation, or the exact methods of procedure in exercising the sexual function'.[16] While adumbrating a new ideology of marriage relations, these writers still forbore to give any exact physiological instructions for rendering the act mutually pleasurable. Providing that the couple were in good health and not vitiated by the corruptions of modern life, and the act was not abused or perverted, it would naturally be agreeable to both. Warnings were reiterated against excess and sexual gluttony, citing their injurious effects. Such warnings were connected to the constant cautions to the husband against abusing his wife and injuring her health through selfishness and overindulgence.[17]

Such ideas were in wide circulation. *Nature's Revelations for the*

Married Only, issued by the Electric Life Invigorator Company around 1904, price one shilling, to advertise its products, included exhortations to 'moderate desire and act with self-control, temperance, and virtuous judgement'. It warned against 'violence or indecent haste', and declared that 'NO MAN IS JUSTIFIED, in the eyes of nature or grace, who commits a *rape* upon his wife under the cover and licence of marriage.' Marriage, it maintained, was constituted for progeny, not selfish pleasure. Intercourse, however, 'if not reciprocal must in a measure be demoralising and unhealthy', and simultaneous orgasm was desirable.[18]

'Any effort demanded is amply justified'

The concept of conjugal love as an art which required to be learnt had to wait for Havelock Ellis. He promoted this ideal not only in *Sex in Relation to Society*, in which he devoted a whole chapter to the topic, but in his pamphlets produced under the auspices of the British Society for the Study of Sex Psychology. These three pamphlets constituted almost a programme in themselves for a new and higher ideal of marriage: they were entitled *The Objects of Marriage*, *The Erotic Rights of Women* (both 1918) and *The Play-Function of Sex* (1921).[19]

It was not until Marie Stopes published *Married Love* in 1918 that such ideas obtained wide currency instead of being confined to a small group of the sexually progressive. The reasons for the success of *Married Love* are not hard to find. It is clear from the response of her readers that Stopes was writing in the right place at the right time, that she was attuned to the spirit of the age in her descriptions of what many couples were seeking in marriage and failing to achieve. *Married Love* had the particular advantage of being short, something that could be read in one evening, and got straight to the problems of human marital sexuality in western society without climbing the evolutionary ladder and covering the globe first. It also advocated, though without giving details (*Wise Parenthood* dealt more explicitly with the matter), the use of artificial birth control, a radical departure in books of this kind. Earlier works had made a token gesture to the need of some couples to restrict their families by recommending a safe period usually based on Mosaic Law and thus even less reliable than the present-day rhythm method ('Vatican roulette'). Stopes's message that sexual fulfilment for both partners was necessary to marriage, independently of reproduction, clearly struck profound chords in her readers, male and female. Above all *Married Love* was technically helpful in explaining what to do to obtain pleasure in the sexual act, although many men were devastated by her recommendation that twenty minutes of coitus was essential for their wives' full arousal and complete satisfaction.[20]

Stopes was not the only successful writer of sexual advice of the period. Numbers of works followed *Married Love* in providing the sexual advice which so many readers sought. So many books on the object were published, some of them exceedingly ephemeral, that it is impossible to discuss them all. A representative sample has therefore been chosen of books all of which had a considerable following, went into several editions and continued to be reissued over a period of many years.

Wise Wedlock: The Whole Truth: A Book of Counsel and Instruction for All who Seek for Happiness in Marriage (c. 1920) by 'Dr' G. Courtenay Beale[21] was alleged by Stopes to be more or less a plagiarism of her own work, and 'G. Courtenay Beale' a pseudonym concealing a syndicate.[22] Certainly no doctor of that name appears in the *Medical Register*. Passages in *Wise Wedlock* echoed the phraseology and general tenor of Stopes's work suspiciously closely. Nevertheless, a later edition of *Wise Wedlock* received the accolade of an introduction by Norman Haire, the Harley Street sexologist, who considered it 'one of the best, if not the best, of its kind available in English'.[23] It was still being reissued well into the 1940s.

'Beale's' medical status remains uncertain. Isabel Hutton was a woman doctor whose career in psychiatry had come to an abrupt end following her marriage to an army officer she had met while serving in the Balkans with the Scottish Women's Hospitals during the First World War. Although her husband was perfectly willing for her to pursue her career, most psychiatric appointments were in institutions operating a marriage bar against women doctors. For some years the couple had a semidetached marriage while he studied at the Army Staff College and she built up a practice in London.[24] In 1923 she took the daring step of publishing *The Hygiene of Marriage*,[25] under her own name. Her work, like Stopes's, evolved out of her own 'past ignorance and difficulties', as well as 'the questions patients had asked me throughout the years'.[26] Though never one of the most notorious works in this field, *The Hygiene of Marriage* enjoyed a certain modest success, being reprinted several times. She believed that it was 'the first of its kind to be written by a medical doctor', and intended it for recommendation to patients by her professional colleagues.[27]

Perhaps Stopes's major competitor in the field was Theo. Van de Velde, Dutch gynaecologist author of the famous *Ideal Marriage*.[28] This work, even though the sale of the earlier British editions was restricted to members of the medical profession,[29] was extremely and enduringly popular, being reissued regularly well into the 1960s, and a paperback edition appearing as late as 1984. According to E. M. Brecher, Van de Velde 'taught a generation how to copulate',[30] and in 1949 the British doctor Eustace Chesser wrote that *Ideal Marriage* was 'still handed to the enquiring husband as confidently as Mrs Beeton on Cookery has been passed to innumerable wives'.[31] If Stopes's works emerged from the sexual failure of her first marriage, Van de Velde's, ironically, appear to have originated in adultery. After ten years of childless marriage, this respectable Haarlem gynaecologist eloped with a married patient and spent several years living in sin with her abroad before he obtained a divorce. He then married his mistress, to whom *Ideal Marriage*, published thirteen years later, was dedicated.[32]

Ideal Marriage emphasized the necessity for mutual sexual pleasure in marriage, with instructions for achieving it, in overwhelming, even wearisome, erogenous detail. Its baroque complexities make the comparison with Mrs Beeton very pointed: it might be doubted how useful that work was to the beginning housekeeper, and Chesser evoked doubts as to the value of *Ideal Marriage* for the learner-lover. He claimed that 'nine readers out of ten have felt cheated' after studying Van de Velde's 'huge inventory of sexual pleasures, all of them carefully inscribed "normal"'.[33] These were embedded in pages of platitudinous aphorisms and dire pseudophilosophical wafflings about love, marriage, manhood, womanhood, etc. ('intermezzos', as Van de Velde called them), which may have reassured some readers about the work's high-minded credentials. There is a misogynist bias to *Ideal Marriage*, at least to the eyes of a modern reader: the 'liability to unpleasant odour' of the female genitals constituting a subheading within the chapter on female sexual physiology is one of the more flagrant examples. Why a feminist such as F. Stella Browne chose to translate it into English is obscure.

Helena Wright was a woman doctor who, after an early career as a medical missionary in China, returned to England and became involved in the birth control movement.[34] Her experiences at the North Kensington Women's Welfare Clinic, a birth control clinic independent of Marie Stopes's organization, led to the writing of her two short, lucid books *The Sex Factor in Marriage* (1930) and *More About the Sex Factor in Marriage* (1947).[35] Both works were much reprinted up to the 1960s, special editions being produced for the use of the National Marriage Guidance Council and the Family Planning Association. Most remarkable in her work was her continued emphasis on the importance of the clitoris in female arousal and satisfaction, throughout the period when many writers were insisting that the only 'right' orgasm was the vaginal and deprecating clitoral stimulation as immature.

A writer who tended to promulgate this belief was E. F. Griffith, in his work *Modern Marriage*, orginally *Modern Marriage and Birth Control*, first published by Victor Gollancz in 1935 and in print for nearly forty years, with some changes of publisher.[36] Griffith was a general practitioner who came to sex-advice through involvement with the establishment of birth control clinics and sex-education centres, and was a founder of the Marriage Guidance Council. He subsequently underwent a Jungian analysis and became himself a psychotherapist of that school.[37]

A. Havil's *The Technique of Sex: Towards a Better Understanding of the Sexual Relationship* (1939: 'the sale of this book is restricted to adult persons')[38] is still obtainable. His medical status is dubious and the name probably a pseudonym. The book is short and the title misleading, since only one chapter might be said to be particularly about technique: eleven pages on 'The Sex Act'. The rest of the book consists of brief summaries of information on the anatomy, physiology and psychology of sex, and chapters on pregnancy and labour, contraception, abortion, venereal disease, prostitution, impotence and sterility.

Eustace Chesser's chatty and exhortatory *Love without Fear* came out in 1941 and was reprinted four times in the ensuing eighteen months in spite of war stringencies. It went on being reissued well into the 1980s. As far as promoting *Love without Fear* went, Chesser was outspoken about the need for reliable methods of birth control, and gave information on getting advice. He created a climate of permission (for married couples) for the deliberate pursuit of sexual pleasure, for attention to foreplay, for experimenting with different positions. But this in itself became something of an imperative:

> Too many people let love's joys largely escape them. They are unwilling to make an effort to retain them. Any effort demanded is amply justified.[39]

He wrote prolifically on matters of sex and psychology during the 1950s and 1960s.

This whole new genre did not merely promote a new idea of the conjugal relationship; it presented a view of the average male which, if not wholly internally consistent, varied very little from book to book and from author to author.

'A man has to revise his whole outlook'

The image of the normal male delineated in these works was, like so much of their teaching, prefigured in the work of Havelock Ellis. The conceptualization of the problem of control over the insurgent force of male sexuality underwent a major shift. No longer was the problem seen as simply one of the 'supposed physiological needs of the husband'. Advice on the subject had been 'framed in the same spirit of exclusive attention to those needs as though the physiological needs of the evacuation of the bowels or of the bladder were in question'. In the new philosophy of conjugal relations, sexual needs were 'the needs of the two persons, of the husband and of the wife'.[40] Unfortunately the male was perceived as ill-fitted to fulfil his wife's sexual needs or even to appreciate what these were, if he believed they existed at all.

Ellis found it 'not easy to form a clear picture of the erotic life of the average man in our society'. The average man failed to realize the profounder possibilities of sexual congress because his ideas in the erotic sphere were reducible to two:

> (1) He wishes to prove that he is 'a man' and he experiences what seems to him the pride of virility in the successful attainment of that proof; (2) he finds in the same act the most satisfactory method of removing sexual tension and in the ensuing relief one of the chief pleasures of life.[41]

Deleterious as such an attitude was for the wife of such a man, it also provided the man himself with a very impoverished sexual life.

Men were depicted as, though ardent, clumsy and impetuous. The image first invoked by the French novelist Honoré de Balzac, of the orangutan trying to play the violin and becoming violently frustrated when he failed to produce music,[42] was constantly cited. Griffith characterized the average man as follows:

> He behaves so frequently like a bull in a china shop, and his conceit prevents him from seeing what a mess he has made of things...a man has to revise his whole outlook before he is in any way fitted to be a suitable mate.[43]

No longer was it simply a matter of control over the emission of the vital seminal fluid. Perhaps simplistically it could be said that the Victorian notion of continence and restraint from performing the sexual act changed to a concept of restraint within the act itself, with a new emphasis on the desirability of mutual pleasure. The male was supposed to contain his urges for as long as it took to arouse the female with foreplay, and then, subsequent to intromission, to continue the act for as long as it took for the elusive female orgasm to be achieved. 'A man may become a worthy lover only with patience, knowledge and practice', Helena Wright wrote, and it was 'necessary to have an atmosphere of peace and leisure; hurried love-making cannot be successful'.[44] One of the few dissenters from the emphasis on male self-control was 'Courtenay Beale', who asserted

> to hold up the climax, which in the nature of things would supervene with imperious force of its own accord, means the imposing of a severe and probably injurious strain upon the nerves and the emotions alike.[45]

On the whole, however, these works assumed that once a man was aware of the need to control the insurgent spontaneity of his own desires, he would be both willing and capable to do so.

Fears were still prevalent that, before a man came to marry, self-abuse might have vitiated his powers and rendered him unfit for marriage and fatherhood, even if it were no longer regarded as the cause of total physical mental and moral wreck. This new school, however, tended to see it not as something having profoundly serious effects on the entire organism but as something which might have set up deleterious patterns of sexual response:

> The sex organs are as susceptible to habit as any other part of the body, and they may become so accustomed to some particular method of self-relief that enjoyment of the normal sex-act may become difficult to establish.[46]

Whatever sex-education literature warning boys continued to allege (and more and more, as the period went on, it became reassuring), these works tended to console their readers that masturbation would not necessarily have unfitted them for marriage.

Male lack of control, impetuosity and clumsiness, were depicted as imperilling the marriage right from the wedding night, unless the man could put some kind of restraint upon himself. It was 'hopelessly wrong for the husband to regard the wedding night solely, or even primarily, as merely an occasion for his own sexual gratification'.[47] Men were warned of the 'fatal blunders...often committed and irreparable mischief done in the first night',[48] and cautioned that if they were 'not specially gentle and considerate in the early days of marriage' they risked endangering 'the happiness of the whole of...married life'.[49] At worst 'there have been not a few brides whom the horror of the first night of marriage with a man less considerate has driven to suicide or insanity.'[50] This wedding night carelessness was not necessarily the result of sheer malice or deliberate brutality. Stopes believed that 'the men who consciously sacrifice their wives are in a minority. Most men act in ignorance',[51] and Isabel Hutton remarked that it was 'very rare for a man to use force intentionally, but he may be too impetuous without realising it'.[52]

The general tenor of wedding night advice was in terms of cautions to the husband. His own anxieties, doubtless exacerbated by such warnings, were less often addressed: was there a fear of putting ideas of failure into men's minds? The image was of the rampant, impetuous male who needed to curb his insurgent desires if the marriage were not be wrecked from the outset. Few writers mentioned, as Isabel Hutton did, that

> Temporary inability to obtain erection, and so perform the marital functions, is of fairly frequent occurence in the early weeks of marriage. Few know that this may happen in perfectly normal and healthy men, and they are consequently very anxious and imagine that there is something seriously wrong...Many a man fears, long before the wedding ceremony, that he will not be able to consummate the marriage...A frequent cause of this trouble is that a man may be afraid of inflicting pain upon his bride.[53]

This view was borne out by the anxieties correspondents expressed to Marie Stopes. The likelihood of a disparity in the speed of male and female sexual reactions in the early days of wedlock was more often ventilated: 'inexperienced men find it difficult not to come to the climax too soon'; 'the inexperienced man has to ejaculate after very short "play".'[54]

Once this traumatic beginning had been safely passed, the couple had to aim for 'mutual adjustment'. The perfect sexual act was coitus culminating in mutual and simultaneous orgasm and 'no couple should be content until they have learnt how to experience orgasm together.'[55] In fact there was 'real harmony only when ejaculation and the woman's orgasm take place at the same time', but to reach this happy nirvana took 'time, patience, and understanding'.[56] This desirable outcome was not expected to occur naturally: it was the result of effort, study and striving; 'both partners should, in coitus, concentrate their full attention upon one thing: *the attainment of simultaneous orgasm.'*[57]

This belief in the sexual rights of women coexisted with continuing commitment to the idea that femininity was essentially passive and responsive rather than spontaneously desirous and active. Female desire was something which had to be carefully awoken and cultivated, laying the burden of ensuring happy conjugality squarely on the male. His desire was seen as much less fugitive and complex than that of his partner, as, 'providing he is really attracted', a healthy man did 'not need nearly so much stimulation as a woman to bring him to the point where he can satisfy his desires'.[58] In spite of all declarations concerning their tendency to thoughtless, selfish clumsiness, men were designated 'naturally educators and initiators of their wives in sexual matters'.[59] At least in the early days of marriage,

> the man is the initiator, the woman the willing recipient; the husband, understanding his wife's nature, has the joy of arousing her gradually, of creating in her an ardour equal to his own. A woman's body can be regarded as a musical instrument awaiting the hand of an artist. Clumsiness and discord will produce nothing but discord, knowledge and skill evoke responses of limitless beauty.[60]

Few writers dared mention that male arousal was anything but a given response, not needing any encouragement. Havil called impotence and sterility 'due to defects in the construction of the body, due to defects brought on by illness, or due to a lack of knowledge'.[61] This hardly covered the common functional disorders. Van de Velde, in particular, was uncharacteristically taciturn about male dysfunction. That male potency could sometimes fail or prove inadequate in normal circumstances was a matter ignored by the Dutch sexologist. He considered 'genuine impotence' to be 'distinctly morbid',[62] dealing only with the temporary impotence due to overexertion and fatigue. Premature ejaculation he barely alluded to at all: 'these cases are on the borderline of disease.'[63] There was little indication in Van de Velde's work that marital sexual failure could be due to anything but the remediable defects of the husband's erotic technique or stubborn frigidity on the wife's part: male sexual inadequacy was 'so serious and complex a condition' that its treatment was 'a matter for the medical specialist'.[64] While Stopes, in *Enduring Passion*, dealt with such subjects as 'The Under-Sexed Husband' and 'Premature Ejaculation',[65] it was only Isabel Hutton who went so far as to suggest that

> The wife must be ready to help her husband if his reactions are slow and if he be tired and unable to achieve erection easily. She must master the subject of love-play, and learn what helps sexual response in him.[66]

Although Stopes was prepared to take issue with problems of male dysfunction or disinclination, she did not recommend a more aggressive approach on the part of the wives.

Exhortations to wives laid more stress on an attitude of responsiveness than on activity: 'no amount of skill and tenderness on the husband's part can be successful unless the wife *is* willing to be aroused.'[67] The standard assumption was that 'initial advances are usually made by the man', although it was 'most misleading to suggest that the woman is merely a passive partner'. She had 'a good deal to contribute to the relationship at the right time...by kissing, by touch, and by active cooperation during coitus'.[68] But only once the delicate period of initiation and adjustment was over could a man even begin to hope for a little more reciprocity, or have any of the responsibility for managing the couple's sex-life taken from him. But, provided he had made no irreparable mistakes in the early years of marriage, the time might eventually come when it was, according to Helena Wright, 'the wife's turn to take the initiative', when she had 'opportunity to show her many-sided nature' and could 'woo her husband and charm him out of his fatigue'.[69]

Much of this new phase of writing about sex could be seen as replacing one set of anxieties with a new set. There was a new performance ethic, with emphasis on getting it right, in the right place (within monogamous marriage, with simultaneous orgasm). Increasingly, there was a differentiation between the right kind of female orgasm (the vaginal) and the wrong kind (the clitoral). Few writers were as practical and non-judgemental on this subject as Helena Wright:

> Theoretically it might be said that the ideal type of female sensation is concerned with the vagina alone, but that idea is seldom realised...

Many wives are unable to reach the climax because their husbands fail to realise that rhythmic friction of the clitoris is necessary right up to the end of the act.[70]

This dichotomy placed a heavy burden upon women, but it was hardly a congenial concept for the male. He too was likely to experience a sense of failure if unable to induce in his wife the more 'mature' satisfaction due to his own weaknesses, and he may well have been subject to intense performance anxiety on that account.

'Designed for people's comfort and happiness'

This new genre of sex-advice burst upon the scene when the very concept of marriage was undergoing re-evaluation. While differences between the sexes continued to be emphasized, there was the suggestion of a new egalitarianism within marriage. 'Companionate marriage', given a specific meaning by the American Judge Ben Lindsay as an agreed and not necessarily permanent, childfree liaison between 'consenting adults',[71] was often taken as a short-hand way of expressing this new ideal, in which partners in marriage were to be companions and comrades – a definite reaction against the 'Victorian' patriarchal household. Husbands and wives were to be lovers, the husband was encouraged to favour his wife's having interests beyond the home and to lend a hand in the domestic sphere. This was a philosophy found in works by religious writers, as well as lay and medical authors.[72] *The Threshold of Marriage* (1932), a specifically Christian manual for engaged couples, sold over half-a-million copies,[73] though many of these may have been to clergymen who had to prepare couples for marriage.

A new spirit among married couples can be seen in autobiographies. The domestic and conjugal arrangements of the Mitchison household or within the menage of Vera Brittain and George Caitlin, as they described them, may have been characteristic of 'advanced' artistic and bohemian circles, but a similar arrangement catering for the needs of both partners was set up by Dr Isabel Hutton and her army officer husband.[74] At a very different social level an army private wrote to Stopes in 1919 that he hoped to find in marriage a 'friend and wife and companion'.[75]

This was a period in which the conditions under which couples lived were changing, with domestic life becoming more central. Real incomes were increasing, families were growing smaller, more and more people were owning their own homes or living in rented accommodation of a better standard. Houses themselves were more agreeable and convenient, with electric light, gas and indoor plumbing becoming standard. Domestic appliances made housework easier and more efficient (carpets hoovered at least weekly rather than beaten every spring). The home was a nicer place to be. There were more recreations to enjoy in domesticity. The radio, gramophone, reading, were all home activities. Outside pursuits were also becoming less gender-differentiated: couples would visit the cinema together, for example, rather than the husband going to the pub while the wife stayed at home. The pub itself was becoming less of an exclusively male precinct, and statistics of drunkenness in all classes were declining. Sex was, perhaps, like the family car, one of the good things of life which the couple should share; and while the driver's seat was the husband's, the wife had increasing say over where they went and what for.

Couples were being thrown back upon each other's company to an increasing extent. Though extended family households were seldom to be found in Britain after the Industrial Revolution or even before, newly married couples would have been most likely to have found accommodation near their parental homes, within a close community. Following the First World War there was a period of considerable social mobility (geographical at least), as men in particular moved around the country in search of a job or to better the one they had. Cut off from neighbourhood networks, couples had each other rather than same-sex groups for company. The patterns of housing development, with the vast explosion of suburbia, also isolated couples. Their house might be their own (on a mortgage) rather than rented, but at the cost of a certain solitude. There was more pressure upon the nuclear couple, in a context of rising living standards.[76]

Symptomatic of changing feelings about marriage was the passing within the space of twenty years of two Acts extending and liberalizing the grounds for divorce. For well over half a century there had been no attempt to eradicate the major inequities of the 1857 Act, in spite of the Royal Commission on Divorce of 1909. The double standard had thus been enshrined in law, with a single act of adultery in the wife sufficient for divorce but only aggravated adultery (infidelity plus other matrimonial offences such as cruelty or incest) in a husband considered adequate grounds for dissolution of marriage. Divorce was also less accessible to the poor than the better-off. Nevertheless, the divorce rate tripled under the stresses of the First World War.[77]

The 1923 Act at last made simple adultery a marital crime for both spouses. It also enabled divorce cases to be heard in certain assize courts, instead of having to be taken before the Divorce Court in London, a condition which had added to the prohibitive expense.[78] In 1930 a Mr Athelstan Riley addressed the Church Assembly, describing this Act as 'cruel and wicked' because there was not and could not be 'equality in matters of sexual morality between men and women', but he appears to have been a lonely voice. By this time the Church of England was firmly committed to the doctrine of a single code of moral responsibility for both sexes.[79]

The defects of the revised law were satirically presented by A. P. Herbert in his novel *Holy Deadlock*. Because adultery was the only acceptable grounds for divorce, couples who wanted to dissolve their marriage had to commit adultery – or rather, one but not both of them had to.[80] Herbert sponsored the Matrimonial Causes Act of 1937, extending the grounds far more widely. Now both husbands and wives could obtain divorce on the grounds of adultery, cruelty, desertion for three years, insanity or imprisonment for over five years. Wives could also gain a divorce for rape, bestiality or sodomy. Grounds for nullity were also extended, to include not only non-consummation but being of unsound mind, epilepsy, venereal disease and pregnancy by another man.[81] Neither Act rejected the concept of matrimonial offence: a couple in which both parties were 'guilty' might not obtain a decree. It continued by no means easy to obtain a divorce, and having been involved in a divorce was still heavily stigmatized socially. Nevertheless, the number of causes for which a marriage could be dissolved suggests that there was in fact a higher standard of what a marriage ought to be.

Class differences in the divorce rate continued, and bigamy remained a working-class crime. There were undoubtedly class variations in the meaning of marriage throughout this period, though the evidence should be regarded somewhat critically. Much of the published writing on working-class marriage came from middle-class observers who found it easier to study and comment upon working-class habits and practices than those of their own class.

Male selfishness and crassness within this specific class context was the theme of several writers. M. Leonora Eyles in *The Woman in the Little House* depicted male lack of consideration in the sexual sphere as one of the greatest trials of poor working-class women. She claimed that five different women had told her 'I shouldn't mind married life so much if it wasn't for bed-time.' In a general context of sexual shame and ignorance it was more 'ignorance than unkindness' that led husbands to misuse their wives. Unfortunately the working man had 'theories, usually formed by and coincident with his desires'. From what the women told Eyles, 'the prevalent idea among men' was 'that continence is wrong', with the result that they made 'exercise of the sex function a nightly occurrence'. The men's attitude to birth control was 'that the use of preventives is bad for them.' Eyles argued that 'this continual pandering to an impulse robs it of thrill or pleasure' and turned 'what should be a feast into a dreary penance'.[82]

These remarks had a strong middle-class bias, exaggerating the failings of the working-class male. Most writers who mentioned any class dimension when discussing male sexual attitudes and behaviour proceeded, implicitly if not explicitly, on the basis of pre-conceptions about the greater effeteness of the middle-class male and the coarseness and brutality of his working-class counterpart. While, as a very crude generalization, Marie Stopes's correspondents from the lower social classes were more concerned about the prevention of unwanted pregnancy, and the more middle class with the quality of the marital relationship, this was in no way an absolute dichotomy. Within the birth-rate from 1870 onwards, which was declining overall, occupational and regional variations were as significant as or even more so than those between classes as such, with some 'working-class' groups restraining their fertility earlier and more effectively than some 'middle-class' groups. Within both middle and working classes in Britain there were wide variations in patterns of marriage and fertility. From the evidence of the Stopes letters, members of the middle class were also anxious about too many and too frequent pregnancies, while men and women of the working class too were concerned about the quality of their marital relationship.

The class-based assumptions, however, were common: the Viennese psychoanalyst Wilhelm Stekel (1868–1940), in his monumental work on *Impotence in the Male*, implied that the more intelligent, cultivated man, because of his higher ideals and aspirations in the sexual sphere, was more likely to suffer from dysfunction, and to worry about his sexual adequacy.[83] Marie Stopes, rightly or wrongly, believed that premature ejaculation as a problem was most prevalent among 'British men of the professional and upper classes'. While seldom a problem for manual workers, 'among Public School and University men it is one of the marital difficulties oftenest brought to my notice.'[84] Arthur Cooper, in *The Sexual Disabilities of Man* (1910), also assigned sexual problems 'fancied or real' to 'honourable men of high intellectual capacity and culture holding positions of responsibility and trust'.[85] The likely subject of sexual disorder was 'a young man perhaps highly educated and of more than average intellectual power'.[86] The class from which his patients were drawn can be deduced from his prescription in cases of wedding-night impotence: 'a single glass of good champagne taken shortly beforehand'.[87]

Male insensitivity was not solely a working-class attribute, and problems of sexual functioning not exclusively a bourgeois defect. Kinsey's evidence in his mammoth study of the sex-life of the American male would seem to bear this out, since he found extreme rapidity in attaining a sexual climax as prevalent, if not more so, among the lower classes as the middle classes. He suggested that the middle-class male took this perfectly normal reaction and turned it into a problem, while it was not perceived as such by the lower-class male.[88]

In the 1940s and early 1950s there were a number of British social surveys investigating marriage. A study of 200 families carried out between 1943 and 1946 by the psychiatrist Eliot Slater and psychiatric social worker and researcher Moya Woodside was published in 1951 as *Patterns of Marriage: A Study of Marriage Relationships in the Urban Working Classes*. While restricted by the method of selection (two groups, one of soldiers who succumbed to neurotic illness while in army service and another of soldiers hospitalized for non-neurotic ailments), Slater and Woodside believed their admittedly small sample to be fairly representative 'of Londoners of working and lower middle-class, married, and between the ages of twenty-two and forty-seven'.[89]

The Mass Observation organization, inspired by Kinsey's work in the USA, embarked upon a survey of attitudes to sex (rather than sexual behaviour itself), in the course of which over 3000 individuals were interviewed. The Mass Observation study included members of their Panel: individuals prepared to survey themselves rather than simply presenting themselves as the subject of others' studies, and to act as observers of social phenomena. However, while Mass Observation noted differences between the (predominantly middle-class) Panel and the general public whose views they sought on sexual attitudes, Mass Observation Panel members were probably in no way typical members of the middle classes.

Marriage, Mass Observation found, was regarded by 'the man in the street' as 'a purely mundane personal arrangement designed for people's comfort and happiness – an arrangement, however, which is easily capable of going wrong'.[90] Both Slater and Woodside and

Mass Observation found a certain complacency amongst men about sexual functioning and the state of marriage. In a preliminary article by Woodside on the survey, she concluded 'women suffer most', while the men found 'their sex lives satisfactory'. Any complaints were 'usually on the score of "coldness" or lack of interest of their partners'. In spite of the apparent level of male satisfaction, Woodside concluded that

> sexual maladjustment is widespread. Ignorance, far from ensuring bliss, has meant embarrassment, fear and misery. Men are lacking in the rudiments of erotic technique, and have been brought up to think that frankness in such matters is improper.

A 'middle-aged brewer's drayman' declared 'I respect my wife. I would never talk intimate to her', and a man of 38, seventeen years married, with five children, 'didn't know' if his wife enjoyed intercourse.[91]

This conclusion was expanded in *Patterns of Marriage*:

> Men seemed to be less troubled on the subject and took it much more for granted. Sexual adaptation was in fact far more successful...Time and again, things were said to be 'all right', and further enquiry was blocked.[92]

Mass Observation reached the similar conclusion that 'men appear to have experienced fewer troubles, on the surface at least', and they seemed

> to be more complacent about their lack of sex instruction; perhaps in any case street-corner bandying of sex facts is more open and casual amongst boys – or perhaps men are less willing to admit to sex doubts and difficulties.[93]

This latter view could be substantiated from the numbers of men who wrote to Marie Stopes reiterating how hard they would find it to tell their troubles to anyone else, how reluctant they were to consult doctors. However willing respondents to these surveys may have been to discuss their general attitudes, the face-to-face questionnaire method of the survey very probably deterred any discussion of personal fears and problems. Continuing male shyness and inhibitions around sex were noted by Dr Joan Malleson in a leaflet on 'Difficulties Commonly Encountered among Men', produced during the 1940s for the Family Planning Association:

It is not at all unusual to find an apparently normal man who is quite limited in what he feels to be 'proper' during sexual intercourse; this limitation will tend to lessen his own sexual satisfaction and also may lead him to misjudge seriously his wife's feelings and necessities.[94]

Apparent confidence might hide severe self-doubts.

E. L. Packer presented a grim picture of 'Aspects of Working-Class Marriage' in 1947:

The attitude of the man's rights and wifely duties is still encountered in many working-class marriages. Although in law a husband is not entitled to seize his rights by force in order to render him conjugal rights, in practice it frequently happens.

He claimed that 'children assume that sexual intercourse is forced on the woman by the man', and that copulation could become 'a weapon whereby the partners in the marriage can attack each other'. The example he gave of this hostile use cited turned on a husband who refused to practise withdrawal (his wife being in serious danger from further pregnancies) in the course of a matrimonial disagreement, and no equivalent female example appeared. Packer emphasized the state of divorce and upheaval, though with the proviso that this might be a transitional stage.[95]

It would seem that the working-class male was seen, both by Kinsey and in the United Kingdom, as being more 'male', in the sense of unthinking, spontaneous and selfish in his desires. The criticism of him on this score by Eyles, Woodside and Packer was consistent with attacks on the impetuous and clumsy male in literature on sex generally. Kinsey rather valorized these qualities as lacking in the effeteness he purported to find among American middle-class males, with their plethora of non-coital 'outlets' and greater liability to sexual anxiety. National differences in notions of 'manliness' as well as differing class biases may be involved here.

Eustace Chesser's *The Sexual, Marital and Family Relationships of the English Woman* (1956), reporting upon surveys carried out in 1954, found particularly noticeable differences between older and younger age groups, especially in discussion of sexual matters both between women and with boyfriends. Two-fifths of the women born before 1904 had discussed sex with other women, and one-seventh with boyfriends. Three-fifths of those born after 1914 had discussed sex with other women, and over one-fifth of those born after 1924 with boyfriends.[96] Moya Woodside also remarked upon the greater willingness to discuss sex among younger couples and their more sexually satisfactory marriages.[97] It would therefore seem that by the 1950s there was some degree of greater sexual openness between the sexes, with beneficent repercussions upon marital satisfaction.

'Taught me more than a lifetime's groping'

Was there any relationship between the state of marriage and the ideas about it which were being advanced in marriage advice manuals? It has been suggested, principally by Sheila Jeffreys, that as woman was becoming more emancipated, politically, economically, socially, there was an attempt to bind her back into conventional domesticity by making orgasmic marital sex of paramount importance in the definition of a real woman and what she should want. The whole genre of marriage advice was about the eroticization of the married woman for her husband's benefit. The 'frigid woman' was constructed as a bogeywoman figure of what wives should not be like, sexually unresponsive and refusing to submit sensually to their husbands and blighting not only their spouses' lives but their children's.[98] It seems probable that there were far more plausible reasons than brainwashing by sex-manuals for the increasing numbers of women marrying even when they could be out earning their own livings. The roles of the sexes had not changed radically by 1950 and certainly marriage manuals embodied concepts of the innate natures of the sexes which were culture-bound and shot through with assumptions about their correct roles. But in order to get a woman to submit to him in this new, eroticized way, a man was also under pressure to do all sorts of things which were not supposed to be at all 'natural' for the unreconstructed, impetuously sexual male. The conditions of domesticity were themselves changing from the Victorian era and required new adaptations from both partners. Did these works promote an intentional programme of oppression or were they simply riddled with unthinking and un-thought-out assumptions?

Sex-manuals manifested considerable ambivalence. Writing about sex in itself was seen as such a dubious project that their authors may have felt particularly anxious to demonstrate that they were not trying to undermine the foundations of society. As social purity writers had written about taboo topics such as fornication and masturbation with impunity because they were clearly against them, writers of sex-advice were able to write about orgasms, pleasure and practices such as oral sex by carefully hedging them about with the institution of marriage and its better preservation. Nevertheless, the works discussed in this chapter were not in any sense official propaganda or altogether approved by dominant social institutions. Isabel Hutton feared prosecution of *The Hygiene of Marriage*, and Chesser's *Love without Fear* was actually tried for obscenity.[99] Sales were often subject to petty restrictions.[100]

It has also been suggested that these works merely replaced one set of anxieties about sex with others, to do with 'normal' sex, with the right person (the one one was married to) and in the right place (in the vagina, with mutual orgasm). If these works were simply a new turn of the screw of moral policing of sexual activity, at least they employed the carrot rather than the stick. The writers themselves saw their project as liberatory: they were well-meaning and risk-taking, their agenda to encourage a more positive approach to sex within marriage, eschewing the punitive and guilt-inducing medico-moral framework of so much earlier sex-advice. Any prescriptive writings on a charged topic like sex may induce anxiety, but this was no explicit part of the programme of these writers. In an atmosphere of shame and inhibition about sex their permission-giving may have made more impact upon their contemporary readers than did their reservations.

The role within society of works of advice and how they were read is a difficult question. Did they make opinion and life-styles or did they reflect them, or is the relationship between advice literature and 'real life' far more complex? People paid good money for these books, and presumably read them. Were they affected by them? The writers believed they were, as did those who aimed to restrict or censor sexual information. But did these books influence behaviour? Did they reflect accepted norms? Or were advice books generally a literary genre whose relation to actual conduct is tenuous to say the least?[101] The very production of such works, impinging, as they do, on matters often supposed 'natural' to humanity, raises interesting questions about the kind of society within which such a manifestation takes place. Nevertheless, it cannot be contended that the writing and reading of such works merely constituted a kind of intellectual exercise, without any influence upon behaviour.

An analogy with cookery books occurs (as it did to Eustace Chesser with his association of Van de Velde and Mrs Beeton). Cookery may be a skill which girls learn (supposedly) at their mother's knee, but in the early twentieth century cooking was taking place in kitchens with gas-stoves in place of the old ranges, with new equipment and new ingredients. Cookery books both reflect and encourage changes in culinary practice. Producers of aids for the cook (for example, baking powder manufacturers) published recipe books explaining how these were most effectively employed. The genre of sex-advice should perhaps be considered alongside guides to household management, social etiquette, home health manuals, as being bound up with changes in social custom and the material surroundings of life. Readers may have been less interested in swallowing such works whole than in picking out tips useful for running their own lives where tradition and upbringing did not help them.

It is possible to study the reactions of a large group of readers to a popular work of sexual advice in the letters received by Marie Stopes. The very fact that so many individuals wrote to her says a good deal about the impact of her books. The number of men who had read and responded to her works is particularly revelatory: sex-advice manuals have been assumed to have been addressed to women, a female genre like the cookery book or the women's magazine. In fact this correspondence confirms Chesser's remark about such works being handed to the bridegroom rather than the bride.

A handful of men found Stopes's flowery style offputting: a Mrs R. suggested they 'find the facts in your books most interesting and helpful, but they do not like your style as it is too emotional for them' and suggested to Stopes that she wrote 'some concise unemotional guide for men.' Stopes replied:

> My experience is that there are such things as men and men. *Married Love* was first appreciated and praised in the very words 'but it is a new gospel of hope and happiness' by men, old, middle-aged, young.[102]

Criticisms (of which there were few) tended to concentrate on her advocacy of birth control and her philosophy of marriage, in which continence and restraint were not necessarily the highest conjugal good:

> A man who does not try to control and subordinate his (unnatural) sensual inclinations is committing a very grave offence...He is an enemy to posterity...Lust, Lust, Lust!!! Such departures expose the lamentible [sic] extent to which humanity has sunk in depravity![103]

By far the most common response was outright praise and congratulation, expressed in such fulsome phraseology as the following:

I have read many books on the sex question and its difficult problems but none written in such beautiful language, unfolding the joy of complete married life as a glorious thing rather than a sordid fact.

We pray that God may richly bless your gloriously straightforward endeavours to further the wondrous beauty of really happy married life.[104]

Many of her correspondents praised the 'cleanness' as well as the lucidity and beauty which they found in her works:

every decent feeling man must thank you for the frankness and courage with which you have dealt with aspects of life usually most unfortunately kept 'veiled' in a kind of miasmatic haze.

Married Love is especially pleasing by its lucidity, its candour and its practical idealism in comparison with the suggestion of semi-pruriency and semi-religiosity which hangs about books of the 'Self and Sex' type.[105]

The books were described as 'courageous and beautiful', gratitude expressed for 'the fearless spirit in which you have issued your books'.[106] They were said to have 'opened my eyes and taught me more than a lifetime's groping could possibly have taught me', in 'expressing the hitherto inexpressible'.[107] Many wished her advice had been available to them 'seven years ago', 'fifteen years ago', '25 years ago' (the longest period given was 40 years previous), 'just after marriage' because it 'might have altered the whole course of my married life'.[108] A not uncommon comment was that it should be in the hands of all young couples about to marry:

I have always avoided 'sex books' but a friend made me buy [*Enduring Passion*]. It has but one fault, namely that it isn't so cheap that every man and woman in the country can have a copy of it!

if these books were read by all who are about to be married and those that are already there would be many more happy unions.

Some went so far as to say 'no marriage certificate should be issued without a copy of your book.'[109]

Stopes's books seem to have been able to break through taboos on open discussion of sex matters and to initiate discussion in army and airforce messes, and among groups of male friends:

This letter is the outcome of many serious conversations with some friends of mine, all of whom, owing to several years having been spent in the Army, have come up to the University at a more mature age than was usual hitherto, three of them are engaged and the perusal of your works has made them deeply sensible of their responsibilities as future husbands and fathers.[110]

This was not always the case. Captain H., of the Indian Army, commented:

Living as I do in messes and clubs, chiefly masculine gatherings, I know something of the manner in which they have been met, and the criticism and remarks they have invoked...As you will know, in such gatherings these are sometimes not a bit pleasant.[111]

Michael Gordon, in a paper on changing trends in marital advice literature in the USA, 1830–1940, has suggested that the growing concern with technique and foreplay during the 1920s and 1930s was due to the new emphasis on the sexual rights of women. As intercourse for the male thus became surrounded by greater anxiety, technique provided a form of 'ritual magic'.[112] However, it would seem that these works of advice aided marriages not by providing husbands with a compendium of erotic skills but by opening up communication within the couple. E. M. Brecher, in *The Sex Researchers*, considered that the success of Van de Velde's *Ideal Marriage* lay in its ability to open up communication on matters of sex between partners, not in the carrying out of his recommendations in grim detail.[113] This was also true of *Married Love*, to judge by readers' comments:

we have both read your works about wooing and the necessity for tender embraces and caresses prior to the sex act.

[*Married Love*] does open one's eyes and wife to as [sic] read the book.

now after reading your book we realise what is wrong in our lives.

We talked matters over, and read your book *Enduring Passion*. My wife then persuaded me to write this letter.

I have just read your book *Married Love* and am sending another copy to my wife.[114]

Several men mentioned sending a copy of her book to their fiancées.[115] Not all men took this attitude: in spite of his own positive reaction to reading *Married Love*, Captain H of the Indian Army declared

> frankly, [I] should not wish the woman whom I shall marry to read some parts of them; it may sound illogical, of the old era of ignorance – but I think any normal healthy-minded young man feels similarly.[116]

This connection between reading the books and communication between the couple was also mentioned by Slater and Woodside, E. L. Packer and Eustace Chesser in their surveys. Woodside noted that the more satisfactory marriages of the younger couples did not seem to depend upon any increased sexual knowledge or expertise on the husband's part.[117] In *Patterns of Marriage* Slater and Woodside commented that 'books on sex have helped, and create a mental background which favours attempts at a planned adaptation', and mentioned examples of books being exchanged between the couple.[118] E. L. Packer found that

> Reading text-books on sex technique has not proved helpful in correcting sexual maladjustment unless both husband and wife have read the book, and have been able to discuss it together.

He adduced in support of this contention the case of a marriage which had reached the point of a consideration of separation. The husband

> came to realise that his part in copulation was deficient in skill, and to remedy this he bought a number of manuals on sex education for marriage. There was no confidence between man and wife at this time, and he did not attempt to impart any of his newly acquired knowledge to his wife before coition. During coition his wife maintained the reserve which was customary, and the maladjustment persisted.[119]

Chesser's results confirmed the important part such literature played. (While his research pertained to women, social changes affecting both sexes can be generalized from his findings.) The highest proportion of those experiencing a lot of satisfaction in marriage was 'among those who obtained their sex education mainly from books and pamphlets'. He therefore extrapolated

Such reading may have helped to allay fears and anxieties and was, presumably, the expression of a desire to know more in order to find greater enjoyment in the sexual relationship; it might also have suggested more satisfactory sexual techniques.[120]

The particular book mattered less than the channel it opened up for married couples to talk about sex. In many cases it must have been only works like *Married Love* or *Ideal Marriage* which provided couples with a vocabulary in which to talk about such matters. The wholesale adoption of Stopes's language and concepts by her readers, which can be seen in their comments, suggests that before reading her works they had had little or no way of articulating their thoughts and feelings on the subject, or at least no way that seemed decent and permissible, suitable for use within such a relationship. This is not to say that the books did not also give helpful tips on erotic technique, as Chesser suggested.

The whole concept of marriage, therefore, was undergoing revision during the early twentieth century. The very criticisms of marital behaviour put forward by writers like M. L. Eyles and E. L. Packer were symptomatic of a belief that marriage should not be the degraded relationship which they described. Much of the blame for troubles in marriage was laid upon the male. Was he as complacent about marriage and as callously insensitive as the writers cited suggested? The way men responded to *Married Love* suggests that this picture is perhaps too black.

4

'Not such a selfish beast': men's problems in marriage

Marriage was changing. The unflattering picture of the average male presented in sexual advice literature and surveys has been described. Was this merely a polemic construct, and did it bear any relationship to the actual experience of men? Marie Stopes specifically dedicated *Married Love* to 'Young husbands, and all those who are betrothed in love'.[1] The fulsome praise of her works contained in the letters she received was usually a preamble to a request for further elucidation of matters touched on in her works, or for advice on some personal problem upon which it was assumed that she, being an authority on sexual questions, might be able authoritatively to pronounce.

Among the problems presented by her male readers there was a dichotomy, by no means absolute, between those men who were writing as solitary beings about a problem which seemed to them of purely individual concern, and those who wrote about problems as part of an existing or potential mutual relationship, or indeed as spokesman for the conjugal couple. Very few correspondents voiced the charge that *Married Love* was 'a book written by a woman for the benefit of women exclusively...its gospel is sacrifice by the man'. Few of them were as convinced as Mr G. that there are a great many women (my wife is one of them) who are so devoted to their husbands that they are quite satisfied and delighted when they know that they are giving joy and pleasure to their loved ones and are indifferent whether they experience orgasm or not.[2]

Most of Stopes's male readers, it would seem, did not regard conjugal pleasure in these terms and were anxious to achieve sexual mutuality. In this chapter evidence is considered relating to the feelings and experiences of men within the marital relationship.

'I write on behalf of my wife'

Men who wrote to Stopes on the whole demonstrated a considerable concern for their wives, or women with whom they were emotionally involved. Many had general queries relating to the health and wellbeing of their wife or fiancée or girlfriend: usually involving 'women's problems'. Presumably because the woman in question was reluctant to seek medical advice, men wrote to Stopes for advice about painful and heavy menstruation,[3] as well as about other problems connected with the menstrual period: 'my wife...for a few days preceding each monthly "period" becomes violent and dangerous',[4] was a rare reference to the premenstrual syndrome. There were also cases of a girl of eighteen who had never menstruated and had other health problems, a fiancée whose scanty periods led to worries about her fertility, a wife who had not had periods for years, a wife who was 'poorly' during her period, and a fiancée suffering from something like fits during her 'poorly times'.[5]

Similarly there were some queries about mysterious female complaints: 'I write to you on behalf of my wife, who is troubled with what she terms "the whites"',[6] as well as about the loss of figure following childbirth, pain after intercourse, and ovarian inflammation.[7] A number of questions related to matters to do with fertility: the case of the female friend with small undeveloped breasts – would she be able to breastfeed; how old could a woman be and still safely conceive a first child; would an appendectomy render a woman sterile; would use of an abortifacient affect future childbearing capacity.[8] Nor were men insensitive to the suffering childbirth caused women:

> I was home on leave when my kiddy was born and so I know what terrible agony my wife had to endure...If I thought my darling had to go through that every 2 years or so I think I should try to stay on foreign service until she was past child-bearing.[9]

In some cases the general state of the wife's health gave cause for concern, as in the case of the man whose wife was in a 'frightfully enemic [sic] condition and is a nervous wreck'.[10] In one case a man ascribed this ill-health to his own past actions, without actually stating what these were,[11] and in several letters the wife's poor state of health was attributed to sexual problems within the marriage.[12] Some correspondents may have sought Stopes's advice because their wives were not covered by any insurance scheme they belonged to and the costs of consulting a doctor were perceived as prohibitive. However, queries about marital relations where one or both partners had tuberculosis or a bad heart suggest the reluctance of doctors to advise or patients to enquire on such a sensitive topic as sexual functioning.[13]

Some of these men may have been moved to write less from concern for their wives than out of the selfish desire to have a healthy one, if the selfish can be differentiated from the altruistic motive in this way. While presumably correspondents wished to present themselves to Stopes as caring husbands, one hardly need doubt that statements such as 'my one aim in life is to give my wife all she deserves and if you cannot help re the points raised I do not know where to turn for help'[14] were sincere. Other men were prepared to state the suffering that their wife's indifference to or refusal of sex caused them:

> It's the problem of the 'cold and unresponsive' wife...it puts me in the greatest despair for the best part of my days...I find it slowly dragging me down to underhand and disgusting thoughts...torture I endure and have withstood for 4½ years.[15]

Given taboos on male expression of emotions or open admission of affection, for a man to declare his warmer feelings about his wife may have seemed as dangerous and threatening as to admit his pain and suffering, but was, like that, something that these writers felt that they could communicate to Stopes if to no-one else (it must surely have helped that she was a stranger).

The problem of birth control is and was often seen as something concerning women alone. The notion that men were reluctant to use birth control or even opposed to its use as diminishing their control over their wives has often been advanced. The idea of men as indifferent, if not wholly hostile, to the use of reliable methods of birth control, or at least methods which did not leave control in their own hands, cannot be substantiated from the letters which men wrote to Marie Stopes. As population in Britain had been declining since 1870, though less in some classes and occupational groups than others, some form of family restriction must have been being used by a large number of couples at least some of the time.[16] Numbers of men, alerted to the existence of methods more reliable and less nervewracking than coitus interruptus and less aesthetically obnoxious than the sheath, wrote to Stopes for further details and the names of reliable suppliers.

Seeking such help, they often mentioned the means they had already been employing to avoid pregnancy. Coitus interruptus was a much-used method involving no appliances: 'I don't see any way to limit conception except by interrupted coitus. This I plead guilty to.' There was a feeling about that its effects on the couple were deleterious: 'have been reduced to withdrawing which I know to be bad for both and am becoming semi-impotent'; though others claimed differently: 'I have been married 12 years and have always used the withdrawal method with success.'[17] Others had been using sheaths but did not like them:

> Only by total abstinence or using rubber specialities can we avoid a child annually. This latter method fails to give pleasure to either.

> From my point of view renders the 'sex act' sordid and destroys the aesthetic side entirely.

> Rubber check pessaries (male) remind me of one having a bath with top hat and spurs on.[18]

Chemical pessaries such as 'safety cones'[19] were known to some couples but there was much doubt as to their general reliability:

> Is there any truth in the statement that by law there must be at least one harmless and ineffective pessary in every box sold?

> I am informed that so many per cent of check pessaries have to be made *defective* else the Government do not allow their sale.[20]

(This belief that there was some obligation upon manufacturers to make a certain percentage defective was not confined to the pessary, it was also averred that so many in any box of condoms had to have holes in them.) Douching was also known: 'the woman has to get up and wash out the bad-smelling liquid the man has injected into her.'[21] Some individuals had come across the concept of a safe period, usually misleading as to actual location within the menstrual cycle. 'There is *only* danger I understand when or about the menses'[22] was a belief often supported by medical opinion prior to the discoveries of Ogino and Knaus (1928) of the actual place of ovulation in the monthly cycle. One man wrote to Stopes (though he did not say he used this expedient himself):

> I was a short time since in the flat in London of a fashionable cocotte...had a talk and was informed that middle-aged married men came to cocottes as a means of keeping down their progeny! So you see that there are other means of birth control![23]

While some correspondents queried whether birth control might not be 'a form of prostitution',[24] this is presumably not what they meant.

Some couples simply refrained from actual penetration:

> Our nearest relations consisted of weekly and bi-weekly love-play in the course of which we both reached high pitches of excitement but never once was intercourse attempted, altho' at times greatly desired.[25]

They managed to satisfy themselves by 'other means' which appears to have meant mutual masturbation or a practice described as 'extra-vaginal intercourse',[26] presumably intracrural intercourse. Anal intercourse as a contraceptive alternative was extremely seldom considered by Stopes's correspondents.[27]

The occasional very bizarre notion of a contraceptive method was put forward by Stopes's correspondents: in at least one case dependent on a total misconception about the reproductive system. The letter itself does not survive, but Stopes replied

> In reply to your question about rendering of the navel air-tight as a possible means of preventing conception I may say I never heard anything more ridiculous in my life. It is an absolutely preposterous notion.[28]

A strange method mentioned by one correspondent would seem to derive from the popular belief that a lactating woman would not conceive. The idea was that the husband should suckle his wife's breasts to maintain lactation and keep away the menstrual flow. The writer remarked 'we married men know that the suckling time is practically a safe period so far but it is a bit too real for the man to do this.'[29]

While the idea of birth control was not new to many of Stopes's readers, nevertheless numbers of them still felt repugnance at the concept or reluctance·to practice it:

> such means and devices are rather abhorrent to me.

> like many others I have always shrunk from enquiring into these matters.

> we neither of us understand... the actual practical method of preventing conception... the idea of wearing artificial means of prevention tends to make us question the rightness of union apart from children.

> I want to maintain our love without degrading it by impure means.[30]

This revulsion from the use of artificial contraceptives, perhaps understandable in the current crude state of the technology, led to enquiries as to how to have intercourse '*without* any risk of conception and without employing any artificial contraceptives, which my friend abhors', a query which was presented to Stopes by a 'Balliol man'. Another man wrote in similar terms:

> my wife and I are anxious to resume cohabitation but without the risk of any more children... but wish to avoid the use of contraceptives.[31]

One man shrank from the idea of birth control 'as from sodomy', while a naval Lieutenant-Commander claimed that employing a birth control device 'shocked my sense of delicacy even more I think than hers'.[32] Another man sought 'methods of course that would be scientific and consistent with decorum and prevention'.[33]

Because of the ambivalent feelings that were aroused by the subject of birth control, some correspondents found it necessary to assure Stopes that they were not actuated by 'morbid curiosity' and to give their credentials for venturing to enquire about it. Some vouched for their own respectability: '[I am] a householder and a family man of limited means and deeply interested in the subject.' Others couched their enquiry in terms of philosophical justification: 'I have become convinced that the practice of self-control in this respect without the use of some artificial appliance, must in time prove injurious to one or the other.' Some claimed 'I do not want the information from a selfish motive but for my wife's.' A few spoke plainly of 'the ever present fear of a woman and the mental agony of a man lest she should have been "caught"' as 'one of the foundations of marital unhappiness. The ecstasy of union is clouded by the subsequent torment.'[34]

There were cases in which, far from birth control being seen as the wife's province and none of the husband's concern, the husband seems to have been forcing a method upon the wife which she was reluctant to employ:

> [My wife] said [the female check pessary] was distasteful and took away the romance of everything...the more I think of this matter the more I think it looks selfish on the woman's part especially if coitus interruptus really does harm to the man.

> I took my wife to you [the Mother's Clinic set up by Stopes] in order to be fitted for an occlusive cap (very much against her will) as I considered it would be a more efficient and beneficial method of birth control.

> I simply cannot persuade her to...adopt the preventive measures recommended by you. At present I simply cannot afford to indulge in parenthood...After three years of married life I am still compelled to be satisfied with the use of a thick preventative.[35]

Most men seem to have been rather more sensitive to their spouse's feelings, one man writing to Stopes for advice 'since my wife feels that the method recommended would be repellent', and others stressing the deleteriousness of coitus interruptus from the woman's point of view:

> I have to practice coitus interruptus which is most unsatisfactory from my wife's point of view and therefore from mine because my climax is reached as a rule just as the pleasure for her is about to begin.[36]

For many couples the only way that they could conceive of to limit births was to abstain, usually from all kinds of sexual activity, a method which could hardly have been practised without the husband's cooperation:

> We tried for some years a life of pretty rigid abstinence and it didn't work and only brought a decrease in happiness.

> Consequently we have had no union ever since the child was conceived over 5 years ago.

I have by the greatest exercise of self-denial kept our family down to three, without any artificial checks but it has been a very great trial.

Some couples even delayed consummation of marriage on this account: 'my wife and I have been married three years and we have not had a union, because we do not want children yet.'[37] Some men felt that practising abstention had other benefits besides the obvious:

> Prior to reading your book I was of the opinion that the one and only course was total restraint and you must admit that it has one great advantage – it enables the man to prove to his loved one that in his desire for marriage there are no selfish or secondary motives, and for that very reason I cling to the idea.[38]

This statement embodies the lingering belief that sex was a pleasurable indulgence on the man's part rather than a mutual experience.

A few of Stopes's readers mentioned the practice of 'karezza' or prolonged intercourse without male ejaculation, a practice which was supposed to have profound spiritual/mystical benefits for the couple as well as having been advocated by certain nineteenth-century writers for its non-reproductive aspect. Most had come across the notion in her own works and were writing for further information; only a few seemed to have been practising it and even fewer found it satisfactory or at all coming up to descriptions of its benefits.[39] Stopes's own comment was

> In my opinion an average, strong and unimaginative Englishman is not likely to achieve success in this type of union, but more sensitive and artistic temperaments and those in which the vitality is not excessive undoubtedly can do so...Whole communities are known to have practised such control successfully and healthily, though I do not know of more than a few British men who have done so.[40]

Even more than birth control, abortion has often been regarded as a particular female concern; indeed, as part of a women's 'underculture', a practice that went on hidden from the male world. While the vast majority of requests for abortion advice received by Stopes (much to her horror) came from women, a significant number were addressed to her by men, suggesting that this was an issue in which both members of the couple were interested, even if the brunt of anxiety and suffering would naturally have been experienced by the woman.

Most of the abortion requests addressed to Stopes by men

concerned unwanted pregnancy occurring within marriage, where there were too many children or conceptions following too closely upon one another or the wife suffering from ill-health. This did not differ greatly from the requests from women. Panic in some cases set in very early, after one act which had taken place unprotected or with contraceptive failure,[41] while others wrote when the woman was already several months along in pregnancy.[42] Some wrote in very veiled, circumlocutory terms which contrasted with the explicitness of others.

The involvement of the men with the problem was very clear. Presumably it was those couples who did not have access to any network which might have put them in touch with an abortionist who wrote to Stopes, but in at least one case the husband wrote 'my wife will not speak to anyone.'[43] The use of folk remedies was mentioned in some letters:

I have heard that a medicine of some kind is allowed to be given to stop things at the early stages.

Are we doing wrong in taking these pills?

My wife has been trying Vegetable Tablets and also syringing herself.[44]

The general ignorance, when it came to practicalities, of what could be done, was very apparent: 'we are ignorant of how to deal with such cases'; 'how to effect menstruation in my wife, who is overdue by about a fortnight'.[45]

Many couples were agitated by the prospect that pregnancy had occurred after a single act of intercourse. This happened not only when courting couples got 'carried away': 'on the 9th, the sex act, we are both afraid to say, was indulged'; 'I have been keeping company with a young lady for a considerable time and nothing happened between us until I lost control of myself on March 9th – the result is that the girl is in a certain condition.'[46] It was also an anxiety for married couples after an incomplete or inadequately contracepted act:

I have always been as careful as I possibly could whenever we had any intercourse not to go too far and although we have two children I can truthfully say we have never yet had one proper full union together. My wife never has any orgasm herself and seems to take if I go near her...she [has] accidentally caught again.

[I] fear that intercourse has been achieved while we were both in a somnolent state.[47]

The terror and sense of disgrace which affected couples faced with undesired pregnancy in or out of wedlock was eloquently described:

> I am afraid I shall lose her if she has another child and she is so frightened herself. I feel afraid to go out to work and leave her. I would give all I possess to have her right again.

> A time of great trouble for me and my young lady...we have got ourselves into very great trouble...may I appeal to you to help us out of the disgrace that has come upon us...it has been like this for three months ever since we made the great mistake and I was wondering if it is possible for you to do anything for us...it is our only hope – just one little ray of light in our darkened lives. I am sure I can never face the terrible ordeal – I know I am a coward.[48]

An associated anxiety sometimes expressed to Stopes was the ease with which conception might take place even without full intercourse: readers wrote to ask how long sperm would survive outside the body, could conception be caused by the deposit of spermatozoa on the labia, through cloth, and could a woman get pregnant from a single drop of sperm. One man wrote on behalf of 'a friend' who had been practising digital stimulation on his girlfriend, through her clothes, and was worried that he might be transferring sperms to her on account of his practice of masturbation.[49] A particularly convoluted contingency was mooted by one enquirer:

> If an ejaculation takes place during the night, and the body is subsequently washed in a bath the next morning, is there any possibility of live spermatozoa remaining in the bath-water, and is there any chance of these spermatozoa impregnating a woman who may happen to use the bath afterwards?[50]

One young man, surprised by the number of couples he knew who had had to get married in the previous eighteen months, and the number of hasty marriages noticed by his fiancée who worked in the Registrar's Office, wrote

> It is inconceivable to my fiancée and myself that they would have had intercourse such as we understand is necessary from your books...Is it possible that an 'accident' could have such serious results, by this I

mean, supposing for example they were in an embrace, the fellow 'became excited', could this soak through their clothing or anything like that. If this is possible I would submit that as so many are running such a grave risk, it would be worthy of mention in one of your volumes...I would like to observe that if conception can take place so easily then life for engaged couples is unbearable, if however it *is* necessary for complete intercourse then it is true that 'still waters run deep'.[51]

One young man brought up in a remote country district of Ireland had no such technical worries: he had feared that if one 'talked too much with girls or made chums with them too much God sent a child'.[52] Men were not indifferent to unwanted conception nor exempt from anxieties on the subject, often becoming profoundly agitated at the prospect.

'Looking ever forward to the complete joy of marriage'

Men brought many other marital anxieties to Stopes besides those to do with anxieties over pregnancy. In spite of all their perturbation at the prospect of conception occurring inconveniently, men also expressed the desire for fatherhood, declaring themselves 'ardently desirous of becoming a father' and mentioning their 'strong desires and aspirations re parenthood'. Others wrote more as part of a couple:

We are both awfully keen on having some topping children.

We would like to have three children; at what intervals should these be born and what books can you recommend on child education and upbringing?[53]

However, most letters which concerned the question of fatherhood were to do with anxieties about its desirability in the particular case of the writer. Although the organized eugenics movement was small, the pervasive influence of eugenic thought can be detected in these doubts about 'fitness' or the desirability of having children in particular circumstances. Some men, intending to marry their cousins, feared that this meant that they should not risk having children.[54] There was also anxiety about potentially hereditary disorders on one or other side of the family: tuberculosis,[55] fits,[56]

club-foot and deafness.[57] Some men feared that they had permanently unfitted themselves for marriage and parenthood through
masturbation.[58]

Worries about problems in marriage and being a satisfactory husband often began well before the wedding, sometimes even without
a prospective bride in view. Numbers of men, young and some less
young, wrote to Stopes concerning their anxieties about marriage.
While some of these involved questions of actual sexual competence, and others were to do with birth control, many of the men
who wrote to Stopes displayed a concern for their wife-to-be and an
idealism about the potential of the conjugal relationship which was
expressed for them by Stopes herself in *Married Love*:

> The young man is often even more sensitive, more romantic, more
> easily pained about all ordinary things, and he enters marriage hoping
> for an even higher degree of spiritual and bodily unity than does the
> girl or woman.[59]

This spirit of idealism was echoed by several of her correspondents:

> I'm in a quandary, how I should act when I'm married, I'm extremely
> passionate but do not want to do anything that would hurt her sense
> of the aesthetic – I want her to be really happy.

> There must be innumerable thousands of husbands like myself who
> wish the marital embrace, that mystical beauty of body and soul, to
> contain the fullest possible joy for their wives.

> It was ten weeks where my affection was sorely tried against human
> passion but I thought then and now that her happiness was most
> important.[60]

Many men took pride in going 'to the altar with what I call "clean
hands"'.[61] In some cases they explicitly expressed morally egalitarian views about the subject:

> I am a young man of 25 years of age, who is to be married soon, and
> who, I am proud to say, will be able to offer his wife, himself,
> uninitiated in sexual intercourse.

> I have not ever known in that sense anyone but my wife as I look
> upon those matters as sacred.

For her sake during the long and hard years of boyhood, youth and manhood (I am now 35) I kept myself clean, looking ever forward to the complete joy of marriage.

Simply it had always been one of my ideals that I should be able to feel that I had been married in the state in which I expected my wife to be.[62]

Other men were less explicit about this and their views seem to convey more of a general sense of fastidiousness about sexual relations: 'Previous to my first marriage [aged 31] I can honestly say I had led absolutely a life free from vice'; 'I am some 32 years old and have not had sex experience before, being anxious to keep myself for the love that is given and not bought.'[63]

It is hard to quantify the prevalence of premarital intercourse and how acceptable it was assumed to be. While illegitimacy rates as such were low for most of this period, this is a less reliable indicator of premarital intercourse than bridal pregnancy. However, the kind of reconstructive work which can be done for earlier centuries, relating date of birth of first child to date of marriage, is unfortunately not possible for this period due to the hundred-year closure period placed on the Registrar-General's records. It might also be argued that in an age of increasing contraceptive awareness the number of pregnant brides no longer corresponds even roughly to the amount of premarital intercourse actually taking place. But given the problems even married couples of the period had in coming to terms with the very idea of contraception, as well as its practicalities, it may be doubted whether it was a significant element for unmarried couples except in fairly sophisticated circles.

Attitudes towards prostitution expressed by Stopes's correspondents have already been quoted in chapter 2; while some men were having or had had sexual intercourse with the woman they were intending to marry. Though this was not always directly stated it can be deduced from statements such as 'my young lady is in trouble.'[64] Others, though this disaster had not occurred, nevertheless expressed a sense of guilt over the occurrence of sexual relations prior to marriage.[65] The young man who declared that 'we have been like most normal couples I presume (that is) guilty of having intercourse'[66] was possibly less 'normal' than he supposed. Another young man was adamant in his determination to 'stem the flood of our natural desires', because 'I love her so deeply it would break my heart if any premarital event took place.' Another young man similarly declared 'passionate devotion has never caused me to over-ride an almost sacred regard for her.'[67]

Besides worries about the consequences of intercourse, there were instances in which premarital indulgence had alerted the man to a state of premature ejaculation:

> I thought to have connections with a woman would cure me [of masturbation] but it did not. Because, in the first place, I could not get properly erected, and in the second place my strength was spent in a few moments.[68]

Anxieties about the sexual relationship can be seen to have commenced well before marriage took place.

Such anxieties were not unjustified. A surprising number of correspondents wrote about unconsummated marriages, some of which had existed in this state for an extremely long period:

> I am 54 years of age my wife being 48 and although we have been married many years, union between us has never been possible.

> We have been married just over 12 years and yet...through a number of difficult circumstances which I will first very briefly indicate – we have not been able to consummate our marriage.[69]

Other lengthy periods mentioned included five, nine and ten years.[70] In other cases the couple had been married a very brief time before consulting Stopes:

> Although we have been married only 3 weeks, we are both unhappy and distressed to find that physical union is impossible.

> Everything has gone wonderfully except for the fact that we have been unable to experience our first coitus [married 1 month].[71]

Most left it a little longer before worrying: two, four or six months being more usual.[72] A number of couples who wrote with this problem had been married between one and three years. 'we have been married 3 years and have as yet been unable to effect coition'; 'our union has not yet been consummated' (in two years nine months); in two-and-a-half years 'there has been no marital relation between us'; 'I have been married for one year and have not as yet been able to have sexual intercourse.'[73] Others did not mention how long they had been suffering from this difficulty but only revealed that 'we have not yet had a normal sex union'; 'we are both healthy and clean-minded but up to now we have made a complete mess of things'; 'when we come together I have never succeeded in making entry. . . I am a strong working fellow'; or that they had found 'entry being so very difficult and it took so little trying on my part to cause such pain'.[74]

Some failures in consummation appear to have arisen following deliberate abstention for contraceptive purposes: '[we] have been holding off from our great mutual experience' (addressed from St John's College, Cambridge).[75] Other couples abstained for reasons of the wife's general health, or her ignorance.[76] One writer (a woman) said that 'the happy companionship of our bodies seemed sufficient' but soon found that her husband wanted union, which they were unable to achieve.[77]

'My greatest wish is to make her happy'

Even if a man succeeded in consummating his marriage there were still numerous difficulties which he might encounter. Many men wrote to Stopes about problems connected with ensuring that their wives were as satisfied with the sexual side of marriage as they were themselves. Many were distressed that their wives seemed to lack sexual desire:

> After nearly 5 years of marriage my wife still appears to be frigid and to scarcely ever desire sex union. . . I am so anxious to make her happy.

> For the whole of that time [11 years] I have been unable to stir her to any passionate interest in our love.[78]

Still more were depressed by their inability to satisfy their wives sexually:

> I am seldom able to satisfy my wife when we do have intercourse . . . my wife is a very pure-minded woman and I deeply regret that I am not able to satisfy her.

> My greatest wish is to make her happy – we are very happily married and are in every way suited to each other but when we have union she is very rarely satisfied.

Never has she been fortunate enough to be satisfied.

My wife can obtain no actual climax to the sexual act. Not by any
stretch of the imagination can she be called frigid – on the contrary
she is *extremely* passionate before and during the act but however long
it lasts she is left feeling unsettled.[79]

Some evoked the concept of pleasure: 'I really want to give some
pleasure to a good wife'; 'although I obtain pleasure every time I
unite with my wife she has had pleasure only twice during this
period...I would do anything if only I could help her.'[80] Men seem
to have found the concept of pleasure difficult to come to terms
with: one correspondent, a clergyman, was obviously much happier
discussing his wife's lack of orgasm in terms of health: 'how is it in
the power of the husband when holding physical union with his
wife to ensure that she receives the full orgasm and thus the full
benefit of union?'[81]

The ignorance of many men about the existence of the female
orgasm was considerable: one man (writing from the Carlton Club)
claimed that before he realized such a thing existed, he 'was frightened and thought it was some sort of fit' when his wife had one.[82]
Numbers of men awakened to the possibility of female arousal and
satisfaction by reading Stopes's works were anxious to learn 'what
natural signs should a woman exhibit that she is in a totally tumescent state?'[83] Some might have had an inchoate idea that mutual
pleasure was a possibility:

> You argue the necessity of the climax of one with the climax of the
> other. I have long felt the necessity of this mutual state but must
> admit the inability...will you please tell me how to arrive at this
> perfect state in the accomplishment of which I consider my duty to my
> wife.[84]

But often her books were the first intimation that that a problem
existed:

> I have not realised till now that I haven't given my wife the satisfac-
> tion to which she has a right.

> You speak of 'rousing a woman's body and soul' and you say that this
> takes time. My wife states that she has never had this experience...I
> should be very grateful for any hints as to how to produce the effect
> which you describe.

I do not believe she has reached anything like the ecstasy portrayed in your book.[85]

Stopes's correspondents described the torment that the lack of mutuality was to them, as well as how distressing for their wives:

She fired me to the extent that I was rarely master of myself and it all seemed to mean so little to her...I seemed bound to give myself up entirely and yet to have no power to fire her in the same way. To my personal esteem alone it was a bitter blow...I felt it for her too.

To speak plainly, my wife can obtain no pleasurable sensation whatever from sexual union...I find it almost repugnant to take advantage of what is hardly more than generosity on my wife's part, she feels that she is missing what is her due.

The only thing that troubles me is that when we have sexual intercourse my wife never receives that pleasure which we expect...it makes me feel such a cad, when I desire this pleasure, and she does not.

I feel it rather badly when I turn away satisfied and see her laid there 'just left' as you might term it...I feel my wife's position rather keenly.

When I found I could not awaken the desire in her it made me feel so selfish and mean.[86]

Men sought various solutions to this problem: some asked how they could identify the 'love-tides' described in *Married Love*: 'I am asking you to let me know the dates of these moments when she may have these welling desires'; 'what noticeable outwards indications does a wife give when she is at her high tides or desires bodily union with her husband?'[87] Others asked for literature to give them guidelines which they had not found in *Married Love*: 'can you not tell me of any literature on the subject which goes into details of the techniques, etc, of the sex act?'; 'would it be too much to ask of you for further enlightenment of the above, to recommend a book showing how this could be controlled?'[88] Others were interested in the possibilities of aphrodisiacs:

In short if you could advise me of some way of rousing her with the aid of drugs etc, I think it might help a lot. I have studied her periods and courted then as advised by you but it has no effect.

Are aphrodisiacs advisable please? and if so, which are the best to use?[89]

Few of these concerned husbands fell into the mechanical-adjustment way of describing their problem used by Mr L.: 'Can you tell me how to get this remedied?', or the man who hoped that an operation would improve his wife's sexual responsiveness.[90]

This widespread phenomenon of female lack of arousal and satisfaction in the conjugal act is less surprising when it is realized how very hesitant most of these men were about using even the most ordinary forms of tactile stimulation, at least with wives: one recently married man aged forty-eight, not altogether lacking in experience, wrote to Stopes that 'but for your advice I should not have hazarded preliminaries, for fear of shocking my wife'.[91] A number of the men who wrote to Stopes for help with the problem of their wives' lack of satisfaction were aware of the role of the clitoris (even if they did not name it or know precisely where or what it was) in the achievement of this elusive state. Some had realized that 'the ordinary act does not seem to touch the seat of pleasure in her at all' and that 'the seat of the most acute and gratifying sensation is far way too high up (not in depth in vagina) to receive the motions necessary to give orgasm from actual union.'[92] Others did employ digital stimulation in order to satisfy their wives:

[I] just lay down beside my wife and cuddled her while I worked gently with my fingers round about the opening with slight pressure until my wife completed her orgasm.

After my own orgasm...I help my wife to achieve her orgasm by digital manipulation.

You say that a woman should have a paroxysm when relations take place between husband and wife. My wife is unable to experience this unless I cause it with my finger.[93]

Most of them were extremely troubled about the use of this expedient, efficacious though it might be. There were fears that it might be somehow impermissible:

Whether it is right or not to do so by fondling with the hand?...what is – perhaps vulgarly, termed 'feeling' – or, is this too indecent to the nicely minded woman.[94]

Other anxieties were that it might be actually harmful:

> Quite by chance my wife and I discovered that considerable stimulation and excitation was afforded her prior to the sex act by some digital stimulation of the clitoris...the thought remains in our minds that perhaps this digital excitation of the clitoris prior to union may savour of perversion or prove harmful.

> I have often adopted the plan of remaining idle myself until I have worked up her enthusiasm with the aid of a little external friction. I am afraid this may not be good for her.[95]

Fears of female disgust were also expressed: 'are most women not likely to object to this form of stimulation?'[96] Those employing this expedient felt that there was something somehow superior or more natural about an orgasm achieved without this intervention: 'although Mrs H has an orgasm artificially we haven't succeeded really'; 'my wife is therefore though always "satisfied" not so deeply thrilled as I would like her to be'; and some deplored 'our inability to reach the crisis together in the natural way'.[97] It was seldom that a man objected on his own account to this practice: 'I can make her get the feeling by tickling her with my finger but this does not satisfy me.'[98]

A fortunate handful, however, wrote to Stopes to tell her the happy news that her works had confirmed principles and practices which they had managed to discover for themselves over years of marriage: 'many of your observations we had marked out for ourselves in 18½ years very intimate married life'; '*Married Love*... fully confirmed our own practice.'[99] For some their procedures had appeared natural:

> I find that I have carried out the majority of the practice which it [*Married Love*] lays down, and these things seemed to come to me as second nature.

> We were children as far as knowledge was concerned and yet I must have approached her as you would have advised, for years after she was grateful to me for the way I acted then. I did what seemed natural.[100]

For some it had been more of a conscious working out: 'things have worked out themselves to the same conclusions as you draw', while others had '"muddled through" to almost exactly the idea you describe'.[101] Even lacking instruction, not all men behaved like lust-crazed beasts when faced with the marriage bed.

Such basic issues as how frequently marital intercourse should take place would appear to have been provocative of considerable anxiety. It was a question often included in letters requesting pre-marital advice or along with other questions with an assumption that there was some kind of acceptable standard:

> I am a young man of thirty contemplating marriage and I cannot decide in my mind what is usually considered the normal amount of intercourse per month between a married couple.[102]

Some men were anxious not in terms of accepted propriety in the matter or out of concern for their wives but for fear of damaging their own wellbeing:

> You... suggest (what appears to me to be extraordinary) that in most cases an average would be 5 or 6 times a week... I would not doubt the *desire* for union as frequently as this but I cannot help thinking that the desire must be suppressed if one wishes to maintain one's health.

> It seems to me to be quite possible to give the reins to the sex impulse at the expense of health and efficiency.[103]

This echoes the anxieties more often expressed in nineteenth-century literature of sexual advice about the depleting effect of sexual activity upon the male.

'The woman did not know that it is not only her arms which should embrace her husband', Stopes wrote in later editions of *Married Love*.[104] From the beginning her correspondence had re-vealed widespread confusion about the correct or acceptable posi-tions for sexual intercourse. The phrase about 'not only her arms' was frequently cited with a request for explication, and often oc-curred along with other queries in letters of premarital enquiry.[105] Questions about positions were seldom to do with a search for variety and exotic stimulation, though in some cases this seems to have been part of the motive for enquiring:

> How can I possibly convince my rather Puritan little wife that there are 'more positions than one' and that '*not* only the arms should embrace'?[106]

Far more frequently such queries sprang from attempts to find a position which actually worked: 'my wife does not assume a position which allows of simple access on my part to her. I do not seem to get full entry';[107] or which was comfortable for both partners:

> My wife is of medium size and perhaps a little frail. I myself am a largely built man. I have found that my unions with my wife are marred by her feeling my weight unduly, particularly on the thighs...
> I fear I must seem very stupid in being unable to solve this problem myself, but I must confess that my love and respect for my wife fill me with a horror of ill-informed experiment.

> Now that I am cured [of hasty ejaculation] we feel that we could be in connections for any length of time...but the ordinary position...is much too tiring and exhausting for her [A man describing himself as being ex-public school and University][108]

The problem of the best position for mutual satisfaction was also ventilated: 'what positions other than face to face would you recommend in view of my previous remark as to the apparent seat of sensation, as likely to give increased gratification to the woman?'[109]
Even the most basic position was sometimes in doubt:

> Would it be asking too much of you to explain fully what the usual position is, how men and women should entwine themselves.

> Although I have read several books on the subject I have never yet learnt what is considered the natural position to adopt during union.

> Would it therefore be too much to ask you to just mention the principal position in which sex union may be accomplished?[110]

Others, though they were aware of the so-called missionary position, were taxed by 'this difficult subject of the ideal position for sexual union', since they had never heard of or thought of 'any but the usual position which suits me but as you say another position might be better'. 'In what position besides face to face should the act be done, will you kindly explain to me some of the various positions?[111] suggests bewilderment in the face of recently revealed erotic possibilities.
These difficulties were perhaps not so remarkable when many married couples indulged in intercourse clothed and in the dark, or so it can be deduced from some of the letters Stopes received:

Can you tell me what proportion of married women refuse to allow their husbands to see them nude?

Though I beg her for coitus just once with both of us naked she completely shrinks from it, even in firelight or dark.

If a woman realised how much her husband liked to see her naked and admire her in that state there would be fewer unhappy marriages to record.[112]

Other problems sometimes raised by Stopes's readers were to do with sexual activity continued into later life, after the wife's menopause:

We are sixty years of age and occasionally like intercourse but of course there is not the cumus [sic] or saliva of former days and often the entrance and passage are difficult.[113]

or with sexual activity during pregnancy, either its permissibility or the practicalities to do with positions.[114]

Whatever their difficulties and anxieties about sexual conduct, however, men regarded themselves as actors and initiators in the sexual act. Even those upon whom this seems to have placed an intolerable burden believed that it should be so. Men might wish that their wives would be more responsive, leave their nightdress off and the light on or wear pretty underwear for their husband's gratification.[115] The possibility that the wife might be the sexual aggressor was never voiced. In one marriage distressing demands for sexual union by a wife in an asylum with puerperal insanity were reported by her husband.[116] Was this normally too rare an occurrence, or was it too wholly unspeakable, in its inversion of the norm, to merit mention? Or maybe those men whose wives did take the initiative had no cause for complaint.

'Pain and unhappiness'

Numbers of men wrote to Stopes expressing distress about various aspects of their married relationship. Some of these have been already cited above in connection with the difficulties of consummation and achieving mutual satisfaction, and problems to do with birth control. In spite of the obvious strains that they described, these men were usually careful to declare that apart from the particular problem they sought remedy for, they had happy marriages and were contented with their wives.

Those who found that their wives were indifferent to sex were sometimes less contented with the overall relationship. In some cases it was a question of simply wanting their wife to be a little more sexually active:

> Whilst I admire her body mine 'leaves her cold'. She never 'handles' me and I never receive those kisses and caresses that I am anxious to bestow on her.

> You refer to the playing of an active part by the woman during the sex act and you speak of certain movements she should make...by what instinct can she know those movements which will most readily promote mutual facility?[117]

A far more profound lack of interest was a more frequent cause of complaint:

> She herself believes that in common with most girls of her class she is incapable of experiencing sexual desire or sensation.

> I am somewhat of a passionate nature and my wife is not. I tell her that the sensual side was left out when she was created. Still I am deeply in love with her and ardently desire her.

> My wife seems quite incapable of any sexual feeling or desire. I have done my utmost to awake this feeling, but have failed to do so.[118]

Men did not hesitate to describe the suffering this indifference caused them: 'I am one I suppose of thousands of ordinary middle-class husbands...I ought to be happy but I am not'; 'as I am fairly virile her attitude causes me pain and unhappiness.'[119] They were not simply deploring the deprivation of intercourse subsequent upon their wives' attitude but the degraded quality of intercourse itself when performed with a reluctant and unresponsive partner:

> I do not force it but general attitude is 'I am your wife I must submit'.

> I think she must have married, as I feel so many women must, with the fixed idea that it was her duty to submit at all times to the whim of her husband's desire...consequently after a time neither she nor I took any real pleasure in the sexual union.

My wife has not the slightest bit of feeling for intercourse which while she never refuses me, as you will understand, one cannot enjoy it to the full extent if their partner as it were hasn't any interest in it.

Loving wives know that it is expected of them and submit or offer themselves from a sense of duty but you will know that there is no satisfaction in that.

[She] seems to be guided by a sense of duty...which I regret to say I am finding just a little nauseating.[120]

Others spoke bitterly of their partner's coldness in terms which suggest that it went well beyond the bedroom:

So many Englishwomen look upon sexual intercourse as abhorrent and not as a natural fulfilment of true love...rock on which so many marriages are split...women often show their cruelty through their coldness.

Mine is a nature which *cries out* for that deep mutual love and passion, that intimate understanding and tender sympathy you so well describe; and it has withered up by being in an atmosphere of too low a temperature.[121]

Nevertheless, few of the current marriages of Stopes's readers and correspondents seemed to have reached the stage of outright breakdown, though some described previous unions which had done so. Rarely, one partner might be engaged in an adulterous affair: one man wrote of his 'very dear friend' who was 'a far greater influence for good than wrong in my life' and had given him 'all that a woman can to the man she loves'.[122] This was the exception rather than the rule, though some men stated that the stress caused by restraint either for contraceptive purposes or on account of their wives' coldness was driving them to consider such action: 'before long – and much against my will – I will be compelled to seek satisfaction elsewhere.'[123] At least one man found his escapades with other women completely inexplicable and a threat to his marriage over which he had no control:

Some six months ago I did a thing which I can never expect my wife to overlook. I made some attempt to take liberties with a maid in my father's employ. What made me do it I cannot say, I must have been mad. I must say that even before my wife found this out she suspected I was fond of other girls. I admit I did flirt but no more than that...[I] have offered to undergo an operation so that I shall never want that sort of thing again. Can you tell me if a doctor will do this for me...I am prepared to do anything if only I can keep my wife that is all I ask.[124]

An almost unique case was that of an army sergeant whose wife was purchasing contraceptive supplies from one of the Mother's Clinics set up by Stopes in order to conduct an adulterous relationship:

the advice and help you gave us should have been a path to happiness but owing to my wife's abuse of it, it has led to anything but happiness. I'm writing to ask you, not to supply her with any more goods, unless the application comes from me, and will you please send me a copy of what purchases my wife has made since March of this year.[125]

(Stopes refused to betray the clinic's confidentiality.) Conversely, one man recounted the story of his marriage, which had included his wife bearing three children by two different men, besides one of his own, all regarded as legally his, a tale told without any condemnation of his wife.[126]

The vast majority of the men who wrote to Stopes seemed committed to their marriages and emotionally bonded to their wives. They often entered marriage with an idealism as to its potential for their happiness which could lead to deep disillusionment, but also to a determination to get the best they could out of the relationship for the couple and any family they might have. Many of them realized upon reading Stopes's works that they had been clumsy and inept, but the type of man to whom these books appealed was less unthinkingly selfish than many writers assumed him to be. The enthusiastic response evoked by Stopes's writings, and the desire for instruction evinced by her correspondents, confirmed the opinion of one of them that the male was 'not such a selfish beast if he only knows'.[127]

5

'The most miserable of all patients': men with sexual problems

There is an assumption that male sexuality is not subject to the problems and complications which are understood to be an intrinsic part of female sexual functioning. As so incisively demonstrated by Naomi Pfeffer, the very male organs are regarded as less complex and less liable to malfunction than those of the female, an illusion maintained in part by labelling, so that the functioning of the male organs is represented in terms of health and that of the female organs in terms of pathology, and in part by an immense ignorance of how, in fact, the male organs work, the mechanisms of spermatogenesis being far more mysterious than the process of ovulation.[1] The impotent male in literature written during the inter-war years was almost always the unfortunate victim of a war wound, like Hemingway's Jake Barnes in *The Sun Also Rises*, or Clifford Chatterley in D. H. Lawrence's *Lady Chatterley's Lover*. At a less exalted literary level, the heroine of Helen Smith's *Not So Quiet* learnt from her fiancé that he had been wounded in such a way that the hoped-for perambulator on the lawn was no longer a possibility.[2] Symbolic these wounds may have been, but they represented a statistically unusual cause of male sexual malfunction. The designation of the male as unproblematic meant that men with problems of sexual dysfunction were 'among the most miserable of all patients that a doctor is called upon to treat'.[3]

'How seldom normal potency is to be found'

The common view of male sexuality might be that it was an impetuous force needing to be held in check, restrained outside marriage and indulged only with caution within it, but in spite of this assumption that only the pressures of civilization succeeded in keeping this force within the bounds necessary to prevent the overthrow of society itself, it was recognized by those who had had the opportunity to discover the experiences of individuals that matters were rather different. Occasional cases became widely known. The dissolution of Ruskin's marriage on the grounds of non-consummation was a high Victorian *cause célèbre*, and that other Great Victorian Carlyle was also widely supposed to have had a *mariage blanc*. Doctors who specialized in the area were aware that men had problems which were not simply those of maintaining control over an impetuous and insurgent force, while quacks preyed on the fears of men anxious about their manhood or fearful that through 'excess' they had wrecked their powers.

In 1870 an anonymous writer in *The Lancet* gave warnings against advising men with 'questionable powers' to marry: 'family practitioners will know how large a number of uterine maladies are directly traceable to ill-assorted unions.' The writer had no compassion for the victims of sexual weakness, describing them as 'as a rule, inexpressibly nasty', the aetiology of such dysfunction being attributed to the effects of long-continued masturbation and excesses.[4] Sir James Paget in 'Sexual Hypochondriasis' described the anxieties and problems which any doctor might encounter among his patients, most of which he assigned to a psychological cause:

> Though the physical causes of impotence and great decrease of sexual power may be thus numerous, yet from all these causes together the cases are less frequent than those due to nervous disorder or to mental defect; and the impotence which is complained of or dreaded without any real reason is more common still.[5]

A venereologist, F. W. Lowndes of the Liverpool Lock Hospital, in 1883 touched upon the problems of sexual hypochondriasis (distinct from the specific problem of venereal hypochondriasis in which the patient believed himself to have contracted a disease which he did not, in fact, have). He attributed fears of a disorder of sex to 'previous excessive intercourse or self-abuse'.[6] D. Hack Tuke in his *Dictionary of Psychological Medicine*, Volume II (1892), under the heading of 'Marriage and Insanity', mentioned that 'young men think of the loss of power and fear they are impotent' during the approach to marriage. As a result 'the idea of impotence may have become so dominant that no congress is possible' and 'probably most of the suicides which take place soon after marriage are due to ideas of impotence'.[7]

Victor G. Vecki, author of a much reprinted work on impotence first issued in 1888, practised in the USA but originated in central Europe, where he had served as a military doctor in the Croatian Army.[8] Thus his experience would seem to have spanned the Old World and the New: he believed that 'impotence besides being a very *serious* disease is also of *frequent* occurrence',[9] so frequent that the 'ideal condition of virility is somewhat rare with men following the customary manner of life of our days, and in any given case it will generally last for but a short time'.[10] While he believed that new instruments such as the urethroscope were illuminating lesions causative of states of sexual dysfunction previously attributed to neurasthenia, he was also convinced of the prevalence of psychogenic impotence with no apparent clinical cause:

> Comparing the number of psychically impotent with those that are affected with real impotence, we shall find that the former constitute a large portion of those applying for relief.[11]

The British doctor Arthur Cooper in *The Sexual Disabilities of Man*, first published in 1908 and appearing in a second edition in 1910, argued that impotence, far from reflecting the strains of modern life, had been 'from time immemorial a matter of anxiety to a vast number of mankind'. He considered that 'psychical impotence probably dates from the time when man first began to think about himself, and evidences are to be found in the writings of all ages.'[12] In his experience it was 'quite common for medical advice to be sought respecting the copulative power'.[13] He was inclined to believe that premature ejaculation was on the increase and a consequence of the strains of modern life:

> These cases of early ejaculation without assignable cause, may perhaps mean that under the nervous stress of modern life the sexual centres are becoming more impressionable and more quickly responsive to stimulation, and thus that the duration of the sexual act may be tending to become gradually shorter.[14]

Unusually he mentioned the role of other men in the aetiology of impotence, citing 'the not uncommon case of a man fancying himself impotent because he is not so vigorous as some friend is – or says he is, for these boasters exaggerate greatly.'[15]

Krafft-Ebing and Havelock Ellis described all sorts of bizarre and flamboyant perversions, nearly all of them ascribable solely to the male. More recent writers have also reached the conclusion that fetishism is an anomaly of sexual functioning almost exclusive to men. While it has been argued that men are responsive to a far wider range of stimuli, and more readily conditioned by them, it also seems entirely probable that a fetish offers reassurance to men with fears about potency, where the fetishism has not grown to exclude normal coital activity. The fetish acts as a form of magic against male anxieties about sexual arousal and functioning. Even in the 'liberated' era fetishism remains a male province, and such deviations have been used to argue for the continuing existence of prostitution, given the need for such unfortunates to find a partner ready to indulge their quirks.[16] But besides these flamboyant oddities of sexual behaviour there was a vast amount of quieter desperation: Freud commented that

> To the uninitiated it is scarcely credible how seldom normal potency is to be found in a husband... what a degree of renunciation, often on both sides, is entailed by marriage, and to what narrow limits married life – the happiness that is so ardently desired – is narrowed down.[17]

These examples suggest that male sexual difficulties were a constant problem likely to appear before the doctor far more often than might be suspected. Twentieth-century, post-First-World-War writers appeared sometimes to imply that sexual disorders were a new phenomenon, produced by the strains and tensions of modern life in the aftermath of the Great War, just as contemporary male problems are attributed to the strains of modern life and the changing roles of the sexes. It is possible that a certain proportion of impotence was caused by the after-effects of shellshock and war strain. Graves and Hodge in *The Long Weekend* (1940), their study of the inter-war era, considered that everyone who had served in the trenches for several months returned to civil life more or less an invalid, suffering from some degree of shellshock, the lingering effects of which took several years to pass off. They also contended that the strains of battle had created numbers of alcoholics.[18] A large number of men did of course suffer from long-term health problems as a result of the war, which could have affected their sexual functioning. A less direct link between the war and sexual dysfunction was the associated increase in cigarette-smoking: heavy nicotine consumption does have some correlation with impotence.[19]

Wilhelm Stekel's work on *Impotence in the Male* (1927) (a companion work to his similarly massive work on frigidity in women)[20] was only available in English in an American edition, but it does seem to have been read and cited by other specialist writers on the problems of male sexuality. It also, like the work of Vecki, demonstrated that male dysfunction was not a problem confined to one nationality or culture. Stekel (1868–1941), born in Vienna, was originally a general practitioner in a working-class area and among the earliest group of Freud's disciples, though he subsequently separated from Freud and psychoanalysis in its classical form.[21] In *Impotence in the Male* he maintained that

> The percentage of relatively impotent men cannot be placed too high. In my experience hardly half of all civilised men enjoy normal potency. Nowadays ejaculatio praecox is no longer a disorder; it is the regular accompaniment of civilisation.[22]

He considered that 'we are not dealing with rare cases and exceptions but with widespread disorders which are characteristic of our age.'[23] He discounted the belief that in ancient times men were more potent and instinctual, and put the prevalence of sexual disorder down to the fact that 'love is becoming more and more deep and profound', with the result that 'in men the struggle between the brain and the spinal cord is much more severe',[24] though he also contended that 'in some individuals the potency is enhanced by increased intelligence.'[25] Both his volumes presented the male sexual impulse as fragile indeed: 'there is hardly another physiological process which can be so easily disturbed by inhibitory ideas as the act of erection';[26] 'no man can say that he is absolutely certain of his potency.'[27]

Dr Siegfried Placzek, a Berlin neurologist, in *The Sexual Life of Man* (1929) remarked that 'imaginary obstacles of the most varied descriptions react on the capacity for coitus far more than is generally believed.'[28] H. W. E. Walther, an American urologist, while emphasizing the significance of physical lesions and the necessity for 'thorough study and examination through the urethroscope', nevertheless pointed out the statistical prevalence of the functional disorders in urological practice, and the frequent lack of 'correlation between the clinical phenomena and the urethroscopic picture'. Even among specialists whose major interest was in the physical lesions of the male genito-urinary system the functional nature of many of the disorders they encountered was recognized.[29] Drs Costler and Willy, and others, in the *Encyclopaedia of Sexual Knowledge*, published in London in 1934 under the general editorship of Norman Haire, also made readers aware that 'the anomalies which can occur in the male genital system are consequently numerous and varied', and noted that

> all unfavourable conditions can induce impotence...Men in general are very sensitive on the subject of their potency...a man, once persuaded that he is incapable of a normal erection, becomes impotent through auto-suggestion.[30]

Kenneth Walker (1892–1966) was the leading British writer on male disorders for several decades. He had a brilliant career in genito-urinary surgery, attending upon 'the highest in the land', but was always something of a maverick. With a sought-after post at St Bartholomew's Hospital, he nevertheless chose to spent three years practising in South America. In spite of his surgical background he was deeply interested in philosophical and social issues and the psychological basis of disorder. He was influenced by the thinking of Gurdjieff and Ouspensky. He also wrote a children's book, *The Log of the Ark*.[31] In *Male Disorders of Sex* (first published in 1930), he implied in the introduction that medical men might well frequently encounter problems of sexual disturbance. These complaints fell inconveniently between the specialisms of neurology and urology, and the busy general practitioner might dismiss them as trivial and non-life-threatening. Walker indicated that the problem was not that doctors did not encounter such cases but that very few had the knowledge to deal with them, even if they had the time to give to them. He acknowledged that these disorders were common, far more so than was popularly believed: '"First night impotence" ...such cases as this are commoner than is usually supposed... there are many men who are frightened of sex.'[32]

Kinsey's evidence in his famous *Sexual Behaviour in the Human Male* (1948), although applying to a sample taken wholly from within the USA, tended to confirm the assumption that lower-class men, while lacking in sexual subtlety, suffered much less than more refined males from problems of sexual functioning: he concluded that 'most cases of impotence... are to be found among upper level, educated males.'[33] However, Kinsey did not regard premature ejaculation as a problem, considering speedy reactions to be an intrinsic part of male response, and characteristic of the lower-class male. Indeed, he concluded that it was not justified scientifically to regard a rapid sexual response as pathological, perceiving it as a problem solely from the point of view of the woman in the relationship. Other evidence indicates that many men found their prematurity not satisfying, a cause for complaint, from their own point of view as well as that of their partners.

The vast prevalence of male sexual dysfunction is borne out by the number of enquiries Marie Stopes received concerning such difficulties. It is not easy to quantify this prevalence, since some correspondents were not very clear about exactly what their difficulty was, and problems might be subsumed under queries relating to birth control methods, requests for help in unconsummated marriages, or pleas for advice over giving wives equal sexual satisfaction. Also types of dysfunction cannot always be differentiated, as Kenneth Walker pointed out:

> If we care to make a preliminary subdivision of these cases into those in which the main symptom is weakness of desire and of erection, and those in which it is irritability and premature ejaculations... we must realise that the division is an arbitrary one and not really fundamental. Irritability and weakness may be different manifestations of the same disease and are often found at different times in the same patient.[34]

'We are the victims of our own natures'

The problem which struck Stopes as almost epidemic in its prevalence on the basis of the enquiries received by her was premature ejaculation, which she therefore dealt with in greater detail in *Enduring Passion*. She, like Stekel and Cooper, regarded it as a disease of civilization, and distinguished it from 'the ordinary haste and carelessness used by too many quite normal men in the marital act'.[35] Complete impotence she considered 'rare, but less rare than is generally imagined'.[36] Irritability or premature ejaculation distressed many men who suffered from it but on the whole they did not, when consulting Stopes, classify it as impotence pure and simple: 'my trouble is that ejaculation takes place simultaneously with erection... I am 42 years of age and strong and healthy and am not in any way impotent;'[37] perhaps because the functions of erection and ejaculation were felt to be there, if somewhat over-hasty in their actions. Many of the men who wrote to Stopes complaining of this disorder were anxious to point out that they were not weaklings in the general sense, but were 'a big man and strong', 'above the average in physical fitness', 'organically healthy', 'well-built, athletic, physically very strong', 'athletic', 'hard and fit', 'healthy and possessed of no defect physically that I know of'.[38]

One reader remarked that 'your book brought great comfort in hearing alone that it is a more or less common complaint.'[39] Many men had only realized that their problem was not a unique curse and might even be treatable on reading Stopes's works – particularly *Married Love*:

> You refer to husbands being cured of too hasty ejaculation. This has always been my trouble.

> You refer to husbands being cured of the habit of too rapid ejaculation.

> You write of husbands being cured of premature ejaculation...how exactly is the cure brought about?

> You say that husbands have been cured of this but not how.[40]

One claimed that 'if some of us men knew how to overcome this difficulty no doubt many of us would take steps to cure it, after all we are the victims of our own natures.'[41] Only one seemed to have discussed the problem with other men: 'I am aware from intimate conversations with other men that it is a common trouble amongst them.'[42] He did not state if these confessions were generated by the discussions of *Married Love* some correspondents mentioned.

Far from being untroubled by this problem of hasty ejaculation except from the point of view of obtaining pleasure and satisfaction for their wives, men often described this over-urgency as being unproductive of pleasure for themselves:

> Neither of us ever feels that satisfaction in the closest embrace which instinct and reason tell me should be the case.

> No doubt accounts for something lacking in my married life.

> This is no good either for myself or for my wife.

> I am unable to control the ejaculation so as to enjoy the perfect orgasm you speak about.

> Mere physical relief for me devoid of all pleasure and love.

> From my own point of view I get practically no satisfaction or relief either...each unsuccessful union leaves me more disgusted with myself and depressed.[43]

In some cases this personal unhappiness about the condition may have been due to the 'growing feeling of inferiority and ineffectiveness' expressed by one man.[44] The fear was also expressed that 'it causes me to desire, I am afraid, more than is temperate, because I never do get proper satisfaction.'[45]

What these men were describing was not just an inability to contain their orgasm for the twenty minutes recommended by Stopes for the achievement of the perfect conjugal orgasm, although considerable bewilderment was expressed at the possibility of such a feat: '[I] do not understand how a man after penetration can control himself for 20 minutes and at the same time bring on the crisis in the woman.'[46] The trouble was often an extreme precipitancy which could occur as soon as or even before intromission had taken place:

> In the case where this occurs almost immediately on entry what would you suggest?

> So hasty is the ejaculation that it frequently occurs before entry is possible, and neither of us benefit.

> I have never been able to keep back the semen during the act, in fact when first married and even now ejaculation would take place before I could nearly penetrate.

> In the endeavour to find the opening the excitement provokes a discharge.[47]

It was a sad irony that several of them described the act of wooing or their wives' own responsive desire as being responsible for these disasters:

> When my wife desires I thrill so terrifically that I find I eject before I have been with my wife many seconds.

I find that in my case by the time my wife is tumescent I have reached such a state of sexual excitement that ejaculation takes place before we have had a union.

When I follow your instructions regarding the preparation by wooing, ejaculation frequently occurs before the act of union can be commenced.

When I feel she does want [connection] I explode in a couple of minutes or so.[48]

Some sufferers had tried to control their hasty reactions by will-power, something which did not, it would seem, enjoy a great deal of success, even when their reactions were not so extremely precipitate:

I've tried to 'put my mind' to restraining the ejaculation, but it just happens – not even 2 or 3 minutes being vouchsafed to the act of union.

I have willed myself to wait, often, but might as well try to dam a torrent with brushwood.

I am unfortunately one of those men who apparently have no power to control the ejaculation and this normally takes place with me within half a minute of insertion.[49]

Others did not see how control over ejaculation could even be feasible:

I do not see how once penetration has begun this can be possible, as, seeing that it is actually possible to experience a reaction through a mere embrace without any actual union taking place, surely the arrival of the climax is bound to be beyond the man's control.

Is not excessively hasty ejaculation due to a congenital irritability of the nerves, and is it not incurable?[50]

In one or two cases mention was made of the (rather counterproductive) use of abstention in the hopes of improvement, in at least one case at medical suggestion.[51] Others had made some kind of approach to an individual solution, but these adjustments were not always satisfactory:

> [I] have found that on some occasions when I do not allow myself to become emotionally excited, a certain amount of movement and a moderately satisfactory union is possible. But quite a small degree of excitement results in premature ejaculation.

> My best time is in the morning when it is not kind to wake a woman up. Besides I don't think morning is the best time.

> Have you any experience as to whether it is harmful or otherwise for the man to wear a small rubber band just sufficiently tight to allow only a portion of the fluid to escape. Does any harm arise from the portion that has been so to speak stirred up but not ejected.[52]

One of Stopes's suggestions to men with this trouble was to pause and then attempt a second union on the same occasion, since the initial sensitivity might be somewhat abated. Even when a man found himself capable of a second erection and another union this was not always regarded as a happy solution, some men fearing that this might lead to debility, and others still being upset at their inability to control their first, hasty ejaculation.[53] Quack remedies were a possible resort, but one in which little confidence was expressed: 'is [there] any possibility that the tablets advertised could be of use – or are they a complete swindle?'[54] Some of Stopes's readers did find some benefit in following her prescription of the application of a lotion to render the glans less exquisitely sensitive. She mentioned this in reply to letters evoked by *Married Love*, and included instructions on how to make it up in *Enduring Passion*.[55] 'Rather less than a month's use of your lotion effected the most remarkable improvement', one reader claimed, and another agreed: 'I have found some benefit from the use of the lotion you describe in your book *Enduring Passion* for premature ejaculation.'[56] It would be hard to estimate how far the benefits were psychological, a question which could also be asked about the hormone preparations Stopes later came to recommend.[57] Another expedient recommended by Stopes to couples in this predicament was for the husband to induce his wife's orgasm manually, so that she was not left 'in the air' as so many feared she would be. This suggestion may have contributed to alleviating 'performance anxiety' by giving explicit permission for an act about which many individuals felt inhibited.

'Unable to enjoy the sexual relation'

The converse problem, that of retarded ejaculation, was either very much rarer or bothered Stopes's readers to a much lesser degree, since few of them consulted her on this problem. The problem received no mention in the 1930 edition of Walker's *Male Disorders of Sex*, suggesting that if not rare, it was not a problem much found in the consulting room. In one case presented to Stopes, a couple had been indulging in 'love-play' but not intercourse. When they attempted to 'commence intercourse' the husband found that

> I am not able to ejaculate – or shall I say, I presume I am unable...the wooing is done by me on each and every occasion but to me (although ardent) there does not come the passion – not even the old passion before we had union at all.

Since it would appear that some form of copulation was neverthe-less taking place this cannot be regarded as a simple case of impotence.[58] Another case was that recounted to Stopes by the wife of a 'universally abstemious, hard-working and self-controlled' man:

> The man is unable (on nearly every occasion) to reach any climax or ejaculate any semen; erection and union occur quite easily but nothing further. This leaves both with a feeling of dissatisfaction and in 'mid-air' as it were.[59]

One man, while continuing subject to the nocturnal emissions he had experienced every few weeks prior to his marriage, found that

> Whenever we have sexual intercourse instead of the sexual excitement increasing more and more until it culminates in the unmistakable emission of semen and the collapse of the penis...the excitement gradually dies down leaving the penis still erect until finally (after say about half an hour) the only thing seems to be to withdraw, feeling somewhat unsatisfied.[60]

Premature ejaculation was pre-eminently a problem among the newly married, and might eventually be overcome by the establish-ment of habit and the decline of the overcharged excitement of the early days of matrimony. Impotence, the failure or uncertainty of actual erection, was more a problem of the middle-aged:

I find that the last few months my power of erectibility is waning so much that penetration is not possible. [aged 60]

We are deeply devoted to each other and my wife more anxious for the pleasures of the bed than ever but alas!...I'm very rarely able to get an erection. [aged 54]

In the last 2 years I have been faced by excessive physical fatigue for no apparent cause and a gradual decrease of sexual prowess now beginning to amount to impotence. [aged 43]

I am a married man 58 years of age and now find myself unable to enjoy the sexual relation with my wife properly.

At the age of 50 while otherwise in abounding health I am finding a deplorable weakness in our sex unions.[61]

It was not necessarily a question of the total disappearance of desire: 'the desire is keen but the reaction is sluggish'; 'I [aged 50] still feel amorously disposed but find that my erections are defective and lack the rigidity of former days.'[62] The waning of desire as such was suffered by some men:

She is 42 and as virile [sic] as ever. Unfortunately, I have lost all desire. [aged 45]

I am beginning to become one of the 'under-sexed husbands' as quoted in your *Enduring Passion*.

I have no pains or trouble, just my normal self, but no desire for the opposite sex. [aged 29, widower][63]

It is not always easy to differentiate between the cases of men who regretted the passing of their virility for their own sakes and those who regretted it on behalf of their wives:

It is very humiliating to me and while my wife bears sympathetically with it, I fear she is disappointed.

My wife being well-sexed suffers as a result. [man aged 40]

I'm not able to do her justice although we lie every night in each other's arms. [aged 54]

This is having a very serious effect on my wife's nerves. [aged 50]

I have never felt for the last twelve years that I really did my duty by my wife. [aged 50][64]

However, few of the men who wrote about this problem and possible solutions expressed it as one man of fifty-five did: 'I am badly in need of something to make me able to face up to my wife.'[65]

Some men attributed their failing to prior indulgence in masturbation: 'this is brought about I expect from unwise habits contracted in youth and even carried on after my married life.' One or two put it down to the prolonged practice of coitus interruptus, or to a general state of fatigue or stress: 'a marked tendency to impotence which I can only ascribe to nervous debility', or simply the expectation of failure after one episode: 'a sudden unusual impotence and since then doubt as to the ability to succeed [aged 57]'.[66] But often they were unable to account for it:

I have not led a fast life nor in our early married life did we exceed the usual limit. My general health is good...PS I rarely touch stimulants.

I have not abused myself in any way and cannot account for it.[67]

Stopes was able to reassure enquirers that some flagging in sexual performance was a frequent experience in men of middle years, and that providing that the sufferer did not fret himself into a state of anxiety about 'declining powers' all might be well.

The difficulties of premature ejaculation and impotence involved a disturbing lack of congruence between desire and performance in those suffering from them. Those who found that lack of interest in sex, or 'sex anaemia',[68] was growing upon them with advancing years nevertheless had some idea of what it was that they were missing. It might be imagined that men who experienced little interest in sex and lacked desire would therefore not consider themselves to have a problem. This was not always the case. Sometimes a man who felt infrequent desire rather than none at all might marry:

My worry is that I feel I am slightly undersexed, at any rate in relation to the sex activities of my wife. Normally we have union every 3–4 weeks...I am sure it would be to her happiness if we had union more frequently, and incidentally, it would also be to my own happiness.

This man did at least enjoy sex when he found himself capable, unlike another who specifically claimed 'I cannot enjoy the sex act.'[69] Sexual anaesthesia was the problem for some men:

> I have always suffered a tremendous lack of desire and virility...The times that I have had intercourse have been more or less satisfactory for her, but for me rather an effort as I find all the time myself trying to *create desire* which is not there, for her or anybody, and this has naturally given me an inferiority complex. Were this not so, I would still lack my 'manhood'...I have always felt that perhaps my glands were lacking.

> Does it not seem strange that in our union, though I succeed in giving my wife intense pleasure, I myself go through the act without *any sensation whatever*? [aged 50, just married, for the first time][70]

Engaging in sexual activity, therefore, was not so very simple an undertaking for the male. Even if totally oblivious to the needs of his partner and his obligations towards her, he was still likely to find that the act was not an automatic and pleasurable success.

'Unable to hold myself in'

The concept of 'spermatorrhoea' does not seem to have continued in prevalence into the 1920s: although one or two of Stopes's correspondents did use the word to describe their disorder,[71] this was not very common. However, the belief in the weakening effects of undue seminal losses still persisted, to create misery in large numbers of young men. It was often not realized that, as Walker pointed out, 'involuntary nocturnal emissions occur in the normal male from puberty onwards.'[72]

The belief that even within legitimate marriage the expenditure of semen could be depleting persisted: a few of Stopes's correspondents touched on this worry.[73] This anxiety was considered by E. F. Griffith (author of *Modern Marriage*) in an unpublished fragment among his later writings after he had undergone Jungian analysis and himself become an analyst: 'it still seems to worry many a man today; his fear of ejaculation.' The often-given reason was that 'he has been told by parent or teacher that the seminal fluid possesses some particular and vital function; that every time he ejaculates he loses strength and vitality.' Griffith hypothesized that the real cause for the anxiety lay deeper, that it was because 'at this moment he loses conscious control; he surrenders himself to the woman.'[74]

The notion that involuntary seminal losses could be deleterious accounted for much of the anxiety which was expressed around masturbation and nocturnal emissions by men who wrote to Marie Stopes. Such losses were not only believed to be depleting in themselves; it was feared that they were a symptom of, or led eventually to, impotence. Stopes's readers certainly expressed extreme perturbation at spontaneous emissions of semen. Some men experienced these in the course of sleep in connection with dreams:

> I had dreams which caused similar occurrences and these became so frequent that I lay the case before a doctor.

> Is there any treatment (otherwise than physical drill) for men with a *too* frequent (natural ejaculation) which affects them adversely (during dreams)?

> [Dreams] which result in unconscious and often very painful emission ... seriously drained my health, greatly weakened my memory and left a continual dread of their constant recurrence.

> I had become a physical and mental wreck, for voluptuous dreams and night losses had added their effect.[75]

One man who had averaged an ejaculation every night for over thirty years wrote to Stopes for advice about this, as he believed it to be weakening him.[76]

Other young men were especially frightened by the fact that, during the course of prolonged engagements, they experienced spontaneous emissions in the waking state:

> the emissions always occur quickly, and complete discharges eventually, when I embrace and kiss my young lady.

> I get an erection whenever my girl kisses me and if we have a long kiss and she is on my knee I often get a discharge. [former army officer, educated at Rugby][77]

They were also worried by the recurrence of nocturnal emissions:

Lately I have felt a sexual longing when sitting on the couch with my fiancée...Since feeling the sexual longing I have occasionally had a discharge of semen when asleep although up till lately I have not had a single discharge for years.[78]

The anxieties caused by the sexual arousal consequent upon courtship and often prolonged but chaste engagements were sometimes severe: one young man was so horrified by the sexual feelings aroused by his fiancée that upon going to the front during the first World War he 'almost hoped I should never return alive'.[79] Another young man, a schoolteacher, found that his bi-monthly meetings with his fiancée rendered him 'nervously excitable and fatigued and sensual in thought'.[80] The strain of lengthy engagements sometimes provoked questions such as the following:

Do you consider it wrong, either from a physical or a moral point of view, for two such persons to give each other relief – provided that actual intercourse does not take place?[81]

Stopes did not believe this expedient to be desirable; her usual suggestion to young people in this state was to marry and to use birth control until they could start a family (she also tended to advocate the wife working until such time as economics permitted childbearing).

Connected to these anxieties around sexual manifestations was the host of fears which many of Stopes's correspondents expressed to do with masturbation. Few elaborated any details about their practice of the habit, except in terms of frequency or how long continued: but one man described the 'sins of my youth' as 'onanism committed with a lady's corset wrapped around a pillow'. Another described his chosen method of self-gratification by rubbing against the bed-sheets.[82] One confessed that 'I in the first place purchased [Married Love] in order to satisfy these promptings' to masturbation, but had undergone a conversion through reading it:

I hope I shall be able to cure myself of I now realise *utterly loathsome cravings*...with your aid I have now realised that there is something fuller and deeper behind it than mere satisfaction.[83]

Marie Stopes received many letters from men who were extremely anxious about masturbation, either because of fears that they had damaged themselves or because of their inability to break the habit.

Sufferers (and it is clear that in their own eyes it was suffering) from the habit often described it in extremely pejorative terms:

The beastly thing.

That pernicious and shameful habit self-abuse.

The abominable habit of masturbation...I have been a weak and miserable rotter.

[I] got into the terrible evil of self-abuse.[84]

Comments such as 'I was a slave to the vile practice of masturbation', 'a terrible craving to give way to self-abuse',[85] suggest considerable internalization of prevalent attitudes towards the solitary vice. Even when descriptions of the habit were less hysterical, it was called 'folly', a 'mistake', a ' "disease" '.[86]

One or two readers did voice some scepticism about how horrendous the effects of self-abuse might be: 'I know it should be discouraged but all boys do it and nothing ever happens.'[87] Some considered it a 'lesser evil' than fornication:

I was told and I believed, that the only possible alternative to this was to go with prostitutes, and that this alternative was more degrading than the other.

I feel sure [it] is not so harmful as generally thought but is obviously unpleasant and undesirable.[88]

This commonsensical approach to the problem, that occasional regulated indulgence in self-abuse was better than a resort to fornication, may possibly have had considerable currency; by the 1930s it was a commonplace concession in works of sexual advice. It was a point of view contrasting with the tales of those men who were so horrified by their practice of self-abuse that they sought fornication as a cure:

Do you think in my case it would be wrong to go to a prostitute?

I thought to have connections with a woman would cure me.

Before I was married I used to have unions three and four times a night, two or three times a week with different girls in the hope of curing myself but it was of no use.[89]

Masturbation was usually presented to Stopes as something of which the sufferer was a victim:

The urge got a great hold on me until finally I was unable to hold myself in.

I formed the habit of masturbation years ago, could not break it when I wanted.

I used to be edected [sic] to this.[90]

In some cases it was said to have been begun or picked up in ignorance of its dangers:

From the age of 18 (I am now 28) until 2 months ago I was foolish enough to masturbate.

So in my ignorance I abused myself, not realising the damage I was doing.

I did not know the dangers of it and became, I suppose, fascinated and practised it for about three years.[91]

Some men felt that they should have been warned:

[I] was denied such knowledge as a boy, abused myself, was never warned and for 20 years was deprived of my manhood's rights.

A weakness which I fell into as a child and which my Victorian parents never noticed or warned me against.[92]

One man declared 'it is only now that I seem able to control myself after having learned about the evil consequences attendant on the practice.'[93]

Men described the feelings and symptoms which they experienced as a result (so they believed) of the practice. For some this was a matter of its effects on the 'nerves':

This has given me a great feeling of nervousness, shame and remorse.

When I was about 22 I had a nervous breakdown and the doctor who attended me said case was taken just in time and that I was on the verge of Petit Mal...It was not until I read that book that I realised what harm I had been doing to my health through self-abuse.[94]

Others believed it had had deleterious effects upon the organ itself, either by restricting its growth – 'my penis is far too small...this I realise...is due to abuse'[95] – or by causing precisely the opposite effect: '"too frequent erection", a certain "flabbiness" and possible "over-enlargement" of the male organ, due probably to youthful indulgence in solitude'.[96] Varicocele (distended veins around the spermatic cord on the scrotum) was widely supposed to be another effect: 'I was operated on, in Africa, for variocele [sic]', 'my left testacle [sic] became swollen and in 1914 I was operated on for variocele [sic].'[97]

At least one of Stope's correspondents (a working-class man) believed self-abuse to have caused the traditional penalty: 'eventually nature's desire and masturbation turned me insane in my opinion.'[98] A railway company clerk produced a compendium of symptoms which reads like a quack pamphlet's warnings on the subject:

As a result I am very pale and awfully depressed, I cannot interest myself in anything, I am unfit for my work, sometimes I feel so depressed that I wish I was dead. I am perfectly certain that my present condition is due to my awful folly as described above...My chief ailments are: – increasing headaches, aching eyes, and I have a throbbing in my body that seems to make my whole being give a little automatic jump, the jump keeping exact time with my pulse and veins, the throbbing is greatly pronounced near the temple and ears.[99]

Another man was so convinced of the deleterious effect of masturbatory practices that he wrote, at the age of 29, to declare that all his troubles were due to self-abuse carried on for a period of five months at the age of 17, since when he had abandoned the habit. Eczema between the legs and a dripping of urine after passing water were also attributed to the habit.[100]

Others, while noticing no particular adverse effects upon themselves, were concerned that it might have affected their capacity to father children:

Would it hinder me in married life as regards being responsible for children as I hope to be some day when means permit.

Would not dream of having children should I marry – which seems impossible.[101]

It was also blamed for sexual dysfunction: 'I am now wondering if it is the cause of my ineffective efforts', '[I was] completely in ignorance that harm would result when I married.'[102]

Fears around the loss of semen caused by an inability to control the spontaneous eruption of sexual desire led some men to beg for a remedy for this ailment, as they perceived it:

> Now will you tell me if vasectomy will cure my loss of semen, for I confess that even yet I get at intervals the terrible craving to indulge in this sin, and sometimes have nocturnal losses.[103]

Circumcision was sometimes thought to be a potential remedy:

> Would you advise me to be circumcised...If you advise circumcision could I do it myself as I don't wish to approach a doctor on the subject as I am thoroughly ashamed of myself.[104]

Few of those who wrote to Stopes mentioned quack remedies: one said that he had been recommended to take 'Damaroids', another enquired of Stopes if there were 'any prescription' for his trouble, and another asked 'is there any treatment (otherwise than physical drill)?'[105] Anti-masturbational devices do not seem to have been in use; however, one man described his own 'efforts to prevent it – extra clothing at night, tying up hands in gloves, all to no effect'.[106]

Stope's usual response to such cries for help was to be reassuring, although she also advocated trying to give up habits of masturbation by cutting down and regulating its use. She was inclined to be scathing about such commonly prescribed remedies as bromides. One young man claimed that he had had a nervous breakdown out of fear for his sexual powers caused by Stopes's remarks about the potential of masturbation to coarsen the nerves and vitiate the male response,[107] but her advice both in her books and to her readers in correspondence was more likely to soothe and encourage than scare.

Masturbation was a practice which for many men was surrounded by guilt and fears, which extended to cover emissions that were not voluntarily produced. The use of the term 'pollutions' to describe these embodied the emotions they raised. So adverse were the feelings about these phenomena that even the sexual feelings roused by contact with an intended wife were sometimes perceived as frightening as well as sinful.

'My organ of sex is slightly below normal'[108]

While the anxieties discussed above were to do with the inability of men to control the activities of their genital organs, other anxieties focused upon the physical conformation of the organs themselves. Men wrote to Stopes for reassurance that they were 'normal', or for means by which they could remedy the matter if they were not.

The most frequent cause of worry in this respect, not surprisingly, was the fear that the sexual organ was too small:

My sexual organ is very much smaller than my wife's and she can scarcely feel me at all. Is there a method by means of which my sexual organ can be enlarged without injury?

I am rather shy and have never discussed the subject actually with anyone but I think my genital organs are below the average size. My erected penis is approx 5½" long and 1½" in diameter.

I am smally made by nature...[is there] any means known to medical science by which I can increase the size of my congenital [sic] organ?[109]

Sometimes this anxiety was based on actual comparison with other men:

Compared with the other men I was equal and more so in physique but my penis is far too small compared with the rest of my body.

I have been laughed at because...my penis has been much smaller than the average...I have taken measurements and normally it is nearly 4" and at other times it is about 5½" long.[110]

Others feared that excessive largeness would have an adverse effect on marital relations,[111] and in some cases failure to consummate was put down to such disproportion.[112]

Varicocele also provoked requests for information: 'What is the best treatment for variocele [sic]? Is it detrimental to marriage?'[113] There were worries over what men perceived as other abnormalities of the testicles:

Both my tisticles [sic] were badly injured matter formed and they had to be lanced to let matter out...do you think I should not marry. Would my children be healthy if I was to have any.

[Dysentery] seems also to have affected my sex organs in particular my testes [I think that is the correct expression) in that they seemed to shrink to considerably less than their normal size.[114]

There was also anxiety in cases where one testicle remained undescended.[115]

Circumcision seems to have aroused a variety of anxieties, from queries as to its value – 'is circumcision really of any moral value, or is it merely a custom delivered to us from the east?' – to problems caused by not having undergone the operation:

I was never circumcised as a baby and as a consequence on entering my wife 'bare' the loose skin at the end of the penis is easily pushed back out of place (except where the skin is grown onto the side of the penis.[116]

In contrast, a Mr F. stated:

with regard to control of ejaculation in my opinion circumcision has a great bearing on this method as I am speaking from personal experience having been served by this inhuman operation...I find that men who have not been circumcised can control ejaculation more than men who have and I firmly believe this business is done solely to increase the population.[117]

One man, although he had already been circumcised in childhood, sought advice as to the advisability of having it done again.[118] Another believed that the odd growth of his foreskin was the reason for his childless marriage.[119] The case of the man who was prepared to circumcise himself as a cure for masturbation and emissions has already been quoted.

Other worries had to do with 'emissions during sleep which have been deeply stained with blood'; a brown spot on the head of the penis; a clear secretion from the penis; spots inside the penis; and large blue veins.[120]

Prostate troubles agitated a number of men. In some cases this anxiety seems to have been aroused by reading Stopes's own works, in particular *Change of Life in Men and Women* (1936), in which she deplored the scant attention given by the medical profession to this problem.[121] Although this may have contributed to the arousal rather than the allaying of worry, one man, whose heart condition made an operation out of the question, had been given hope by reading her work that amelioration might be gained without surgery. Another, who had just had a prostatectomy, complained that he felt very rundown and weak and asked Stopes for her advice. Certainly the idea of the operation was frightening for men: one, a doctor himself, wrote to Stopes of his fear of such intervention and described a failed catherization.[122]

Very few men wrote to Stopes concerning venereal disease: perhaps this was a problem which they felt the medical profession was adequate to cope. Nor did they write to her with phobic fears of having contracted venereal disease, a condition which according to venereologists was far from rare, and found 'mainly in men', seldom if ever in women.[123] Presumably individuals who feared this would take their symptoms to a clinic or their own doctor.

Stopes did not receive confessions pertaining to the more bizarre sexual variations: far from being fetishists of the exotic kind detailed in the pages of Krafft-Ebing or Havelock Ellis, Stopes's correspondents were more likely to enquire as the permissibility of spouses seeing one another in the nude,[124] or to comment that 'I'd love her to slip on a pretty slip or brassiere for me yet she has no idea of the joy it would give me.'[125] This was a rare reference to women's underwear, which had undergone radical changes (the brassiere itself was not invented until about 1916), becoming much less cumbersome and utilitarian, much lighter and much prettier, and an increased focus of erotic interest.[126] One man deplored the 'Corslet Brazziers' worn by his wife to 'hide her figure' so that she would 'appear slim in order to be fashionable' (presumably she had a full and buxom figure, unfashionable in 1926). Though it appears he preferred her with uncorseted bosom, he expressed this complaint in terms of damage to her health, not erotic preference.[127]

The expectation of sympathy which Stopes aroused in her readers did lead to a few men writing to her on the subject of their homosexuality. One man, who had been led to read Edward Carpenter's *Love's Coming of Age* by learning of its existence in the pages of *Married Love*, declared it to be 'one of the greatest revelations of my life' and wondered 'if only Dr Marie Stopes would write a book on the subject'. Another asked for her opinion as to whether 'perpetual restriction of the sex side' would be 'as harmful for the homosexualist as it is for the normal man?' Another felt able to confess to her 'I am a man but I am equally sure...that there is another side to my nature which is effeminately inclined.'[128] Such comments were rare, and men who had undergone seduction or 'degradation' while at school[129] usually mentioned this in connection with problems to do with masturbation, not as having initiated them into a lifetime of homosexual inclination.

The major source of anxiety for most men, at least those who wrote to Stopes, was clearly dysfunctions affecting the actual sexual union. A good deal of the worry around masturbation, emissions and defects of the genitalia had to do with fears of unfitness for marriage and fatherhood. The importance which many men placed on the marital relationship and the success of the sexual relation within it has already been demonstrated in the previous chapter. Failures in potency were not simply failures in 'manhood' in the abstract, but threatened a relationship which men valued. These dysfunctions, and the anxiety caused by them, were remarkably prevalent. Such difficulties troubled the highest in the land; it has been suggested, on perhaps meagre gossipy evidence, that sexual dysfunction may have been at the heart of the abdication crisis.[130]

6

'I shouldn't care to face the experience again': male sexual problems in the consulting room

Years of studying the intricacies of the human organism, it has been, and often still is, assumed, give doctors a particular and peculiar advantage in the sexual realm. There has always been a complacent supposition among the medical profession (shared by others) that medical training constitutes an essential preliminary to a true understanding of the mysteries of sex, and that doctors are uniquely qualified to assist those troubled in these matters. According to *The Lancet* in 1889, 'ours is a very responsible profession. Young men are looking to us as men looked to the old type of priests who combined moral and medical functions.'[1] In 1931 the Reverend T. W. Pym regretted that the educator could not 'speak of the physical side of sex in that matter of fact manner which we find and envy in those who profess the science of medicine',[2] while in 1935 the *British Medical Journal* was of the opinion that 'no walk in life engenders more sympathy with human frailty than does the practice of medicine.'[3]

Millais Culpin, professor of medical and industrial psychology at the London School of Hygiene, however, took a very different view. He declared in 1935 that 'the first sex problem in practice' was the practitioner himself. Just as there were practitioners temperamentally incapable of evaluating psycho-neurotic symptoms and who therefore never heard them, there were practitioners who, by their attitude, warned off any attempt to seek their advice on sex difficulties.

He further suggested that 'a practitioner who said he had never met a case of sexual perversion confessed to a personal inhibition.'[4] This depiction of the way the average general practitioner deflected, perhaps not even consciously, enquiries to do with sexual difficulties is confirmed by the reminiscences of Dr George Day, who much later became consultant physician to the Samaritans. Describing himself as a young doctor in the later 1920s and early 1930s, he wrote

> When I spotted the conversation veering in that direction I went cold and adroitly steered it elsewhere. I was both intolerant and ignorant. My medical education had not prepared me for that sort of thing.[5]

The correspondence received by Marie Stopes supports Culpin and Day. There is little in these letters to substantiate boasts such as the following, made in the The Lancet in 1901: 'most of what [Ellis] has written will be familiar to medical men because of the confidences that have been reposed in them',[6] or to corroborate assumptions underlying practitioners' complaints about 'the undesirability of undermining a patient's confidence in the ability of the family doctor'.[7] The doctors mentioned in letters received by Stopes can be assumed, where not explicitly stated, to be male, given the small number of women in the profession as a whole, and the tendency to ghettoize them into work with their own sex or with children. Even when active in family planning and sex education, women doctors tended to be primarily orientated towards the problems experienced by their own sex.

'So am extremely shy'

Writers on medical sociology have shown that the doctor–patient encounter is emotionally fraught for the patient even when the consultation does not involve so 'degrading' an ailment as sexual dysfunction. James McCormick, professor of community health at Trinity College Dublin, has commented that

Those disadvantaged in terms of status and social class still feel the need to behave in ways that will be approved by their doctors, because lacking that approval their prospect of gaining their objectives is substantially diminished. This need to be approved extends beyond behaviour to matters of dress and personal cleanliness.

Approaching a doctor for help on such a tabooed subject as sex would therefore be particularly productive of anxiety given the stigma surrounding it. This is not merely a lower-class reaction: as McCormick has pointed out, this 'need to be thought well of by the doctor is not confined to those whose status or class is different, and it stems, in part at least, from the supplicant posture.'[8]

The power relations of the doctor–patient encounter are such that men who might regard themselves as the social equals or even superiors of doctors find the strain of consulting one about a sexual difficulty considerable. In *Enduring Passion* Marie Stopes suggested that 'British men of the professional and upper classes', among whom such problems were rife, were often 'the very men who would never be suspected of any lack of normal sex capacity even by their medical attendants'.[9]

Stopes's correspondents who wrote of their reluctance to consult a doctor or of the humiliation they had encountered in doing so included admirals, high-ranking army officers and the 'twice-born' members of the Indian Civil Service. These were men not easily intimidated nor likely automatically to feel any sense of inferiority. The impression gained is that they had found going over the top or governing the Empire a far less harrowing and taxing experience than exposing a less than ideal sex-life to their medical practitioners.

There was certainly a general reluctance to consult doctors on problems relating to sexuality: the great majority of correspondents made no mention at all of having consulted, or even considering consulting, a doctor. They had been moved to write to Stopes by reading her books or through having heard of her work at the time of the Sutherland libel suit. *Married Love* or her other works had revealed to them that the difficulties and problems they had been encountering in sexual matters did not need to be endured with resignation. Having been told that their troubles were not either the natural course of events or a peculiar and unique personal failing, but were common difficulties and capable of remedy, they wrote to the author of this revelation for further assistance. The group writing to Stopes may have been a self-selecting sample attracted to her writings precisely because of her lack of unquestioning belief in the contemporary medical profession. Their opinions, being not therefore representative, may not constitute valid criticism upon the way doctors dealt with sexual problems.

However, in *Male Disorders of Sex* (1930), Kenneth Walker pointed out that

> The consciousness of sexual impotence brings with it a feeling of intense humiliation. The sufferer stands degraded not only in his own eyes but in the eyes of the world; he is robbed of every illusion and left without hope or purpose.[10]

The reluctance disclosed by Stopes's correspondents even to contemplate consulting their doctor suggests that the very prospect was attended with this consciousness of personal unworthiness. As Walker also stated,

> A man suffering from impotence is deeply ashamed and wounded. Loss of virility seems to him a disgrace. He feels that he is inferior to his fellows...In such circumstances the efforts of his medical advisers are handicapped from the start.[11]

Some of Stopes's correspondents, aware of something wrong prior to encountering her works, had contemplated consulting a doctor but had been unable to bring themselves to that point. It does not seem to have been the expense aspect which deterred them, since this was seldom mentioned: 'I am *not* trying to avoid the payment of a doctor's fee'[12] was an almost unique comment, though one or two considered that they could not afford a specialist or that, although competence was essential, any specialist would have to be 'inexpensive', or declared 'of course I had to give up trying to right myself as I could not afford it.'[13]

Others remarked bitterly on doctors' willingness to take fees for giving unhelpful advice and regarded doctors as financially exploiting their patients. An army sergeant seeking advice on the calculation of the safe period reported 'two family doctors' as 'willing to accept fees for the statement that they do not know!'[14] Another man wrote to Stopes giving a detailed account of what he perceived as a racket being operated by several doctors whom he encountered in the process of seeking a remedy for the sterility of his marriage, all of them, in his view, in collusion to extract the maximum profit from a desperate patient.[15]

Class factors entered into this anxiety: patients who were on the 'panel' of a doctor's practice under the national insurance scheme, rather than free contractors for his services, sometimes seemed to feel that with this humble status they could not expect to take up a doctor's valuable time with their sexual problems:

> I am only a panel patient and as you are doubtless aware doctors have neither the time nor in many cases the inclination to advise on such matters.

> I have a panel doctor but... should not care to approach him in this matter.[16]

However, even those who were accustomed to pay doctors for their services displayed a good deal of hesitation over consulting a medical practitioner upon sexual matters. The expense involved in consulting a registered medical practitioner does not seem to have constituted a prime consideration among Stopes's correspondents for writing to her, and many expressed a willingness to pay her for advice or a personal consultation. Some of them subscribed to her Society for Constructive Birth Control, thus aiding the establishment and support of birth control clinics for poor women.

From the tenor of their letters many of those who wrote to Stopes would seem not to have had one single doctor to whom they regularly went for all their problems, since they wrote not of 'my' or 'our' doctor but of 'a' or 'any' or 'a local' doctor whom they might consult but would rather not:

> I have a panel doctor but have never had occasion to visit him.

> I have not seen any doctor for six months.

> I shrink from the idea of calling on the nearest practitioner.[17]

This whole correspondence rather contradicts the cosy image of bygone medical practice with its reassuring figure of the friendly family doctor, sympathetically concerned for his patients and with an intimate knowledge of their lives, turned to in every crisis.

Many men simply felt a shyness about raising the matter at all:

> I cannot for the life of me ask this question of any doctor out here [the Malay States] as have never seen one about that (or about any disease) so am extremely shy about it.

I have never had the courage to speak to my doctor about it.

I *write* as I have not got the nerve to interview a doctor on so intimate a point.

When the doctor examined me I would not tell him the trouble.

I have tried to muster sufficient courage to go to a local doctor but somehow I cannot do it.[18]

Doubts were voiced as to whether a doctor would give them a sympathetic hearing:

They would probably put me off by some incomprehensible jargon (you know what doctors are!) or else take a pitying attitude at my lack of knowledge.

I hesitate to ask my family doctor owing to his orthodox ideas.

Not being sure of sympathetic hearing I do not care to consult our own doctor.

One is somewhat chary of applying to medical men and the like for advice on such a delicate point.

I am not sure that a doctor would appreciate my difficulty.[19]

Others specifically stated their reasons for writing to Stopes rather than seeking a doctor's advice. In some cases her sex seems to have led them to regard her with expectations of sympathy:

I would rather confide in a woman like you after reading your book than any man...somehow I feel could not tell any doctor what I feel I could tell you...I would *much rather meet you than one of your doctors.*

The idea of explaining my difficulty to another man is somehow very distasteful.[20]

However, one at least had felt some initial hesitation upon precisely this account: 'I feel somehow more at ease, writing to you, in spite of your sex, than discussing the matter with the usual medical men.'[21] The sympathy which her readers deduced either from the fact of her sex or from the evidence of her books, and in apparent contrast to their expectations of doctors, was an important factor in motivating them to write to Stopes:

> It is only the extraordinarily sympathetic manner in which you have dealt with these subjects that makes me explain what I would never dream of telling an ordinary practitioner.

> I prefer to write to you...than consult my own medical practitioner both because I feel that you will deal with the matter more sympathetically and on account of other reasons which I need not go into here.[22]

At least one correspondent gave the following reason: 'I feel it would somehow be less difficult to unburden myself to you, a total stranger, than to someone I know slightly.'[23]

Some general prejudices were expressed against doctors:

> I ask you this question in preference to our...doctor because I have most faith in your teachings.

> I don't want to address you – as doctor – as I don't want – a doctor's advice.

> I know that [my wife] is very much prejudiced against doctors and not without reason. I myself think many of them not the equals of experienced old women.[24]

Some writers were explicitly cynical about the capabilities of doctors to deal with such sensitive matters:

> There are things about which one cannot ask a doctor, even if the doctor knew anything about it when asked.

> I do not feel like going to my medical man on the matter, and am afraid he (and others) know little of these subjects.

> The usual medical practitioners...seldom have any practical advice to give.[25]

Some correspondents, however, were not so much generally disillusioned with doctors as dubious about the competence of those immediately available to them to help in such delicate cases:

I shrink from the idea of calling on the nearest practitioner, who might be dense and lacking in understanding.

I could not think of consulting any of our local doctors on this particular question, as I am of the opinion that they are nearly as ignorant as most other people on the subject.

I would go to a local doctor about the matter if I had any confidence in them.[26]

Even a local doctor described as 'good' was 'not the man to whom I could turn in a case of sexual trouble'.[27]

The particular geographical location in which the writer found himself was sometimes blamed. Some men purported to believe, with some justice, that they were residing somewhere where they could not expect to find a doctor in touch with the latest sexological developments:

My medical practitioners are *Army doctors*, who have probably little knowledge of the subject, and I do not know of a suitable civilian practitioner to go to in Shanghai.

I have no confidence whatever in any local practitioner here for it is only a remote country district.

There is not *one* doctor in this country town whom I could honestly expect sound advice from.

I live right away up in the north east of Scotland where doctors who give advice on sexual matters are hard to find.

We are now living right out in the wilds of Cornwall... neither of us care to mention the subject to our doctor – and we very much doubt if he would be able to enlighten us if we did.[28]

This desire not to consult local doctors was sometimes grounded in fears of gossip and social embarrassment:

I do not like to consult any of the doctors here as it is a small place and talkative.

They do not feel that they could consult a doctor, partly because they do not wish to go to a local one.

I live in a very small place in India and I do not care to go to our only doctor because everyone knows everyone else.[29]

It was not merely the 'local' practitioners who were scorned, for the above reasons, but the 'ordinary' doctor in general (which may have had to do with the feelings men had about the rarity and intractability of sexual disorders):

I do not believe the ordinary medical man knows enough to help.

The ordinary medical man, not having made any special study of this matter is unable to give any useful advice.

I feel that my difficulty is not one that can be dealt with by an ordinary doctor.

I do not put any confidence, I am afraid, in the ordinary practitioner on this matter.

I consider the Doctor [Stopes] a 100 years ahead of her time and if I consulted an ordinary doctor he would not approach the difficulty in the same way.

I want of course to put myself only in competent hands, and am doubtful whether the ordinary family doctor could achieve the desired result.[30]

While all these reasons for not consulting the doctors available to them may have been deliberate or unconscious mechanisms for not doing so, a corollary to the distrust of the average practitioner was a belief that somewhere there was a doctor who was capable of dealing with sexual difficulties to the patient's satisfaction. Stopes's enquirers were sometimes seeking a doctor whose thinking was along the lines they found and responded to in her works:

I wish to seek the advice of a physician. At the same time I realise that all medical men do not hold your views.

Some doctor who approved of your work would command my confidence.

I should be most grateful if you could put me in the way of a medical man in London to whom I could go with some chance of gaining understanding treatment and possibly some such help as you prescribe.[31]

Others were simply in search of a 'qualified' specialist:

If you would be so kind as to recommend me the name of an inexpensive but really competent (male) specialist on sexual questions.

I would rather apply to a doctor I knew dealt with such complaints.

[I] am anxious to go straight to a specialist who can advise treatment.

What I should like is a quiet talk with someone who is able to advise sympathetically and who specialises in these matters.[32]

One man requested the name of 'an up-to-date doctor. . . if possible within easy reach'.[33]

The desire to take their problems to a stranger may indeed have been one reason for people to avoid consulting their usual practitioner. One couple suffering from problems in their marriage had actually been to see a doctor 'in a strange town', where 'he looked on us as a newly married couple.'[34] However, from the correspondence cited above it would seem that those who wrote to Stopes were perhaps more concerned about the incapacity of the medical practitioners available to them to deal authoritatively with sexual problems.

'Worse than useless'

As well as expressing disillusionment with or lack of faith in the medical profession, men also recounted to Stopes discouraging experiences they had had in the consulting room. They deplored the reception they had met with, substantiating the fears of those who described their hesitation in even seeking help for that reason. Some doctors were said to have displayed a perfunctoriness and lack of interest from which their patients shrank:

They only asked a few perfunctory questions.

My doctor seems to treat the matter very lightly.

Before marriage I consulted a doctor who treated the subject with such indifference that it rather disgusted me.

I was informed that there was nothing that could be done for me.[35]

Other doctors were not perceived as sympathetic, particularly (as mentioned above) in contrast to Stopes herself:

I didn't feel the atmosphere sympathetic.

I always feel you have the great sympathy and *'understanding'* which the average medical man lacks.[36]

Numbers of men complained that they had actually been treated with scorn by the medical men they consulted. It is possible that they were misinterpreting attempts to reassure the patient by not taking his problem too seriously. The following comments suggest that this rather hearty approach was not appreciated:

He quite missed my point and treated the matter as a joke and the only result was we had a row, and I shouldn't care to face the experience again. [a commander in the Royal Navy]

I consulted the best doctor available and explained the whole position to him. He examined me and appeared to laugh at my fears. [a mining engineer employed in India]

I have approached my own doctor, an Edinburgh man, but he either seems not to know anything about it, or rather laughs at it.

Questions on the subject are apt to receive rather heavy-handed replies from the General Practitioner.

He even ridiculed the idea of my thinking I was impotent...I went to another and he only laughed at me.

The ordinary doctor smiles and makes a joke of difficulties in the way I mean...I went to the old Family Doctor...but he made light of it.[37]

Even if doctors were not actually offensive to their patients when dealing with sexual matters, it would seem from the experience of Stopes's readers that they were seldom at all helpful:

I consulted a local doctor on the subject but obtained absolutely no advice of any use whatsoever from him

You are quite right in saying men cannot get any help from their own family medical advisers.

I have consulted my doctor and he says he is unable to help me.[38]

According to the men who had futilely consulted them, doctors were as ignorant as or more so than themselves:

I decided he probably knew less about marriage than I did.

The surgeon who operated on me...although very free with me in conversation, could not give me any idea what caused this trouble, and I can see that they are not at all clear on this subject.

I have already consulted our family doctor, himself a married man, without gaining light or guidance obviously for the reason that he had none to give.

I have already consulted my own doctor on the subject but he seems to know practically nothing about it.[39]

It might have been hoped that even if doctors had no particular remedies to provide to sexual sufferers, they could have provided sympathetic listening and reassurance, and created such confidence in their healing abilities that even their ineffectual bromides and tonics would have had a potent placebo effect. It has been suggested that prior to the advent of 'scientific medicine' and effective chemotherapy for a wide range of disorders, doctors were much better at listening to their patients because this was something that they could do, and thus were able to generate a powerful placebo effect to ameliorate if not cure many ailments.[40] Stopes's correspondents, however, were bitter about their experience of doctors' lack of sympathy and inability to inspire confidence in their therapeutic competence.

A few even mentioned unsatisfactory behaviour from their practitioners in cases involving venereal disease: one man had accidentally made his wife pregnant while suffering from uncured syphilis contracted during the war: 'I have put the case to my doctor – as you know they are always retisent [sic] to tell you anything concerning this', and a man suffering from gonorrhoea and under doctor's treatment thought it 'seems to be getting worse.'[41]

Those seeking for information about sexual conduct while suffering from some other complaint were also badly served: one woman with a husband who had tuberculosis wrote

> Perhaps it is not advisable for my husband to have sexual intercourse while he is suffering from this complaint. He was examined by a specialist last week but he did not mention the matter at all.[42]

In other cases the advice given was too vague to be of much help: a man with heart disease was told by the 'heart specialist' 'to have no children and to avoid any abuse of sexual intercourse, undue straining would have serious consequences'.[43]

'Nothing seems to have any effect at all'

Some doctors did at least make some kind of physical examination, although not all of them bothered: 'I consulted a doctor but I was not examined physically.'[44] Reassurance about their general state of fitness did not set men's minds at rest:

> Although he examined me most thoroughly he was unable to find anything wrong with me.

> Three different doctors, all of whom seem to confine their examination to the physical condition and all with the same finding, i.e. 'physically sound' but none offer any real advice on the point at issue.

> My panel doctor...after examination could find nothing wrong with me. He suggested I might be a little 'rundown' in general health.

> I was assured that I was quite normal, except for my nervous system which was in a bad state...marriage would be beneficial.[45]

Transatlantic urologists such as Walther and Vecki lauded the 'vistas undreamed of' opened up by developments in urethroscopy.[46] There was scant allusion by Stopes's correspondents to any such deep probing. One clergyman had been recommended cytoscopic examination, but found 'the doctors are not agreed' and it is not clear if the examination actually took place.[47]

Some doctors were inclined to dismiss the whole matter with references to 'nature':

All the doctor can say is that is natural.

My medical men...both think these things should be 'left to nature', say I shall 'find out in due course'.

Doctor says don't worry...condition natural...some men start chasing flappers and small boys.[48]

Others invoked the healing properties of time: 'my doctor merely suggested waiting on developments'; 'as to this state of semi-impotency he says time is a great healer.'[49]

If the doctor bothered to prescribe at all, the medicaments given, according to the recipients, were perfectly useless. The very variety of things given suggests the therapeutic desperation of the medical men concerned, although few men underwent so poly-pharmaceutical a course of treatment, to so little avail, as this mining engineer, employed in India:

They prescribed various things [for impotence]. I took Easton Syrup steadily for six months. I took 5000 tabloids of Hormotone at the rate of three a day and I have taken Iron Jelloids and all kinds of tonics and nothing seems to have any effect at all.[50]

In some cases tonic preparations were prescribed to pep the patient up:

One suggested the use of strychnine, which I have taken for some months.

The ordinary doctor seems satisfied with giving a tonic and saying it will probably be alright.

All I could get out of him was a tonic for nerves, phosphates or something I think, but it made no difference.[51]

In other cases a bromide was given to calm the patient down:

No (4) prescribed bromide saying my husband's sexual centres were too excitable – no benefit.

I have consulted my physician who prescribed bromide but the effect was so slight as to be negligible.[52]

Some doctors (possibly the more up-to-date ones) employed 'glands' and 'hormones', but with no greater success:

> The Gland Specialist said that I could be cured by injections of pro-state gland extract, I paid 3 gns for the interview and 12 injections cost me 6 gns.

> He also gave me a prescription for Hormones and Chalones.

> He treated me with 'hormones' without much success it seems.[53]

Injections, which seem to have been combined with more usual medication, were administered by some doctors, but to little effect:

> All he did...was prescribe injections of 'Testogan' with which I care-fully followed his instructions but without any result.

> I told him my case and was under his treatment for about 2 months, during which time he gave me about a dozen injections and tonic.[54]

Some correspondents mentioned apparently patent preparations (for example, 'Testogan', above) given them by doctors:

> Two of them gave me pills (aphrodyne [sic]) [?or a mishearing of aphrodisiac] to take but they did not seem to have any effect at all.

> [I] consulted a Harley Street specialist who advised me to take Homoir [? sic] a French preparation.[55]

A surprising number of cases did not mention what kind of medi-cine it was they were given, whether it had been meant to have a tonic effect or a calming one: all they recorded was that the medicine did not have the desired effect:

> They simply give me medicine which does no good.

> He gave me medicines and pills and treatment but to no effect.

> He ordered me a course of phisic [sic] and tablets for about 8 weeks...this is some time ago but I am still the same.

> I have been to a doctor who gave me tablets and am sorry to say that they have not done the necessary.

The medicine doctors gave me did not help at all.[56]

In a review of *Sexual Disorders of the Male* (1939) by Kenneth Walker and E. B. Strauss, it was remarked:

> as a rule the practitioner is quite helpless and is driven to the administration of either bromide or strychnine without even the confidence in his administrations which might make for good suggestion.[57]

This verdict is amply confirmed from the Stopes correspondence. Patients appear to have been fully cognisant of their medical attendants' lack of confidence.

Other doctors, in what seems to have been therapeutic desperation, recommended circumcision:

> The doctor told me that I had an unusually tight foreskin, that it would have been better if I had been circumcised but that he did not think it was really necessary, although he added that it would of course be better.

> I was circumcised as I wanted to leave nothing unturned.

> One said circumcision may cure him.[58]

Another was recommended to see a certain Dr W. 'for the "Tapelights" [sic] the idea being to see inwardly',[59] though what the presumed benefit of this was is not clear. Norman Haire was reported to have given one man electrical treatment but 'without effect', and another was prescribed 'electrical treatment to lower part of back and crutch – no benefit'. This latter patient had also been recommended, by another doctor, to try 'cold hip baths morning and evening – result failure'. Another of the doctors seen by the same man made the suggestion 'to make the attempt not on retiring at night but in the morning or daytime, and that [his wife] should take the position on top'.[60]

If the patient were unmarried the doctor might have the solution to his problems in advocating marriage:

> When I was 21 I remember mentioning some little trouble to my doctor and he told me 'marriage was all I needed'.

> They both suggested that I should marry again and said that they were convinced that if I did so I would immediately see an improvement.

I was told that marriage would be beneficial.[61]

This, of course, was not a feasible diagnostic option when dealing with the problems of married men, which might indeed have only arisen or become apparent as a result of marriage.

Surprisingly few doctors seem to have recommended 'having a woman' to their patients as a solution to their problems. However, one elderly man (aged 76 in 1924) wrote anonymously to Marie Stopes with the following account from his own youth (he had contracted 'a clap' while seeking to cure masturbation through fornication with a prostitute):

> The doctor...strongly advised me to drop masturbation. He even suggested certain houses where I might meet women of a better class, and advised the use of sheaths or injections...The doctor even advised woman as a lesser evil than the risk of disease in masturbation.[62]

A retired naval surgeon from New Zealand wrote to Stopes around the same time arguing the case for 'licensed houses', on the basis that masturbation was increasing in prevalence as reflected in physical deterioration. He claimed that 'the number of young men crippled by masturbation is appalling.'[63] These were, however, men of a previous era, and hardly evidence of widespread prescription of such remedy by the medical profession.

The response of Stopes's correspondents to those doctors who did recommend fornication suggests that they were not a group of patients seeking medical authority for this. One patient would seem to have had this intention:

> A doctor in Egypt and one in Stockholm both said I should do so soon or I should go mad but English doctors have always gravely warned me against women unless I marry...any English doctors I have approached on the subject have given me rather evasive advice.[64]

A man whose wife was undergoing medical treatment which made intercourse impossible was told by his doctor 'find someone else, just what most men would, but I thank god I am in this not like other men'. Others reported:

> So I went to see a doctor...and in the end he told me the only thing that would do any good was to take Nature's remedy, well, that is all very well for him to say so, but I could not bring myself to do so, for

you see, I have the pleasure of being engaged to one of the best of girls.

He refused to tell me any remedy, except to say, jokingly I think, you'd better get a woman.

I have asked for information from a doctor of my own sex, who merely advised me to spend a night with a prostitute.[65]

Doctors faced with a man suffering from a sexual disorder did little more at best than make reassuring noises. Many of the correspondents who complained of the treatment they had received from their doctor nevertheless implied that the doctor had tried, however ineptly, to convey some kind of reassurance. Those doctors who were accused of having treated their patients' problems 'lightly' may have been endeavouring to set their minds at rest by suggesting that it was not quite such a major tragedy. Clearly, these attempts at reassurance were not enough.

Medical sociologists have indicated that saying 'not to worry' does not reassure and often appears insensitive to the patient, implying that he is fretting about nothing.[66] This was a point Kenneth Walker made in 1930, specifically referring to men having sexual problems: 'on no account must it ever be said that there is nothing wrong. This is the most certain method of losing a patient's trust.'[67] The futility of such reassurances is substantiated by the accounts given by Stopes's correspondents: it is clear that many of them had been given precisely such empty exhortations 'not to worry', which had done no good whatsoever, leaving them feeling if anything worse. Statements such as the following, given subsequent to a course of treatment, cannot have conduced to any great optimism: 'he said I must hope for the best but keep my mind off it, and eventually I may come alright.'[68] Such bet-hedging actually undermines statements intended to reassure.[69]

'He advised me to read your book'

It is true that a few of Stopes's correspondents dissented from this tide of fear and condemnation of doctors and reported that they had found their own, or particular, practitioners helpful and reassuring:

I saw a local doctor whose general ability I have no reason to doubt. His advice was that it was quite common and no harm resulted.

One medical man with whom I discussed the question gave it as his opinion that the sufferer from this habit need fear no serious physical results.

Other doctors took their patients sufficiently seriously to 'put me in touch with a Harley Street specialist, who consented to see me without a fee'; '[send] me to a specialist'.[70] However, helpful and reassuring though these doctors had been, they had not produced the results their patients had wanted from them, leaving them still in a sufficiently anxious state to seek Stopes's advice.

The help some doctors gave was a recommendation to their patients to consult Stopes's own writings:

> At my doctor's suggestion have just read your *Married Love* and much wish I had done so before.

> On the advice of a doctor (when he ascertained we had no children) I purchased *Married Love*.

> [My doctor] recommended me to read *Married Love* which I did, and I have also read *Wise Parenthood*.

> I asked my doctor, and he advised me to read your book.

> I was given your other two books to read by my doctor.[71]

Several correspondents wrote of reading her books 'on the advice of a young doctor friend'; 'acting upon advice of a doctor friend of mine'; or that 'a doctor friend advised her to get the books and send them along to me if she thought fit.'[72] Presumably the advice was not given in the course of a formal medical consultation, but as from friend to friend. It is significant that doctors could think of no more helpful thing to do than to prescribe the reading of works by a notorious laywoman.

Some doctors actually wrote to Stopes for help with their own problems. Some were young men, fresh from medical education, about to marry, who confessed 'you must know how abysmally ignorant even a medical man like me is in these matters'; 'although I know anatomy and physiology being a medical student my knowledge of psychology especially of women is very crude.'[73] Long-married medical men who had read her books revealed:

> I was utterly ignorant of how the sex impulse acts in the average healthy woman.

I find these things puzzling. How to obtain mutual satisfaction is the point.

I knew little or nothing of the abstruse problems of sex...Thus I was incompletely equipped...to enter the married state.

Having spent nearly thirty years in the practice of medical psychology I did not think that anyone could teach me anything about myself, but I was mistaken.[74]

Doctors explicitly deplored the defects of medical education in this respect when writing to Stopes. Some of them treated this as an impersonal fact:

Our Assistant MOH here in Chesterfield told me that the books now in question supplied the missing link in the education of a medical student.

Many doctors are unaware of the intricacies of the sex act.

Too little of anything is taught in our medical schools on such subjects, and yet who needs more than the medical man to know about the psychology of men and women in relation to each other, seeing that he is the one who is most often consulted.[75]

Others had sufficient courage and humility to admit their own personal ignorance on the topics dealt with in her books:

Although I am a physician 95% of what I read in your book is new to me, and I am certain that the knowledge obtained will be of great benefit to me in my practice.

Although a medical man myself I must confess to a most woful [sic] ignorance of all essential points bearing on a subject of such importance.

I have frequently to advise patients upon the subjects dealt with in your books, and am only too aware of how little we medical men know with any degree of authority how to deal with such enquiries.

Although a practitioner of 12 years and a married man with 4 children it has taught me many things that I did not know before of which many of our profession are ignorant.[76]

No wonder they were reduced to recommending her books. Several requested the aid of her expertise for the benefit of patients presenting with problems of dysfunction they had no idea how to treat:

> I as a Doctor am often consulted about the chapter on sleep, especially by those who have been continent before marriage. They say that their reaction is so quick that they are quite unable to bring satisfaction by one connection. Can you give me any information about the curing of this condition or refer me to any authority on the matter. . . [I] don't feel competent to give the necessary advice myself.

> Hundreds of women have come to me and hundreds of men and I did not know how to put things right. . . the ignorance of some men is appalling.

> [I am] struck by the frequency of sexual neuroses that affect happiness in married life. There seems to be a widespread disorder among young men.[77]

One doctor, working in a military hospital in 1919 and seeing many neurasthenia cases, presumably attributed the number of cases of premature ejaculation he was consulted about to the effects of shellshock.[78] Other doctors wished to know how to advise their patients on the desirable frequency of marital intercourse, a question which also troubled lay readers:

> A matter on which doctors at clinics are constantly being asked for information is this: how often may intercourse occur consistently with the man and woman both keeping their working capacity.

> I have been asked in my practice how often conjugal intercourse should happen where both parties are healthy and mutually affectionate but desire in this matter to be temperate. Before expressing an opinion I wanted the opinion of someone with wider experience along this line.[79]

'I have enquired of several doctors'

Many men, therefore, were reluctant to consult their doctors, and would only contemplate such a course when reassured of the credentials of any medical man they might consult, while others were completely deterred by one encounter with an unsympathetic or unhelpful practitioner. Others seem to have shopped around, fruitlessly, for relief from their sexual problems. These men lacked any trust in the opinions and advice of the doctors they saw: medical authority did not satisfy them.

Some merely indicated that they had not been contented with a single medical opinion:

> I find general practitioners and even specialists very unhelpful I am sorry to say.

> The doctors I have been to never really come to the point.

> Not being satisfied with one doctor I went to another.[80]

Others enumerated more specifically (obsessively?) the exact number they had consulted:

> Four doctors have been consulted with no benefit.

> I have seen two medical men in the last few years on the matter.

> I mentioned the matter to my Panel doctor...further examination and treatment by two or three medical men have produced no improvement.

> I have asked two family doctors for information.

> I have been to 3 doctors of my own sex.

> I have been examined by 4 doctors.[81]

Yet others seem to have lost count among the 'several', 'various' and even 'numerous' practitioners they consulted:

> I have enquired of several doctors as to such a cure.

> I tried to gain advice from several doctors.

> I have consulted numerous local doctors in different parts of the country.

> I sought advice from various doctors previous to our marriage, as I was in doubt as to my fitness for it.[82]

Writing to Stopes was itself a form of shopping around, of seeking help which the medical profession had failed to supply. Her correspondents' comments betrayed the lack of confidence doctors' counsel on sexual matters inspired:

> The opinion of a single medical man who is not an expert places or leaves one in a very doubtful position.

> I have heard of a doctor in Belfast who will [they] tell me give me a *definite* and *decided* answer, a thing I have been unable to get up to date.[83]

Some of these correspondents would have been very hard to satisfy: one man felt anxious and deformed in spite of reassurances from several medical men that having one testicle undescended would not affect his sexual performance,[84] and others not only wrote of the numbers of doctors they had already consulted but bombarded Stopes with demands for a definite answer or reassurance which she was no more able to give than the doctors. One young man had a copious correspondence with Stopes in the early 1930s, showering her with lengthy letters while simultaneously consulting several other doctors (including Kenneth Walker), and concurrently spending some time as a psychiatric in-patient. The case cannot be regarded as at all typical: he was a considerably disturbed and rather manipulative individual, trying to play the various specialists he consulted off against one another.[85] There were some patients whom it was unlikely that any doctor could have helped.

'He appeared unwilling to speak about it'

It is believed that doctors in the 1920s were likely to give to husbands the birth control information they withheld from wives. However, men who wrote to Stopes begging for contraceptive advice told many grim tales of attempts to seek such advice from their doctors. A number reported outright refusal to give it.

> He refused to advise me on the subject, perhaps because he was uncertain himself.

> We endeavoured to obtain the assistance from our doctor but were politely told that prevention was not in accordance with the medical profession.

> He flatly refused to enter into any discussion on birth control, and in addition said a few choice words of his own, with the result that my wife came away very much upset.

> There is unfortunately the opposition of a class of medical men – one such in our own instance has refused the assistance indicated in *Wise Parenthood*.[86]

Other doctors greeted such requests with dire warnings:

> My doctor is the oldfashioned sort who warned me not to use preventives you know the sort.

> We have been told by a doctor that the use of preventive methods may endanger the probability of children when we do want them.[87]

Many doctors held vague or contradictory ideas about methods of birth control and their advice could not be relied on:

> I have spoken to three different doctors, and they appear to have little knowledge of the subject, or are prejudiced, or in too great hurry to be bothered.

> I have asked two family doctors for information in respect to an auxiliary preventive but have had no satisfactory answer.

> He knew of the sheath, but the small pessary seemed unfamiliar to him. Anyhow he gave me no help, save that he suggested union only during the time least likely to have consequences.[88]

Some medical men were sufficiently aware of their deficiencies in this field to advise their patients to write to Stopes:

> My doctor gave me your address.

> I have been recommended by my doctor to write to you to enquire the name of the 'satisfactory cap' mentioned in your article in the *British Medical Journal* of Nov 19th.

> I am directed to write to you through Dr P— whose treatment I am under.[89]

Much more common, however, were cases in which a medical man advised his patients that they should have no more children, without stating whether either childbirth or coitus as such was the deleterious exertion to be avoided, and without making any mention of birth control:

> My doctor told me my wife should not have any more children.

> Our doctor advised me strongly at this time that it would be very unwise for her to have any more children at this time on account of her health, he did not, however, give me any practical advice.

> After my wife's last confinement our doctor definitely said 'No more' but left us entirely in the dark as to how this was to be achieved.

> Our doctor said it would be better if she had no more children, *But* he did not tell us how to prevent them.[90]

If prevention was mentioned the advice was unhelpful: one man, asking 'quite naturally' for 'such information as would enable me to carry out his instructions', found the doctor's answers 'so vague that I was left after the interview in much the same position as before it took place'. Another, whose wife was told 'after her second child was born not to have any more children', was told only 'that there are plenty of "preventatives" on the market'. At the time of writing they had five children.[91]

This unsatisfactory response by doctors was presumably due to their own ignorance. In 1922 Marie Stopes circulated a questionnaire on contraceptive practices to members of the medical profession. One hundred and twenty-eight completed forms survive, also a few which were torn up or otherwise defaced by indignant recipients. While this is a statistically unsatisfactory sample, some useful and suggestive impressions may be gleaned. Doctors as much as their patients were seeking a satisfactory and reliable method. Several of the respondents claimed abstention for greater or lesser periods as the only method of deliberate limitation employed. One couple had abstained for fifteen years following the birth of their only child. None of them considered any one method superior to the rest. Scepticism was expressed about the 'safe period': 'What are "safe periods"?'; 'Personally I do not recognise safe periods'; 'Dare not trust this.' Even today the safe period is regarded as 'Vatican roulette': it is not surprising that, in the early 1920s, when calculations were based upon the injunctions of Mosaic law and not the researches of Ogino and Knaus, it was found such an unsatisfactory method of restricting conceptions. By chance or design, however, most of the respondents to this survey had small families.[92]

Contraception was not a subject covered in the medical curriculum; those doctors who wished to acquire competence in its application applied in large numbers to Stopes to come for training to her clinic.[93] Nor were doctors exempt from such current superstitions as the belief in the existence of one defective pessary or condom in every packet, which one doctor was said to have stated was in accordance with an Act of Parliament.[94] T. W. Hill, a medical officer of health, was reproached by Stopes for stating (incorrectly) in *The Health of England* (1933) that the law prohibited the spread of birth control knowledge and advice.[95] There was considerable ambivalence as to whether contraception should be a medical concern at all.

Birth control was an issue which involved all sorts of social and emotional aspects affecting doctors' responses to the subject. Some welcomed it for the good of the overburdened working-class mother but had reservations about its 'selfish' employment by the more privileged. Many, of course, shared the common feeling of repugnance. One doctor was alleged to have expressed the forceful sentiment that he

> could understand a man overmastered by desire raping a woman; but could not understand any man being so low and vicious as deliberately to make use of any anti-conceptional method.[96]

It is not clear whether this was stated as a professional opinion during a consultation.

Birth control might be dismissed as not part of the appropriate sphere of the doctor, but other matters to do with fertility and reproduction did impinge more obviously upon medical expertise. Sterility, for example, was seen as very much falling within the medical purlieu. How did doctors react to couples coming to them asking for assistance in ending their barrenness? The male factor in a sterile marriage could be discovered readily by non-invasive means, examining his semen to see if it were potent. According to Stopes's correspondents most doctors continued to regard sterility as the wife's 'fault', and if consulted about a childless marriage their reaction was to suggest that the wife undergo treatment. Kenneth Walker remarked 'occasionally even doctors fail to distinguish in their minds' between impotence and infertility in the male.[97] He was perhaps optimistic in believing that 'the doctor...no longer starts with the assumption that the wife is to blame' and was aware that 'for the proper solution of the problem an examination of both is required'.[98]

Many doctors were unwilling to accept that responsibility for barrenness might lie with the husband or be the result of factors affecting both members of the couple. This neglect of the male in questions of sterility still continues. Few men receive advice on sterility and there is considerable encouragement for them to deny that it is they who are infertile, even to the point where the wives pretend that the 'fault' is theirs.[99]

Some doctors in the 1920s and 1930s were unaware of the possibility of performing investigations upon semen. A Mr B. wrote to Stopes in 1931 that only after several operations on his wife did the doctor test his semen, and that the doctor had not even known that this was possible. Similarly a Mr H. B. declared 'the doctor at *my* suggestion has made a sperm test' but appeared to be 'a little out of his depth in this matter'.[100] One woman reported that her husband had seen two doctors, neither of whom had suggested examining his semen: the husband, although said to object to going to a doctor for a sperm test, was 'strongly of the opinion that medical men know little about sex troubles'.[101] According to Mrs G., to whom Stopes had suggested that a test should be performed on her husband's semen,

the doctor is quite convinced that is is my fault I cannot have a baby. He says that *very occasionally* it is the man's fault but in the *great majority of cases* the female is to blame . . . [it was her] *duty* to undergo the operation first and then if nothing happened he would test him six months afterwards.[102]

Some doctors were unwilling to do anything to assist infertile couples, maybe because they did not know what to do:

We had a talk with our own doctor but he appeared unwilling to speak about it so we did not pursue the matter further.

I then asked the doctor about the matter I am now submitting to you but he was not at all disposed to give me information.

Both my wife and myself have at different times seen our doctors and they say there is no apparent reason for it.[103]

In some cases it might have been the man's own reluctance to undergo even so non-invasive an investigation which influenced the doctor's decision, though only one of Stopes's correspondents actually admitted 'I feel shy to ask a doctor to examine my seminal fluid', but claimed 'with you I feel different.'[104] Others had tried to get their doctors to perform the examination, but most doctors proved either ignorant of this test or reluctant to perform it. Possibly there was some squeamishness about the means of obtaining samples.

Doctors had little idea of what to do if the man's sperm count did turn out to be below par: one woman wrote 'my husband was told to go for a six months holiday without me, eat oysters and drink stout and probably things would come right.'[105] This sounds like a folk remedy rather than the latest in scientific medical thinking. Another man's 'well-known London specialist' had in fact tested his seminal fluid, finding very few live spermatozoa, but 'gave neither counsel or advice and made no suggestion as to how lack of fertility might be treated'.[106]

Confusion between the two separate capacities of potency and fertility was also demonstrated by doctors' notions on the subject of vasectomy. Correspondents writing to the Eugenics Society for information about the operation reported:

> He was horrified...it was obvious to me that he was entirely unfamiliar with the modern method...he would not have it that the man would not be affected in some very serious way.

> The family doctor insists that all sorts of mental and physical upset will follow a double vasotomy [sic] in a man of twenty-one.[107]

Stopes's correspondents had similar experiences: one said that his doctor alleged that vasectomy would make him 'a sexless [sic], or useless'.[108] Even when doctors did not come out with such misleading statements, it was a common thing to find

> my own medical man unable to help me in this matter.

> I have broached the matter of sterilisation to both my Panel Doctor and the local Tuberculosis Officer but on each occasion nothing resulted from the conversation.

> neither know about vasectomy, although young and up to date are entirely ignorant.

> He would not give me any information as he does not approve of sterilisation.[109]

'A reproach rather than a challenge'

The average lay perception of doctors' capacity to assist in matter of sexual dysfunction was not particularly flattering to the profession, and was in many cases borne out by patients' experience if they did get themselves into a consulting room. Most of Stopes's correspondents were presenting her with problems for which it seems reasonable that they could have expected some kind of help from their doctor, but she concluded that 'there are few medical practitioners experienced enough in all the subtleties of such a case to be really helpful.' She was aware that 'the tendency of most men toward another male in this predicament is to laugh or be incredulous.' 'Such physiological needs of mankind', she stated, 'have been but little studied or discussed, save by a few experts.'[110]

In 1919 Stopes contacted Dr E. B. Turner, whom she had heard well recommended, asking if she might refer male patients with dysfunctions to him. She felt that there was little that could be done by correspondence and she shrank 'from thrusting them back into the arms of the profession'. Turner replied that although by no means a specialist he had 'seen and come across a good many' such cases. The methods he had evolved for treating them were as follows:

> You can lay down no absolute rule of treatment for general application. Each case requires most careful consideration on its own merits...I always see if there is any physical reason for it, and go thoroughly over the nervous system, and try and put right anything which may be a cause. I lay down rules for each person as to diet, exercise, bathing, etc. In some cases I have found surgical procedures necessary such as circumcision...They are all difficult cases but I have had fair results, on the whole.[111]

This way of dealing with the problem, which must have derived much of its efficacy from the giving of time and attention to the patient and by doing so convincing him that he was not the degraded weakling he supposed himself, was similarly advocated by Kenneth Walker in *Male Disorders of Sex*. Walker was of the opinion that 'even when an organic lesion exists the psychological handling of the patient is of importance, since he is almost certain to be suffering from certain fears and lack of confidence.' Walker was by no means complimentary to the rest of his profession:

It is more than likely that the patient has already sought medical help and been told that there is nothing the matter with him, or else has been given some pills with the assurance that all will be well. As a consequence he comes full of suspicions which must be allayed before any help can be given.

It was therefore essential for the doctor to 'overcome his patient's distrust and despair', which required time and patience. Walker urged an attitude of open-minded tolerance, and an attempt at empathy with the patient and his sufferings: 'he must make every effort to place himself in the patient's position.'[112]

Walker did not minimize the psychological value of physical investigations in convincing the patient that 'his case is being dealt with thoroughly', because 'unless he knows that he has been carefully examined he will never listen to any suggestion that organically he is sound.' Difficulties lay in the doctor's way, as it was 'difficult for some men to understand that their impotence is psychological rather than physical. They will cling to the idea that something is wrong with the organs of sex.'[113] While his general line was a therapeutic optimism, he also warned that 'the strain on the doctor's patience is likely to be severe.'[114]

Twenty years before Walker, Arthur Cooper had also indicated to the practitioner, in *The Sexual Disabilities of Man*, that these cases were by no means straightforward to deal with. He emphasized that 'it is of the first importance that the doctor should gain the full confidence of the patient if treatment is to be successful' and 'whoever thinks these cases can be cured by the mere writing of a prescription' should 'leave them alone altogether'.[115] By the third edition (1916) he was convinced that 'it is essential that the patient have faith in the man who suggests': the aim of treatment was 'so to combine suggestion with other treatment that they mutually help and enforce one another'.[116]

It is not surprising that doctors were reluctant to involve themselves with such cases. General practitioners consider to be troublesome patients presenting a vague, psychological illness, hard to diagnose and manage and unlikely to get better. They regard those who take up time, present the problem vaguely, neither trust the doctor nor accept limits to his skill, and are critical and uncooperative, as difficult. If the general social competence of men presenting sexual disorders was high and therefore in their favour in the doctor's eyes, the very nature of their complaint must have marked them as unhappy, insecure, inadequate and possibly malingerers as well.[117] As patients, therefore, they would have been unwelcome to doctors. As cases they could demand an investment of time and attention which a busy doctor might find it hard to spare, for a therapeutic outcome he might well consider uncertain. Being unable to prescribe an immediate remedy might also tend to undermine a doctor's faith in himself. McCormick has suggested that the 'inability to cure is a reproach rather than a challenge: it is in conflict with his role; he tends to believe that he has nothing to offer'.[118]

In 1932 the *British Medical Journal* published the following remarks by Dr W. J. Mayo, of the world-famous Mayo Clinic, on doctors:

> Having himself a disciplined mind and being in good health, he may be disposed to regard with some degree of contempt the emotional reactions of the patient...The trained physician, in his natural contempt for sham and make-believe, is perhaps apt to forget that he is dealing not with a cool, logical, self-controlled individual, but with one disturbed by uncertainties and doubts and fears; part of the treatment is to banish these, and the agency for the purpose is the attitude of the doctor. If this attitude is not appropriate to the situation, how can success be expected?[119]

This ideal of the doctor divided him sharply from the patient: the doctor had a disciplined mind, good health, logic, self-control, all of which the patient lacked. If banishing the patients' fears was even part of surgical treatment, how much more so would this be the case with functional disorders?

Doctors, being men, and professional men of a class Stopes found peculiarly subject to the 'civilised disease' of premature ejaculation, might have found it particularly difficult to maintain this sharp distinction from the patient who presented himself with a disorder of sexual functioning. Especially if this patient were himself of a similar status in society, turning the medical gaze upon him may perhaps have been too much like looking into a mirror for the average doctor to feel confident and at ease in dealing with the problem. The defensive retreat from a sense of therapeutic impotence into a brusque medical authoritarianism must have been a constant temptation, and one to which, from the plaints of Stopes's correspondents, many doctors succumbed. One way or another, the sexually dysfunctional male was not the kind of patient presenting the sort of problem with which doctors felt most comfortably equipped to deal.

Conclusion

By the time the National Health Service came into existence, sex in Britain was an area less fraught with horror and stigma than it had been in 1900. Changes in attitudes to sex had reduced some of the shame and horror with which the subject had been surrounded, at least for the 'normal heterosexual', and increased the possibility of open discussion on sexual topics. With the advent of antibiotics, venereal diseases, already in decline before the Second World War sent statistics of infection spiralling upwards once again, seemed finally in retreat. Professional prostitution on the Victorian scale had disappeared, even if the double standard had and has hardly vanished entirely from male–female relations. In responsible, respectable sex-education literature nocturnal emissions were decreed a normal phenomenon of adolescence, and masturbation less dangerous than fears of its dire consequences. Birth control was more widely available, more reliable and more used, even though family planning services continued to remain outside the NHS for over twenty years.

The possible improvement in the quality of life created by the decline in venereal disease, the rise of birth control, and access to sources of sexual information which were neither mercenary nor furtive and superstitious, should not be dismissed, though there must be reservations and qualifications as to how far it went and how great the benefits were. If too much can be claimed for the significance of sex in human life, it is nevertheless true that it can be a potent source of happiness or misery for the individual and the couple. Clean air, good drains, adequate nutrition and an un-polluted food supply are usually regarded as good things for the communities which enjoy them, if not the whole source of human happiness and wellbeing. The same may surely be said of conditions which make it possible for more individuals within a community to have (an admittedly hard to quantify) less worried, more enjoyable sexual life.

The roles of the sexes had not, however, been radically redefined as at 1950. If the double standard was in retreat, the male was still expected to be the pursuer and initiator. Heterosexual marriage based on complementary rather than egalitarian roles remained the norm. The continuing emphasis on the importance of female sexual satisfaction, and debates about the vaginal versus the clitoral orgasm, whilst anxiety-provoking for women, must also have aroused worries in men about the capacity of their performance to produce the 'mature' variety. If casual sexual liaisons were on a moral level above the resort to prostitutes, they must have laid more of an obligation upon the man to be sexually competent than purchasing an 'outlet' for male lust. Overt prostitution was still sufficiently widespread and problematical in the 1950s to lead to government action, with the setting up of the Wolfenden Committee to investigate and make recommendations, and eventual legislation. The divorce laws still enshrined concepts of guilty and innocent parties: even after revisions, divorce remains an adversarial process.

Male sexual problems were still something that men found it hard to mention and which still, because of this secrecy with which they were surrounded, provided a thriving market for remedies such as 'Damaroids'. At the height of the 'sexual revolution' of the late 1960s and early 1970s, the most consistent advertiser in the pages of the underground press was 'Magnaphall', which promised bigger and better erections.[1] The existence of the common male dysfunctions and their prevalence in the community continue to be a well-kept secret. This is true of the psychosexual disorders generally, which are still neglected by the medical profession. Recent textbooks for the general practitioner faced with sexual problems in the surgery indicate that most doctors, embarrassed and ignorant, choose to avoid the subject rather than reveal their therapeutic failings.[2] Those who take such troubles to the average practitioner find that doctors either do not know how to help, or do not want to know about sexual difficulties.[3] A leader in *The Lancet* in 1988 remarked that more is known about the behaviour of the HIV virus than what people actually do in the privacy of their bedrooms.[4] In 1989, government funding was refused for a survey of sexual behaviour which had, in the era of AIDS, very obvious epidemiological importance.

Male problems in particular are still a blank spot. In 1989 the *British Medical Journal* commented upon the neglect of the problems of the prostate which affect so high a percentage of men once they reach their middle years.[5] If quacks no longer press pamphlets upon passers-by threatening the dire consequences of 'spermatorrhoea', 'private clinics' advertise in quality newspapers offering treatment for impotence and premature ejaculation. (The naming of the problems, instead of subsuming them under the name of 'male weakness', is perhaps an advance?)[6] If not a product of the strains of modern life, these problems do continue to exist, and sufferers still feel chary of taking them to their general practitioners as men did in the 1920s and 1930s when writing to Marie Stopes. The inclination to regard them as organic in origin continues.

Writers on sex-education have pointed out the neglect of boys not merely in debates about adolescent sexuality but in actual provision for sex-education. Girls usually receive some kind of instruction, though this tends to centre around menstruation and its management and the risks of pregnancy. The changes the male body undergoes at the same epoch are ignored, as is any need for male enlightenment on sexual issues. While sex-education literature is reassuring about masturbation, and even advocates it as a process of learning about one's body, myths still circulate and even present-day boys believe that it may cause impotence.[7]

Refusal to engage with the sexuality of the male and its failings is bound up with the tendency to define the male as healthy and the female as pathological. However, this refusal cannot be completely separated from attitudes towards sexuality in general. The medical disdain of the male dysfunctions described in this study was allied to a general revulsion from the problems of sexuality. Only when the pill meant that the provision of contraception could be separated from any close involvement with actual genitalia did many doctors who were not either family planning specialists or gynaecologists prescribe it.

Persistent perceptions of the male and his sexuality were involved during debates on the inclusion of condoms if contraception in general were to be free under the NHS. Although use of a condom must often have been, in context, an act of caring and responsibility, press debates and medical fulminations cried out against the encouragement of the promiscuous male. The image put forward was that of 'Jack the Lad' popping into the surgery on Friday to equip himself for the weekend's sport, rather than of male assumption of responsibility for birth control.[8] The idea that the male is, by virtue of his sex, randy and irresponsible lives on. While the condom, in the era of AIDS, is becoming more visible, self-preservation as much as caring is involved in its promotion.

The notion of the male as unthinkingly and crudely potent, needing control, has been taken up in recent feminist debates. The entire male sex has been assumed to be constantly and dangerously potent, thrusting continually erect phalluses before them. Certainly the distribution of power in the world today operates to a grotesque extent in favour of the male sex. There are serious and searching questions to be asked about the frailty of sexual potency and its connection with the search for potency in other senses: a topic for investigation beyond the parameters of this study. The penis itself is a fragile, fleshly organ which, unlike the tools and weapons with which men equip themselves in pursuit of worldly domination, is very seldom completely under a man's conscious control. Whatever the social potency of men (and not all of the sex have that to any degree that matters), their actual sexual potency is always dubious and open to question.

Notes

A number of the works referred to in these notes were either constantly reissued over lengthy periods, or have complex, even indecipherable, publishing histories, partly due to the nature of the subject. As far as possible the details of original publication have been given, when this can be established. If not, where this is known to be much earlier than or in another country from that of the edition cited, this has been indicated. In most cases citations are from later and more readily accessible editions (for example, even the British Library does not have early editions of Drysdale's *Elements of Social Science*). Where there are two or more references given, therefore, the last is the edition actually quoted in the text. The place of publication is London unless otherwise stated.

INTRODUCTION: DECONSTRUCTING THE MONOLITHIC PHALLUS

1 Michel Foucault, *The History of Sexuality. Volume I: An Introduction*, tr. Robert Hurley [first published in France as *La volonté de savoir* (Editions Gallimard 1976)] (Allen Lane 1979, Penguin Books paperback edn, Harmondsworth 1981), pp. 104–5.
2 One of the classic works on this subject from an anthropological perspective is Margaret Mead's *Male and Female: A Study of the Sexes in a Changing World* (first published in the USA 1950, Pelican paperback edn, Harmondsworth 1962). John H. Gagnon and William Simon, *Sexual Conduct: The Social Sources of Human Sexuality* (Aldine Book Co., Chicago 1973, Hutchinson 1974), is perhaps the most often cited sociological work of the social interactionist school. For some recent discussions on

sexual diversity, see, e.g., Kenneth Plummer, *Sexual Stigma: An Interactionist Account* (Routledge and Kegan Paul, London and Boston 1975); Alice Schlegel, ed., *Sexual Stratification: A Cross-cultural View* (Columbia University Press, New York 1977); Sherry B. Ortner and Harriet Whitehead, eds, *Sexual Meanings: The Cultural Construction of Gender and Sexuality* (Cambridge University Press 1981); Kevin Howells, ed., *The Psychology of Sexual Diversity* (Basil Blackwell, Oxford 1984, paperback edn, 1986); Pat Caplan, ed., *The Cultural Construction of Sexuality* (Tavistock Publications, London and New York 1987).

3 Valerie Fildes, *Breasts, Bottles and Babies: A History of Infant Feeding* (University of Edinburgh, Edinburgh 1986); Christina Hardyment, *Dream Babies: Child Care from Locke to Spock* (Jonathan Cape Ltd 1983).

4 Havelock Ellis, *Studies in the Psychology of Sex. Volume III: Analysis of the Sexual Impulse; Love and Pain; The Sexual Impulse in Women* (F. A. Davis Co. Ltd, Philadelphia 1910, Random House, New York omnibus edition 1936), p. 189.

5 G. R. Freedman, *Sexual Medicine* (Churchill Livingstone, Edinburgh 1983); C. G. Fairburn, M. G. Dickson and J. Greenwood, *Sexual Problems and Their Management* (Churchill Livingstone, Edinburgh 1983); J. Bancroft, *Human Sexuality and Its Problems* (Churchill Livingstone, Edinburgh 1983).

6 Kenneth M. Walker, *Male Disorders of Sex* (Jonathan Cape 1930), p. 7.

7 L. W. Harrison, 'The Public Health Services and Venereal Diseases', *British Journal of Venereal Diseases*, 1, no. 1 (1925), pp. 12–22, table on p. 13.

8 'DHSS: Sexually Transmitted Diseases: Analysis of the Total Number of New Cases at the Clinics in England only during the Quarter ended 31 December 1972'; from a file in the Birth Control Campaign archives held in the Contemporary Medical Archives Centre at the Wellcome Institute for the History of Medicine, CMAC: SA/BCC/E.54, 'Press-cuttings: Venereal Disease; News, 1972–1974'.

9 Gloria Steinem, 'If Men Could Menstruate', in Steinem, *Outrageous Acts and Everyday Rebellions* (Holt, Rinehart and Winston, San Diego 1983, Jonathan Cape 1984, Flamingo paperback edn, 1984), pp. 337–40.

10 Foucault, *History of Sexuality. Vol. I*, p. 103.

11 A critique of this approach to the history of medical treatment of the problems of women was put forward by Gail Pat Parsons in 'Equal Treatment for All: American Medical Remedies for Male Sexual Problems: 1850–1990', *Journal of the History of Medicine and Allied Sciences*, (1977), pp. 55–71, which includes references to a number of works in which she found it. Examples are Barbara Ehrenreich and Deirdre English, *For Her Own Good: 150 Years of the Experts' Advice to Women* (Doubleday, New York 1978, Pluto Press 1979); Gena Corea, *The Hidden Malpractice: How American Medicine Mistreats Women* (Harper and Row, New York, updated edition 1985); Elaine Showalter, *The Female Malady: Women, Madness and English Culture, 1830–1980* (Pantheon Books, New

York 1985, Virago 1987). See Charlotte Mackenzie's review of the last of these in *Social History of Medicine*, 2, no. 1 (1989), pp. 103–5.

12   Lady Isabel Hutton, *Memories of a Doctor in War and Peace* (Heinemann 1960), pp. 88–9, mentioned this from her own experience as a young doctor before the First World War; the subject is discussed by Naomi Pfeffer in 'Pronatalism and Sterility', unpublished PhD thesis, University of Essex, 1987, p. 275, from an analysis of gynaecological case records of certain London hospitals between the wars.

13   Jane Lewis, *Women in England 1870–1950: Sexual Divisions and Social Change* (Wheatsheaf, Brighton 1984), p. 117.

14   Ann Oakley, *Telling the Truth about Jerusalem: A Collection of Essays and Poems* (Basil Blackwell, Oxford 1986), p. 58.

15   William Cooper, *You're Not Alone: A Doctor's Diary* (Macmillan 1976).

16   Naomi Pfeffer, 'The Hidden Pathology of the Male Reproductive System', in Hilary Homans, ed., *The Sexual Politics of Reproduction* (Gower, Aldershot 1985), pp. 30–44.

17   *The Times*, 15 October 1987.

18   Marie Stopes, *Married Love: A New Contribution to the Solution of Sex Difficulties*, with a Preface by Dr Jessie Murray, and letters from Professor E. H. Starling FRS, and Father Stanislaus St John, SJ (A. C. Fifield 1918 [7th and later edns G. P. Putnam's Sons Ltd], 4th edn 1918), Author's Preface, p. xiii.

19   Biographical details from Ruth Hall, *Marie Stopes, A Biography* (Andre Deutsch 1977).

20   Stopes, *Married Love*, Author's Preface, p. xiii.

21   Peter Eaton and Marilyn Warnick, *Marie Stopes: A Checklist of Her Writings* (Croom Helm 1977); Billie Melman, *Woman and the Popular Imagination in the 1920s* (Macmillan 1988), p. 3.

22   *The Lancet*, ii (1918), p. 886.

23   *British Medical Journal*, i (1918), p. 510.

24   Marie Stopes, *Wise Parenthood. The Treatise on Birth Control For Married People. A Practical Sequel to 'Married Love'* with an Introduction by Arnold Bennett (G. P. Putnam's Sons Ltd [first published 1918], 11th edn 1923), p. 31.

25   Ruth Hall, *Marie Stopes*, pp. 237, 242; also Ruth Hall, ed., *Dear Dr Stopes: Sex in the 1920s* (Andre Deutsch 1978), appendix, pp. 216–17; the proceedings of the trial have been published in Muriel Box, ed., *The Trial of Dr Stopes* (Femina Books 1967).

26   Marie Stopes, *Enduring Passion: Further New Contributions to the Solution of Sex Difficulties, being the Continuation of Married Love* (G. P. Putnam's Sons Ltd 1928, 2nd edn 1929), p. 20.

27   Lesley A. Hall, 'The Stopes Collection in the Contemporary Medical Archives Centre of the Wellcome Institute for the History of Medicine', *Bulletin of the Society for the Social History of Medicine*, no. 32 (June 1983), pp. 50–1; Ruth Hall, *Dear Dr Stopes*, statistical appendix compiled by Christopher Stopes-Roe, pp. 215–18.

28 Hutton, *Memories of a Doctor*, p. 217; Barbara Evans, *Freedom to Choose: The Life and Work of Dr Helena Wright, Pioneer of Contraception* (Bodley Head 1984), mentions correspondence received by her, p. 154.

1 'A VERY DELICATE AND DIFFICULT SUBJECT': ORTHODOX AND RESPECTABLE VIEWS ON SEX TO 1920

1 *Proceedings of the Royal Medical and Chirurgical Society of London*, VIII, no. 1 (1876), pp. 74–6, obituary of William Acton, MRCS.
2 Steven Marcus, *The Other Victorians: A Study of Sexuality and Pornography in Mid-Nineteenth Century England* (Weidenfeld and Nicholson 1966, Book Club Associates edn 1970), chapter 1, 'Mr Acton of Queen Anne Street, or, The Wisdom of our Ancestors', pp. 1–33.
3 William Acton, *The Functions and Disorders of the Reproductive Organs in Youth, Adult Age and Advanced Life, considered in their Physiological, Social and Psychological Relations* (John Churchill 1857, 3rd edn 1862).
4 F. B. Smith, *The People's Health, 1830–1910* (Croom Helm [1979]), Section 4, 'Adults', Part 4, 'Venereal Diseases, Contraception and Sexuality', pp. 294–315; M. Jeanne Peterson, 'Dr Acton's Enemy: Medicine, Sex and Society in Victorian England', *Victorian Studies*, 29, no. 4 (1986), pp. 569–90; Peter Gay, *Education of the Senses: The Bourgeois Experience, Victoria to Freud, Volume I* (Oxford University Press, New York 1984); F. B. Smith, 'Sexuality in Britain, 1800–1900: Some Suggested Revisions', in M. Vicinus, ed., *A Widening Sphere: Changing Roles of Victorian Women* (Indiana University Press, 1977), pp. 182–98; M. Jeanne Peterson, 'No Angels in the House: The Victorian Myth and the Paget Women', *American Historical Review*, 89, no. 3 (1984), pp. 677–708; see also for a critique of this school Carol Z. Stearns and Peter N. Stearns, 'Victorian Sexuality: Can Historians Do It Better?', *Journal of Social History*, 18, no. 4 (1985), pp. 625–34.
5 Havelock Ellis, *The Erotic Rights of Women and The Objects of Marriage* (British Society for the Study of Sex Psychology, publication no. 5 1918), p. 9.
6 *The Lancet* i (1862), p. 518.
7 James Copland, *A Dictionary of Practical Medicine: Comprising General Pathology, the Nature and Treatment of Diseases, Morbid Structures and the Disorders especially incident to Climates, to the Sex, and to the Different Epochs of Life*, (Longman, 3 vols in 4 1844–58), 'Pollutions', pp. 441–8.
8 *British Medical Journal*, ii (1881), p. 904.
9 Sir James Paget, 'Sexual Hypochondriasis', *Clinical Lectures and Essays* (Longmans Green 1875, 2nd edn 1879), pp. 275–98.
10 George Drysdale, *Elements of Social Science: or Physical, Sexual and Natural Religion, an Exposition of the True Cause and Only Cure of the Three Primary Social Evils: Poverty, Prostitution, and Celibacy, by a Doctor of Medicine* (E. Truelove 1854 [anonymously], G. Standring 1905), pp. 80–81.

11   Ibid., p. 78.
12   Ibid., p. 87.
13   Phyllis Grosskurth, *Havelock Ellis: A Biography* (Allen Lane 1980), p. 39.
14   Havelock Ellis, *Studies in the Psychology of Sex. Volume VI: Sex in Relation to Society* (F. A. Davis Co., Philadelphia 1910, William Heinemann Medical Books 1937, War Economy edn 1946), p. 356.
15   C. Knowlton, *Fruits of Philosophy: an Essay on the Population Question, New Edition, with Notes* [first published in the USA 1847], ed. G. Drysdale, printed by Charles Bradlaugh and Annie Besant (The Freethought Publishing Co. [1877]); for an account of the trial of this work see S. Chandrasekhar, *'A Dirty Filthy Book': The Writings of Charles Bradlaugh and Annie Besant on Reproductive Physiology and Birth Control, and an Account of the Bradlaugh–Besant Trial* (University of California, Berkeley, CA 1981).
16   H. A. Allbutt, *The Wife's Handbook: How a Woman Should Order Herself during Pregnancy, in the Lying-In Room, and After Delivery. With Hints on the Management of the Baby, and Other Matters of Importance Necessary to be Known by Married Women* (W. J. Ramsay 1886); for an account of the trial see *British Medical Journal*, i, (1889), p. 270, ii, (1889), pp. 1162–3, 1221–2. This work had gone into over forty editions by the time of the First World War, and was still widely available in the 1930s, according to Norman E. Himes, *The Medical History of Contraception* (Williams and Wilkins Co., Baltimore 1936), p. 326n.
17   *British Medical Journal*, ii (1889), p. 88.
18   C. H. F. Routh, 'On the Moral and Physical Evils Likely to Follow if Practices Intended to Act as Checks to Population be not Strongly Discouraged and Condemned,' originally given as a paper before the obstetrical section of the British Medical Association, and first published in the *Medical Press and Circular* (October 1878), reprinted from the same, Baillière, Tindall and Cox 1879.
19   *British Medical Journal*, i, (1902), pp. 339–40.
20   Grosskurth, *Havelock Ellis*, pp. 114–15.
21   Prof. Patrick Geddes and J. Arthur Thomson, *The Contemporary Science Series. Volume 1: The Evolution of Sex*, ed. Havelock Ellis (Walter Scott 1889), introduction to the 2nd edn, 1901, p.v. (The first edition only said 'such unity as our present knowledge renders possible'.)
22   Ibid. (1st edn 1889), p. 267.
23   Ibid., p. 17.
24   Ibid., pp. 257–8.
25   Ibid., pp. 270–1.
26   Ibid., p. 269.
27   *British Medical Journal*, i, (1893), pp. 1325–6; Richard von Krafft-Ebing, *Psychopathia Sexualis: with Especial Reference to the Antipathetic Sexual Instinct. A Medico-forensic Study* [first published in German 1886, first English edition 1893, numerous subsequent editions] (Staples Press 1965 [based on 12th German edn]).

28 *The Lancet* ii, (1898), pp. 1344–5, 'The Question of Indecent Literature'.
29 *British Medical Journal*, ii, (1898), p. 1466.
30 Biographical details from Grosskurth, *Havelock Ellis*.
31 *Lives of the Fellows of the Royal College of Physicians* ('Munk's Roll'), Volume V, p. 121; obituaries in the *British Medical Journal*, ii, (1939), pp. 203–4, and *The Lancet*, ii, (1939), pp. 164–5, 229.
32 *The Lancet* i, (1933), p. 1348; *British Medical Journal*, i, (1933), p. 1057.
33 Grosskurth, *Havelock Ellis*; Arthur Calder-Marshall, *Havelock Ellis: A Biography* (Rupert Hart-Davis 1957).
34 Havelock Ellis, *Studies in the Psychology of Sex: Volume I: The Evolution of Modesty; The Phenomena of Sexual Periodicity; Auto-Erotism* (Leipzig and Watford 1899 [first published as Volume II]), F. A. Davis Co., Philadelphia 1900, 3rd edn 1910, Random House, New York, omnibus edition, Volume I, 1936).

Volume II: Sexual Inversion, with J. Addington Symonds (Wilson and Macmillan 1897 (withdrawn), F. A. Davis Co., Philadelphia 1901, 3rd edn 1915, Random House, New York, omnibus edition, Volume I, 1937).

Volume III: The Analysis of the Sexual Impulse: Love and Pain: The Sexual Impulse in Women (F. A. Davis Co., Philadelphia 1903, Random House, New York, omnibus edition 1937).

Volume IV: Sexual Selection in Man (F. A. Davis Co., Philadelphia 1905, Random House, New York, omnibus edition 1937).

Volume V: Erotic Symbolism: The Mechanism of Detumescence: The Psychic State in Pregnancy (F. A. Davis Co., Philadelphia 1906).

Volume VI: Sex in Relation to Society (F. A. Davis Co., Philadelphia 1910, first English edn William Heinemann Medical Books 1937, War Economy edn 1946).

Volume VII: Eonism and Other Supplementary Studies (F. A. Davis Co., Philadelphia 1928).
35 Ellis, *Analysis of the Sexual Impulse; Love and Pain; The Sexual Impulse in Women*, p. 189.
36 Ellis, *The Evolution of Modesty; The Phenomena of Sexual Periodicity; Auto-Erotism*, p. 98.
37 Ibid., p. 261.
38 Sigmund Freud, ' "Civilised" Sexual Morality and Modern Nervous Illness' [first published in German 1908, English translation, Standard Edition, 1959], included in *Civilisation Society and Religion* (Pelican Freud Library 12, Harmondsworth 1985), pp. 33–55; ref. to p. 51.
39 Ellis, *The Evolution of Modesty; The Phenomena of Sexual Periodicity; Auto-Erotism*, p. 263.
40 Ellis, *Sex in Relation to Society*, p. 310.
41 Marie Stopes, *Enduring Passion: Further New Contributions to the Solution of Sex Difficulties, being the continuation of Married Love* (G. P. Putnam's Sons 1928, 2nd edn 1929), p. 76.
42 *The Lancet*, i, (1910), p. 1207.

43   Sigmund Freud, *Three Lectures on the Theory of Sexuality* ('The Sexual Aberrations', 'Infantile Sexuality', 'The Transformations of Puberty'), [first German edition, Leipzig and Vienna 1905, English translation by James Strachey for the *Standard Edition* 1952], included in *On Sexuality* (Pelican Freud Library 7, Harmondsworth 1977), p. 45.

44   Ibid., p. 57n.

45   Ibid., p. 59.

46   *The Lancet*, i, (1917), pp. 912–14.

47   *The Lancet*, ii, (1920), p. 404.

48   Prof. Patrick Geddes and J. Arthur Thomson, *Sex*, Home University Library (Williams and Norgate 1914), pp. 118, 138, 144, 150; Arthur Cooper, *The Sexual Disabilities of Man and their Treatment* (H. K. Lewis 1908, 3rd edn 1916), pp. 78, 182.

49   Dean Rapp, 'The Early Discovery of Freud by the British General Public, 1912–1919', *Social History of Medicine*, 3, no. 2 (1990), pp. 217–43.

50   F. M. L. Thompson, *The Rise of Respectable Society: A Social History of Victorian Britain, 1830–1900* (Fontana 1988), pp. 59, 69; John D'Emilio and Estelle B. Freedman, *Intimate Matters: A History of Sexuality in America* (Harper and Row, New York 1988), pp. 66–73, describes similar developments in the USA.

51   Edward Bristow, *Vice and Vigilance: Purity Movements in Britain since 1700* (Gill and Macmillan, Dublin 1977), p. 138.

52   'JEH' (J. Ellice Hopkins), 'True Manliness', in *The Blanco Book* (White Cross League 1913), pp. 115–43.

53   Rev. E. Lyttelton, *The Causes and Prevention of Immorality in Schools* (Social Purity Alliance, printed for private circulation, 1887).

54   Sylvanus Stall, *What a Young Boy Ought to Know*, Self and Sex Series (Vir Publishing Co., Philadelphia and London 1897), pp. 25–72.

55   Ibid., pp. 80–1.

56   Ibid., pp. 82–3.

57   Ibid., p. 113.

58   Sylvanus Stall, *What a Young Man Ought to Know*, Self and Sex Series (Vir Publishing Co., Philadelphia and London 1897; revised and reprinted as late as 1929).

59   Lord Baden-Powell, *Scouting for Boys: A Handbook for Instruction in Good Citizenship* (C. Arthur Pearson 1908, 2nd imprn), p. 279.

60   Ibid., (10th edn 1922), p. 209.

61   Lord Baden-Powell, *Rovering to Success: A Book of Life-Sport for Young Men* (Herbert Jenkins Ltd 1922, 13th printing, n.d.), p. 103.

62   Ibid., p. 104.

63   Ibid., p. 107.

64   Norah March, *Towards Racial Health: A Handbook for Parents, Teachers, and Social Workers on the Training of Boys and Girls*, with a foreword by J. Arthur Thomson (George Routledge and Sons Ltd 1915, 4th edn 1920), p. 33n., also p. 35.

65   Ibid., pp. 97–143.

66 Ibid., pp. 175–7.
67 Lyttelton, *The Causes and Prevention of Immorality*, p. 15.
68 Arthur T. Barnett, 'The Testimony of Medical Men', in *The Blanco Book* (White Cross League 1913), testimony of F. Le Gros Clark, p. 223.
69 Ibid., testimony of C. G. Wheelhouse, p. 226.
70 T. J. Wyke, 'The Manchester and Salford Lock Hospital, 1818–1917', *Medical History*, 19 (1979), pp. 73–86.
71 Judith R. Walkowitz, *Prostitution and Victorian Society: Women, Class and the State* (Cambridge University Press, Cambridge and New York 1980); Paul McHugh, *Prostitution and Victorian Social Reform* (Croom Helm c.1980). F. B. Smith, 'The Contagious Diseases Act Reconsidered', *Social History of Medicine*, 3, no. 2 (1990), pp. 197–215, takes a revisionist look at the subject.
72 Myna Trustram, *Women of the Regiment: Marriage and the Victorian Army* (Cambridge University Press, Cambridge and New York 1984).
73 Keith Thomas, 'The Double Standard', *Journal of the History of Ideas*, 20 (1959), pp. 195–216.
74 *Royal Commission on Venereal Diseases, Final Report*, Cd 8189, 1916, §137–8.
75 Wyke, 'The Manchester and Salford Lock Hospital'; *RC on VD, Final Report*, 134; *Departmental Committee on Sickness Benefit Claims under the National Insurance Act*, Cd 7687, 1914, §134–41.
76 L. W. Harrison, 'Those Were the Days! or Random Notes on Then and Now in VD', *Bulletin of the Institute of Technicians in Venereology* [n.d. ?1950s]), Wellcome Institute Library Reprint Collection, pp. 1–7; Michael Adler, 'The Terrible Peril: a Historical Perspective on the Venereal Diseases', *British Medical Journal*, ii (1980), pp. 202–11.
77 Harrison, 'Those Were the Days!'.
78 R. V. Rajam, 'Progress in the Treatment and Control of Venereal Diseases', *The Antiseptic*, 5, no. 4 (1954), pp. 345–66; ref. to p. 356.
79 Harrison, 'Those Were the Days!'.
80 Local Government Board, *Report as to the Practice of Medicine and Surgery by Unqualified Persons in the United Kingdom*, Cd 5422, 1910, p. 15.
81 *RC on VD, Final Report*, §188.
82 Ibid., §133.
83 E. B. Turner, 'The History of the Fight Against Venereal Disease', *Science Progress*, 11 (1916–17), pp. 83–8.
84 *RC on VD, Final Report*, §144.
85 *History of the Great War Based on Official Documents; Medical Services: Diseases of the War* (HMSO 1923), volume II, chapter III, 'Venereal Diseases' by L. W. Harrison, pp. 118–60; ref. to p. 119.
86 Ibid., p. 118.
87 Adler, 'The Terrible Peril', no supporting reference, possibly anecdotal.
88 *History of the Great War*, p. 72.
89 Ibid., p. 74.
90 Ibid., p. 121.

91   Ibid., p. 121.
92   Jay Cassel, *The Secret Plague: Venereal Disease in Canada, 1838–1939* (University of Toronto Press, Toronto 1987), p. 122.
93   *History of the Great War*, p. 121.
94   Marie Stopes papers in the Contemporary Medical Archives Centre at the Wellcome Institute for the History of Medicine, CMAC: PP/MCS/A.166.
95   CMAC: PP/MCS/A.60 (2nd/Lt RAF).
96   Bridget Towers, 'Health Education Policy, 1916–1926: Venereal Disease and the Prophylaxis Dilemma', *Medical History*, 24 (1980), pp. 70–87; ref to p. 77.

2 EVIL COMPANIONS, SCARLET WOMEN AND PERNICIOUS QUACKS: THE SUBCULTURES OF SEX

1   Sir James Paget, 'Sexual Hypochondriasis', *Clinical Lectures and Essays* (Longmans Green 1875, 2nd edn 1879).
2   T. L. Nichols, *Esoteric Anthropology (The Mysteries of Man) A Comprehensive and Confidential Treatise on the Structure, Functions, Passional Attractions, and Perversions, True and False Physical and Social Conditions and the Most Intimate Relations of Men and Women. Anatomical, Physiological, Pathological, Therapeutical and Obstetrical. Hygienic and Hydropathic. From the American Stereotype Edition, Revised and Rewritten* (Dr Nichols at the Hygienic Institute, Museum St, London WC [*c.*1873]), p. 280.
3   Sylvanus Stall, *What a Young Boy Ought to Know*, Self and Sex Series (Vir Publishing Co., Philadelphia and London 1897), p. 85.
4   Marie Stopes papers in the Contemporary Medical Archives Centre at the Wellcome Institute for the History of Medicine, CMAC: PP/MCS/A.220, A.43 (a missionary).
5   CMAC: PP/MCS/A.146, A.64.
6   CMAC: PP/MCS/A.210 (L-Bdr).
7   CMAC: PP/MCS/A.115, A.244.
8   Mary Scharlieb and F. A. Sibly, *Youth and Sex: Dangers and Safeguards for Girls and Boys* (T. C. and E. C. Hack [1913]), p. 48.
9   Arthur T. Barnett, 'The Testimony of Medical Men', in *The Blanco Book* (White Cross League 1913) p. 224.
10   Dr A. R. Schofield and Dr P. Vaughan-Jackson, *What A Boy Should Know* (Cassell 1913), p. 50.
11   CMAC: PP/MCS/A.107, A.157.
12   Both cited in a review in *The Shield*, 3rd series, 2 (1919–20), p. 228.
13   CMAC: PP/MCS/A.32.
14   T. E. Shaw (Lawrence), *The Mint: A Day Book of the RAF Depot between August and December 1922, with Later Notes by 352087 A/c Ross* (Jonathan Cape 1955), and even then allocated to 'Cupboard' by the British Museum Reading Room; F. Manning, *Her Privates We* (Peter Davies

1964) [version published anonymously in 1929 as *The Middle Parts of Fortune: Somme and Ancre 1916* (Piazza Press)].

15 CMAC: PP/MCS/A.57, A.135.
16 *The Lancet*, i (1884), p. 963.
17 *RC on VD, First Report: Appendix: Minutes of Evidence (1913–1914)*, 1914, Cd 7475, §2822.
18 CMAC: PP/MCS/A.145.
19 CMAC: PP/MCS/A.132.
20 CMAC: PP/MCS/A.44, A.54, A.32.
21 CMAC: PP/MCS/A.63.
22 *The Shield*, 5th series, 2 no. 1 (1933), p. 34.
23 CMAC: PP/MCS/A.222, A.88, A.83.
24 For a description of Mass Observation, its aims and achievements, see Tom Harrisson, *Britain Revisited* (Victor Gollancz Ltd 1961); Angus Calder and Dorothy Sheridan, eds, *Speak for Yourself: A Mass Observation Anthology 1937–1949* (Oxford University Press, Oxford 1985) has a briefer account; Tom Harrisson–Mass Observation Archive at the University of Sussex: 'Sexual Behaviour 1929–1950', A.9 'Sex Survey 1949'.
25 Ibid., file 3/C 'Report on Sex: Chapter Two: Discovering Sex'.
26 Ibid., completed questionnaires, file 10/C.
27 Ibid., completed questionnaires, file 10/B.
28 Ibid., completed questionnaires, file 10/A.
29 Ibid., completed questionnaires, file 10/A.
30 Ibid., completed questionnaires, files 10/A, 10/B.
31 William Acton, *Prostitution* (first published London 1857; new edn, ed. Peter Fryer, MacGibbon and Kee 1968), pp. 61–74; Judith R. Walkowitz, *Prostitution and Victorian Society: Women, Class and the State* (Cambridge University Press Cambridge and New York 1980), chapter 10, 'The Making of an Outcast Group: Prostitutes and Working Women in Plymouth and Southampton', pp. 192–213.
32 G. W. Johnson, 'The Injustice of the Solicitation Laws', *The Shield*, 3rd series, 3 (1920–2), pp. 267–9; anonymous editorial, 'Woman, Where are Thine Accusers?', Ibid., pp. 307–9.
33 H. R. E. Ware, 'The Role, Recruitment and Regulation of Prostitutes in Britain, 1800–1969', unpublished University of London PhD thesis, 1969, p. 303.
34 Ibid., pp. 446, 466.
35 *The Shield*, 3rd series, 3 (1920–2), p. 116.
36 Wilhelm Stekel, *Impotence in the Male: The Psychic Disorders of Sexual Function in the Male*, 2 vols (authorized English version by Oswald H. Boltz, first published in German 1927, Liveright Publishing Co., New York 1927), vol. I, p. 170; Abraham Flexner, *Prostitution in Europe* (first published by Bureau of Social Hygiene, New York 1913, abridged edn Grant Richards Ltd 1919), pp. 40–1, also mentions this attitude.
37 Dr R. Arthur, 'Some Aspects of the Venereal Problem', *The Shield*, 3rd series, 1 (1916–17), pp. 302–8; ref. to p. 308.

38   Flexner, *Prostitution in Europe*, p. 233.
39   Winfield Scott Hall, MD, assisted by Jeannette Winter Hall, *Sexual Knowledge: In Plain and Simple Language; Sexology or Knowledge of Self and Sex for both Male and Female; especially for the Instruction of Youths and Maidens, Young Wives and Young Husbands, All Fathers and All Mothers, School-teachers and Nurses, and All Others who Feel a Need of Proper and Reliable Information on Sex Hygiene, Sex Problems and the Best Way and the Best Time to Impart Sexual Knowledge to Boys and Girls about to Enter into Manhood and Womanhood* (International Bible House 1913, T. Werner Laurie [1926]), pp. 184–5; Norah March, *Towards Racial Health: A Handbook for Parents, Teachers, and Social Workers on the Training of Boys and Girls*, with a foreword by J. Arthur Thomson (George Routledge and Sons Ltd 1915, 4th edn 1920), p. 175.
40   Havelock Ellis, *Studies in the Psychology of Sex. Volume VI: Sex in Relation to Society* (F. A. Davis Co., Philadelphia 1910, first English edn William Heinemann Medical Books 1937, War Economy edn 1946), p. 305.
41   Marie Stopes, *Married Love: A New Contribution to the Solution of Sex Difficulties* (A. C. Fifield 1918 [7th and later edns G. P. Putnam's Sons Ltd], 4th edn 1918), p. 28.
42   CMAC: PP/MCS/A.129.
43   'British Troops in France: Provision of Tolerated Brothels', *The Shield*, 3rd series, 1 (1916–17), pp. 393–7; 'The Maisons Tolerées', *The Sheild*, 3rd series, 2 (1918–20), pp. 53–64.
44   A. Neilans, 'The Protection of Soldiers', *The Shield*, 3rd series, 1 (1916–17), pp. 216–23.
45   Alison Neilans, 'Has Moral Teaching Failed?', *The Shield*, 3rd series, 3 (1920–2), pp. 257–65.
46   *British Medical Journal*, i (1920), p. 273.
47   Sir Arthur Newsholme, 'The Decline in Registered Mortality from Syphilis in England. To What is it Due?', *Journal of Social Hygiene*, 12, no. 9 (1926), pp. 514–23; ref. to p. 522.
48   CMAC: PP/MCS/A.252 (Indian Civil Service), A.193, A.94.
49   CMAC: PP/MCS/A.121 (Lt Cdr), A.168 (Capt).
50   CMAC: PP/MCS/A.88, A.109 (Major, Sudan).
51   CMAC: PP/MCS/A.129, A.109 (Lt Cdr, RN).
52   CMAC: PP/MCS/A.213, A.183, A.246, A.168, A.144.
53   CMAC: PP/MCS/A.144, A.208.
54   John Stevenson, *The Pelican Social History of Britain: British Society, 1914–1945* (Penguin Books, Harmondsworth 1984), pp. 82–5, 383, 386.
55   Prof. John H. Stokes, 'The Future of Syphilis', *British Journal of Venereal Diseases*, 4, no. 4 (1928), pp. 274–89; ref. to p. 275.
56   G. L. M. McElligott, 'The Venereal History: Truth or Fiction?', *British Journal of Venereal Diseases*, 8 (1932), pp. 292–7; ref. to p. 294.
57   Robert Sutherland, 'Some Individual and Social Factors in Venereal Disease', *British Journal of Venereal Diseases*, 26 (1950), pp. 1–15; ref. to p. 3.

58 *The Shield*, 5th series, 5, no. 3 (1937), p. 99; 5th series, 9, no. 1 (1942), pp. 3–7.
59 'Compulsory Methods and the Treatment of Venereal Diseases', *The Shield*, 5th series, 9, no. 2 (1942), pp. 55–8.
60 'The Social Background of Venereal Disease: a Report on an Experiment in Contact Tracing and an Investigation into Social Conditions: Tyneside Experimental Scheme in Venereal Disease Control, October 1943 to Mach 1944', *British Journal of Venereal Diseases*, 21 (1945), pp. 26–34.
61 *The Shield*, 5th series, 6, no. 3 (1938), p. 125.
62 Douglas White, 'The Basis of a New Moral Appeal', *The Shield*, 5th series, 7, no. 1 (1939), pp. 1–4; ref. to p. 2.
63 Major G. O. Watts and Major R. A. Wilson, 'A Study of Personality Factors among Venereal Disease Patients', *Canadian Medical Association Journal*, 53 (1945), pp. 119–22.
64 Lt Col. T. A. Ratcliffe, 'Psychiatric and Allied Aspects of the Problem of Venereal Disease in the Army', *Journal of the Royal Army Medical Corps*, 89 (1947), pp. 122–31.
65 E. D. Wittkower, 'The Psychological Aspects of Venereal Disease', *British Journal of Venereal Diseases*, 24 (1948), pp. 59–67.
66 Eustace Chesser, *Grow Up – and Live* (Penguin Books, Harmondsworth 1949, reprinted 1951), p. 237.
67 *The Lancet*, i (1857), pp. 556–7.
68 For example, *The Lancet*, i (1870), pp. 880, 889; ii (1870), pp. 89–90; *British Medical Journal*, i (1879), pp. 823–4.
69 F. M. L. Thompson, *The Rise of Respectable Society: A Social History of Victorian Britain, 1830–1900* (Fontana 1988), pp. 135–51.
70 *The Lancet*, i (1857), pp. 556–7.
71 Ibid., i (1862), pp. 518–19.
72 Ibid., ii (1870) pp. 89–90, 124–6, 159–60, 224–5.
73 Samuel La'mert, *Self-Preservation: A Medical Treatise on Nervous and Physical Debility, Spermatorrhoea, Impotence and Sterility, with Practical Observations on the Use of the Microscope in the Treatment of Diseases of the Generative System*, ('Published by the Author and sold at all Booksellers', '64th edition', c.1850s–60s): contains credentials pertaining to La'mert's career and qualifications. His licence (1833) to practice as an apothecary is held in the Guildhall Library, ref. Guildhall Mss 8241/6, 8241B/1.
74 *British Medical Journal*, i (1863), p. 567; ii (1863), pp. 586–7; *The Lancet*, ii (1863), pp. 634–5.
75 La'mert, *Self-Preservation*, p. 23.
76 O. S. Fowler, *Creative and Sexual Science; or, Manhood, Womanhood and their Mutual Interrelations; Love, its Laws, Power, etc; Selection, or Mutual Adaptation; Courtship, Married Life and Perfect Children; their Generation, Endowment, Paternity, Maternity, Bearing, Nursing and Rearing; together with Puberty, Boyhood, Girlhood, etc, Sexual Impairments Restored, Male Vigour and Female Health and Beauty Perpetuated and Augmented, etc, as*

Taught by Phrenology and Physiology (first published New York 1870, later edn O. S. Fowler [n.d.] *c.*1900), pp. 801–4.

77 Nichols, *Esoteric Anthropology*, p. 180.
78 *The Lancet* ii (1870), p. 159.
79 Ibid., ii (1857), p. 537.
80 Ibid., i (1929), pp. 1202–3.
81 Ibid., ii (1885), p. 350.
82 *British Medical Journal*, ii (1885), pp. 303–4.
83 British Medical Association Groups files in the Contemporary Medical Archives Centre at the Wellcome Institute for the History of Medicine, 'Medico-Political' files, CMAC: SA/BMA/C.483 'Birth Control and Indecent Advertisements: correspondence, *c.*1929–1955'.
84 Nicole Ward Jouve, *'The Streetcleaner': The Yorkshire Ripper Case on Trial* (Marion Boyars, London and New York 1986), p. 117; Deborah Cameron and Elizabeth Frazer, *The Lust to Kill: A Feminist Investigation of Sexual Murder* (Polity Press, Cambridge 1987), p. 137.
85 *British Medical Journal*, i (1879) pp. 823–4.
86 *British Medical Journal*, ii (1892), p. 753.
87 *The Lancet*, i (1870), pp. 889, 880.
88 Sir T. S. Clouston, *Clinical Lectures on Mental Diseases* (J. A. Churchill 1883, 6th edn 1904), 'The Insanity of Masturbation', pp. 535–46; ref. to pp. 538–9.
89 CMAC: SA/BMA/C.436 'Patent Medicines: Australian Commission on Secret Drugs 1907'.
90 CMAC: SA/BMA/C.429: 'Patent Medicines: Documents used by Dr Crosse in the compilation of evidence to be presented before the Select Committee, 1912'.
91 *British Medical Journal*, ii (1892), p. 753.
92 Mass Observation, A.9 'Sex Survey 1949', file 4/G Report on Sex: 'Miscellaneous unsorted draft material and notes'.
93 Ibid., file 16/G 'Advertising and Publications: Proprietary Medicines and Tonics'.

3 'MOST MEN ACT IN IGNORANCE': THE MARRIAGE MANUAL AND CHANGING CONCEPTS OF MARRIAGE

1 *Aristotle's Works. Medical Knowledge. The Works of Aristotle the Famous Philosopher, Containing his Complete Masterpiece and Family Physician, his Experienced Midwife, his Book of Problems and his Remarks on Physiognomy* ([n.d.] *c.*1890, and other editions, also n.d., of 19th–20th centuries); for a discussion of this work in an eighteenth-century context, see Roy Porter, ' "The Secrets of Generation Display'd": Aristotle's Masterpiece in Eighteenth Century England', in Robert P. Maccubin, ed., *Unauthorised Sexual Behaviour during the Enlightenment*, special issue of *Eighteenth Century Life*, IX, no. 3 (May 1985), pp. 1–21.

2   See notes 15 and 16 to chapter 1.

3   O. S. Fowler, *Creative and Sexual Science* (first published New York 1870, later edn O. S. Fowler [n.d.] *c*.1900), pp. 603, 620.

4   S. Nissenbaum, *Sex, Diet and Debility in Jacksonian America: Sylvester Graham and Health Reform* (Greenwood Press, Westport, CT, and London 1980), pp. 158–73, discusses Nichols and his wife Mary Gove Nichols in the context of health reform and free love movements in the USA.

5   Havelock Ellis, review article in *Reynolds News* (26 April 1936), E. F. Griffith's press-cuttings scrapbook in the Contemporary Medical Archives Centre at the Wellcome Institute for the History of Medicine, CMAC: PP/EFG/A.41; similar opinions appear in Havelock Ellis, *Studies in the Psychology of Sex. Volume VII: Eonism and Other Supplementary Studies* (F. A. Davis Co. 1928), p. 156.

6   T. L. Nichols, *Esoteric Anthropology* (Dr Nichols at the Hygienic Institute, Museum St, London WC [*c*.1873]), p. 120.

7   Ibid., p. 119.

8   Ibid., p. 115.

9   Lyman Beecher Sperry, *Confidential Talks with Husband and Wife: A Book of Information and Advice for the Married and the Marriageable* (Oliphant Anderson and Ferrier, London and Edinburgh 1900), pp. 101–6.

10 Ibid., p. 119.

11 R. T. Trall, *Sexual Physiology and Hygiene: An Exposition Practical, Scientific, Moral, and Popular of Some of the Fundamental Problems in Sociology*, (first published *c*.1888, T. D. Morison (Glasgow) Simpkin, Marshall, Hamilton and Kent Co. 1908), p. 226.

12 Sperry, *Confidential Talks*, p. 113.

13 Trall, *Sexual Physiology*, p. 222.

14 Sperry, *Confidential Talks*, p. 119.

15 Trall, *Sexual Physiology*, p. 232.

16 Sperry, *Confidential Talks*, p. 110.

17 Ibid., pp. 117–20; Trall, *Sexual Physiology*, p. 226.

18 *Nature's Revelations for the Married Only*, Printed for Private Circulation. Only (Electric Life Invigorator Co., G. W. Ventnor, The Limes, Painswick Road, Gloucester [?1904]), pp. 88–9.

19 Havelock Ellis, *The Erotic Rights of Women* and *The Objects of Marriage* (British Society for the Study of Sex Psychology 1918); *The Play-Function of Sex* (British Society for the Study of Sex Psychology, publication no. 9, 1921).

20 Marie Stopes, *Married Love: A New Contribution to the Solution of Sex Difficulties* (A. C. Fifield 1918 [7th and later edns G. P. Putnam's Sons Ltd], 4th edn 1918), p. 50.

21 'Dr' G. Courtenay Beale, *Wise Wedlock: The Whole Truth: A Book of Counsel and Instruction for All who Seek for Happiness in Marriage* (Health Promotion Ltd, 2nd edn [*c*.1922]).

22 Marie Stopes papers in the Contemporary Medical Archives Centre at

the Wellcome Institute for the History of Medicine, CMAC: PP/MCS/ A.22, includes correspondence 'Re Dr Courtenay Beale' in which Stopes voiced her suspicions as to 'Beale's' identity in the light of the fact that she had been unable to track him down in order to serve upon him a writ for plagiarism.

23 Beale, *Wise Wedlock*, new revised edn with an introduction by Norman Haire (The Wales Publishing Co. 1944), p. 5.

24 Lady Isabel Hutton, *Memories of a Doctor in War and Peace* (Heinemann 1960).

25 Isabel E. Hutton, *The Hygiene of Marriage* (William Heinemann Medical Books Ltd 1923, 4th edn 1933).

26 Hutton, *Memories of a Doctor*, pp. 214–15.

27 Ibid., p. 217.

28 Th. H. Van de Velde, *Ideal Marriage: Its Physiology and Technique* (first published in Dutch 1926, English translation William Heinemann Medical Books Ltd 1928, 39th impression 1962).

29 *The Lancet*, ii (1929) p. 177.

30 Edward M. Brecher, *The Sex Researchers* (Andre Deutsch 1970), pp. 82–103.

31 Eustace Chesser, *Sexual Behaviour: Normal and Abnormal* (London Medical Publications Ltd [1949]), pp. 16–17.

32 Brecher, *The Sex Researchers*, p. 86.

33 Chesser, *Sexual Behaviour*, p. 17.

34 For details of Helena Wright's career see Barbara Evans, *Freedom to Choose: The Life and Work of Dr Helena Wright, Pioneer of Contraception* (Bodley Head 1984).

35 Helena Wright, *The Sex Factor in Marriage: A Book for Those Who Are or Are About To Be Married*, with an introduction by A. Herbert Gray (Williams and Norgate Ltd 1930, 2nd edn 1937); Helena Wright, *More About the Sex Factor in Marriage: A Sequel to The Sex Factor in Marriage* (Williams and Norgate 1947, 2nd edn 1954).

36 Edward F. Griffith, *Modern Marriage*, with forewords by Lord Horder, Canon Pym and Claud Mullins [originally published by Victor Gollancz as *Modern Marriage and Birth Control*, 1935] (Methuen and Co Ltd 1946), p. 149.

37 For details of Griffith's life and career see his autobiography, *The Pioneer Spirit* (Green Leaves Press, Upton Grey 1981).

38 Anthony Havil, *The Technique of Sex: Towards a Better Understanding of the Sexual Relationship* (Wales Publishing Co. 1939).

39 Eustace Chesser, *Love without Fear: A Plain Guide to Sex Technique for Every Married Adult* (Rich and Cowan Medical Publications 1941), July 1942 edn, p. 85.

40 Havelock Ellis, *Studies in the Psychology of Sex. Volume VI: Sex in Relation to Society* (F. A. Davis Co., Philadelphia 1910, first English edn William Heinemann Medical Books 1937, War Economy edn 1946), pp. 314–15.

41 Ellis, *The Play-Function of Sex*, p. 5.

42 Honoré de Balzac, *The Physiology of Marriage* (first published in France 1826, English edn privately printed 1904), pp. 56–8.
43 Griffith, *Modern Marriage*, p. 194.
44 Wright, *The Sex Factor*, p. 68.
45 Beale, *Wise Wedlock*, p. 87.
46 Wright, *The Sex Factor*, p. 83.
47 Chesser, *Love without Fear*, p. 61.
48 Beale, *Wise Wedlock*, p. 69.
49 Hutton, *The Hygiene of Marriage*, p. 49.
50 Stopes, *Married Love*, p. 22.
51 Ibid., p. 39.
52 Hutton, *The Hygiene of Marriage*, pp. 49–50.
53 Ibid., p. 54.
54 Wright, *The Sex Factor*, p. 74; Havil, *The Technique of Sex*, p. 40.
55 Wright, *The Sex Factor*, p. 74.
56 Havil, *The Technique of Sex*, p. 40.
57 Chesser, *Love without Fear*, p. 58.
58 Havil, *The Technique of Sex*, p. 39.
59 Van de Velde, *Ideal Marriage*, p. 6.
60 Wright, *The Sex Factor*, pp. 67–8.
61 Havil, *The Technique of Sex*, p. 105.
62 Van de Velde, *Ideal Marriage*, p. 238.
63 Ibid., p. 165.
64 Ibid., p. 248.
65 Marie Stopes, *Enduring Passion: Further New Contributions to the Solution of Sex Difficulties, being the Continuation of Married Love* (G. P. Putnam's Sons Ltd 1928, 2nd edn 1929), chapters IV & V, pp. 54–84.
66 Hutton, *The Hygiene of Marriage*, pp. 65–6.
67 Wright, *The Sex Factor*, p. 68.
68 Griffith, *Modern Marriage*, pp. 155–6.
69 Wright, *The Sex Factor*, p. 76.
70 Ibid, pp. 72–3.
71 Judge Ben B. Lindsey and Wainwright Evans, *The Companionate Marriage* (Boni and Liveright, New York 1927); the concept is discussed (from a radical feminist perspective with which I do not wholly agree) in Christina Simmons, 'Companionate Marriage and the Lesbian Threat', *Frontiers*, 4, no. 3 (1979), pp. 54–9. (I am indebted to Barbara Brookes for this reference.)
72 For examples, see Rev. A. Herbert Gray, *Men, Women, and God: A Discussion of Sex Questions from the Christian Point of View* (Student Christian Movement 1923); A. Maude Royden, *Sex and Commonsense* (Hurst and Blackett Ltd, 8th edn [?1920s]); Mary Borden, *The Technique of Marriage* (William Heinemann Ltd 1933); Dr Margaret Marriner, *First Aid to Marriage* – 'A successful marriage should be an enchanted garden, in which two people can play together long after childhood has passed': note on cover – (Williams and Norgate 1933).

73   John Stevenson, *The Pelican Social History of Britain: British Society, 1914–1945* (Penguin Books, Harmondsworth 1984), p. 179.

74   Naomi Mitchison, *You May Well Ask: A Memoir 1920–1940* (Victor Gollancz Ltd 1979, Flamingo paperback edn 1986); Vera Brittain, *Testament of Youth: An Autobiographical Study of the Years 1900–1925* (Victor Gollancz Ltd 1933, cheap edn 1948); Vera Brittain, *Testament of Experience: An Autobiographical Story of the Years 1925–1950* (Victor Gollancz Ltd 1957, Virago Press paperback 1979); Hutton, *Memories of a Doctor.*

75   CMAC: PP/MCS/A.112 (Pte).

76   Stevenson, *British Society, 1914–1945, passim,* but particularly chapters 4, 5, 8, 15.

77   O. R. McGregor, *Divorce in England; A Centenary History* (Heinemann 1957), p. 28.

78   Ibid., p. 33.

79   *The Shield,* VI, no. 3 (July 1930), pp. 131–2.

80   A. P. Herbert, *Holy Deadlock* (Methuen and Co. Ltd 1934).

81   McGregor, *Divorce in England,* p. 30.

82   M. Leonora Eyles, *The Woman in the Little House* (Grant Richards 1922), chapter 7, 'The Sex Problem', pp. 129–51.

83   Wilhelm Stekel, *Impotence in the Male: The Psychic Disorders of Sexual Function in the Male,* 2 vols (authorized English version by Oswald H. Boltz, first published in German 1927, Liveright Publishing Co., New York 1927), vol. I, p. 57 ('with increasing intelligence...the psychic disturbances of potency become more numerous').

84   Stopes, *Enduring Passion,* p. 76.

85   Arthur Cooper, *The Sexual Disabilities of Man and Their Treatment* (H. K. Lewis 1908, 2nd edn 1910), p. 94.

86   Ibid., p. 127.

87   Ibid., p. 152.

88   Alfred C. Kinsey, Wardell B. Pomeroy and Clyde E. Martin, *Sexual Behaviour in the Human Male* (W. B. Saunders Co. Ltd, Philadelphia and London 1948).

89   Eliot Slater and Moya Woodside, *Patterns of Marriage: A Study of Marriage Relationships in the Urban Working Classes* Cassell and Co. 1951), p. 21.

90   Tom Harrisson–Mass Observation Archive at the University of Sussex: 'Sexual Behaviour 1929–1950', A.9 'Sex Survey 1949', file 3/F 'Report on Sex: Chapter Five: Marriage'.

91   Moya Woodside, 'Courtship and Mating in an Urban Community', *Eugenics Review,* 38, no. 1 (1946), pp. 29–39.

92   Slater and Woodside, *Patterns of Marriage,* p. 167.

93   Mass Observation, A.9 'Sex Survey 1949'; file 3/C 'Report on Sex: Chapter Two: Discovering Sex'.

94   Family Planning Association, 'Difficulties Commonly Encountered among Men', c.1940s, cited in 'Medica' (pseudonym of Dr Joan Malle-

son), *Any Wife or Any Husband; A Book for Couples who have Met Sexual Difficulties and for Doctors* (William Heinemann Medical Books 1950), pp. 25–9.

95 E. L. Packer, 'Aspects of Working-Class Marriage', *Pilot Papers: Social Essays and Documents*, 2, no. 1 (March 1947), pp. 92–104. This short-lived periodical was edited by Charles Madge, one of the founders of Mass Observation. He described 'Mr Packer' as 'an experienced probation officer' (ibid., p. 8).

96 Eustace Chesser, Joan Maizels, Leonard Jones and Brian Emmett, *The Sexual, Marital and Family Relationships of the English Woman*, with the assistance of an Advisory Committee comprising Professor F. A. E. Crew, Professor Alexander Kennedy, Kenneth Walker, Doris Odlum and Canon Hugh Walker (Hutchinson's Medical Publications Ltd 1956), chapter 14, §15, pp. 165–6.

97 Woodside, 'Courtship and Mating'.

98 Sheila Jeffreys, *The Spinster and Her Enemies: Feminism and Sexuality, 1900–1930* (Pandora Press 1988); Sheila Jeffreys, *Anti-Climax* (The Women's Press 1990).

99 Hutton, *Memories of a Doctor*, pp. 216–17; Alec Craig, 'Recent Developments in the Law of Obscene Libel', in Dr A. Pillay and Albert Ellis, eds, *Sex, Society and the Individual: Selected Papers, Revised and Brought up to Date, from 'Marriage Hygiene' (1934–1937) and 'The International Journal of Sexology' (1947–1952)* (The International Journal of Sexology, Bombay 1953), pp. 302–27, gives an account of the trial of *Love without Fear*.

100 Walter Gallichan, *The Poison of Prudery: An Historical Survey* (T. Werner Laurie 1929), p. 147, and letter to Marie Stopes CMAC: PP/MCS/A.158 on self-restriction by booksellers during the 1920s; the July 1942 edition of *Love without Fear* bears the message 'The author has written this book for those who are married or about to be married, and in this connection the bookseller's cooperation is requested' on the dust-jacket.

101 Jay Mechling, 'Advice to Historians on Advice to Mothers', *Journal of Social History*, 9, (1975–6), pp. 45–57.

102 CMAC: PP/MCS/A.210 (Mrs).

103 CMAC: PP/MCS/A.180.

104 CMAC: PP/MCS/A.151, A.297 (Rev.).

105 CMAC: PP/MCS/A.146, A.239.

106 CMAC: PP/MCS/A.134, A.135 (Capt., Indian Army).

107 CMAC: PP/MCS/A.235 (Lt-Col.), A.190.

108 CMAC: PP/MCS/A.173, A.120, A.250, A.123 (Carlton Club), A.240, A.246.

109 CMAC: PP/MCS/A.239, A.254, A.208 (Major).

110 CMAC: PP/MCS/A.201 (RAF), A.152.

111 CMAC: PP/MCS/A.135 (Capt., Indian Army).

112 Michael Gordon, 'From an Unfortunate Necessity to a Cult of Mutual

Orgasm: Sex in American Marital Education Literature 1830–1940', in J. Henslin ed., *Studies in the Sociology of Sex* (Appleton-Century Crofts, New York 1975), pp. 53–77; ref. to p. 71n.

113 Brecher, *The Sex Researchers*, p. 102.
114 CMAC: PP/MCS/A.188, A.112 (Pte), A.128, A.185, A.202.
115 CMAC: PP/MCS/A.160 SL, A.136 Capt. LDAH (RGA), A.129 FH.
116 CMAC: PP/MCS/A.135 Capt. BH.
117 Woodside, 'Courtship and Mating'.
118 Slater and Woodside, *Patterns of Marriage*, p. 173.
119 Packer, 'Aspects of Working Class Marriage'.
120 Chesser et al., *The Sexual, Marital and Family Relationships of the English Woman*, chapter 14, §22–3, p. 177.

4 'NOT SUCH A SELFISH BEAST': MEN'S PROBLEMS IN MARRIAGE

1 Marie Stopes, *Married Love: A New Contribution to the Solution of Sex Difficulties* (A. C. Fifield 1918, [7th and later edns G. P. Putnam's Sons Ltd], 4th edn 1918), p. iv.
2 Marie Stopes papers in the Contemporary Medical Archives Centre at the Wellcome Institute for the History of Medicine, CMAC: PP/MCS/ A.180, A.113.
3 CMAC: PP/MCS/A.250, A.245, A.193, A.117, A.120, A.44, A.105.
4 CMAC: PP/MCS/A.188.
5 CMAC: PP/MCS/A.164, A.77, A.42, A.6, A.98.
6 CMAC: PP/MCS/A.248.
7 CMAC: PP/MCS/A.189, A.73, A.88, A.26, A.208, A.70.
8 CMAC: PP/MCS/A.191, A.140, A.150, A.98, A.146.
9 CMAC: PP/MCS/A.44.
10 CMAC: PP/MCS/A.240 (ex-Sgt RAF).
11 CMAC: PP/MCS/A.41 (Major).
12 CMAC: PP/MCS/A.87, A.89, A.89, A.5, A.26, A.27, A.114. (Major).
13 CMAC: PP/MCS/A.202, A.158 (Capt.), A.28.
14 CMAC: PP/MCS/A.218 (Sgt).
15 CMAC: PP/MCS/A.113.
16 J. A. Banks, *Prosperity and Parenthood; A Study of Family Planning among the Victorian Middle Classes* (Routledge and Paul 1954); Angus McLaren, *Birth Control in Nineteenth Century England* (Croom Helm 1978), p. 116 for statistics of population decline; Richard A. Soloway, *Birth Control and the Population Question in England, 1870–1930* (University of North Carolina Press, Chapel Hill, NC, and London 1982).
17 CMAC: PP/MCS/A.209, A.198, A.168 (Capt.).
18 CMAC: PP/MCS/A.208, A.145, A.46.
19 CMAC: PP/MCS/A.187 (Lt-Cdr).
20 CMAC: PP/MCS/A.247 (Capt.), A.206.
21 CMAC: PP/MCS/A.243.

22 CMAC: PP/MCS/A.234.
23 CMAC: PP/MCS/A.128.
24 CMAC: PP/MCS/A.14.
25 CMAC: PP/MCS/A.113.
26 CMAC: PP/MCS/A.202.
27 CMAC: PP/MCS/A.15, A.66.
28 CMAC: PP/MCS/A.189.
29 CMAC: PP/MCS/A.237.
30 CMAC: PP/MCS/A.235 (Lt-Col.), A.211, A.153 (and wife), A.140.
31 CMAC: PP/MCS/A.155, A.148.
32 CMAC: PP/MCS/A.15, A.187 (Lt-Cdr).
33 CMAC: PP/MCS/A.249.
34 CMAC: PP/MCS/A.135, A.11, A.139, A.128, A.131.
35 CMAC: PP/MCS/A.196, A.153, A.238.
36 CMAC: PP/MCS/A.189, A.168 (Lt-Col.).
37 CMAC: PP/MCS/A.183 (Capt.), A.148, A.147, A.89.
38 CMAC: PP/MCS/A.140.
39 CMAC: PP/MCS/A.28, A.30, A.56, A.68, A.100, A.98, A.109, A.161, A.213.
40 Stopes, *Married Love*, 12th edn, revised 1923, Appendix, n. III, p. 190.
41 CMAC: PP/MCS/A.178, A.160, A.160, A.163, A.109, A.74, A.65.
42 CMAC: PP/MCS/A.174, A.89.
43 CMAC: PP/MCS/A.182.
44 CMAC: PP/MCS/A.179, A.166, A.89, see also A.222.
45 CMAC: PP/MCS/A.182, A.160.
46 CMAC: PP/MCS/A.178, A.196.
47 CMAC: PP/MCS/A.182 (skilled working-class), A.163.
48 CMAC: PP/MCS/A.182, A.174.
49 CMAC: PP/MCS/A.230, A.231, A.232, A.168.
50 CMAC: PP/MCS/A.173.
51 CMAC: PP/MCS/A.169.
52 CMAC: PP/MCS/A.166.
53 CMAC: PP/MCS/A.89, A.232, A.115 (2/Lt), A.238 (F/Lt).
54 For a brief discussion of the Eugenics Society, with suggestions for further reading on the subject, see Lesley A. Hall, 'Illustrations from the Wellcome Institute Library: The Eugenics Society Archives in the Contemporary Medical Archives Centre', *Medical History*, 34, no. 3 (1990), pp. 327–33; CMAC: PP/MCS/A.221, A.232, A.58, A.64, A.35, A.173 (Capt.).
55 CMAC: PP/MCS/A.250, A.70, A.2, A.172, A.206.
56 CMAC: PP/MCS/A.180, A.98, A.190.
57 CMAC: PP/MCS/A.67, A.230.
58 CMAC: PP/MCS/A.182, A.17.
59 Stopes, *Married Love*, 4th edn 1918, p. 9.
60 CMAC: PP/MCS/A.246 (Lt., RAMC), A.173, A.50.
61 CMAC: PP/MCS/A.42.

62 CMAC: PP/MCS/A.161, A.232, A.126, A.220 (Capt.).
63 CMAC: PP/MCS/A.183, A.70.
64 CMAC: PP/MCS/A.130.
65 CMAC: PP/MCS/A.67, A.233.
66 CMAC: PP/MCS/A.28.
67 CMAC: PP/MCS/A.160 (schoolmaster), A.211.
68 CMAC: PP/MCS/A.176.
69 CMAC: PP/MCS/A.222, A.250.
70 CMAC: PP/MCS/A.180, A.152 (Mrs), A.147 (Mrs).
71 CMAC: PP/MCS/A.185, A.179.
72 CMAC: PP/MCS/A.213, A.76, A.60, A.104, A.92, A.208 (Mrs), A.252, A.223, A.126.
73 CMAC: PP/MCS/A.223, A.241, A.202 (Mrs), A.142.
74 CMAC: PP/MCS/A.28, A.80, A.179, A.252.
75 CMAC: PP/MCS/A.238.
76 CMAC: PP/MCS/A.297 (Rev.), A.241, A.197.
77 CMAC: PP/MCS/A.174 (Mrs).
78 CMAC: PP/MCS/A.238, A.220.
79 CMAC: PP/MCS/A.239, A.226, A.226, A.220, A.193.
80 CMAC: PP/MCS/A.202, A.160.
81 CMAC: PP/MCS/A.297 (Rev.).
82 CMAC: PP/MCS/A.123.
83 CMAC: PP/MCS/A.197.
84 CMAC: PP/MCS/A.208 (Pte).
85 CMAC: PP/MCS/A.222, A.248, A.222.
86 CMAC: PP/MCS/A.220 (Capt), A.220, A.218 (2/Lt.), A.158, A.158 (S/sgt, India).
87 CMAC: PP/MCS/A.169, A.166.
88 CMAC: PP/MCS/A.140, A.124 (Cpl, Royal Engineers).
89 CMAC: PP/MCS/A.167, A.232.
90 CMAC: PP/MCS/A.157, A.219.
91 CMAC: PP/MCS/A.129.
92 CMAC: PP/MCS/A.248, A.183 (Capt.).
93 CMAC: PP/MCS/A.161, A.211, A.164.
94 CMAC: PP/MCS/A.220.
95 CMAC: PP/MCS/A.88, A.134.
96 CMAC: PP/MCS/A.205 (Lt Col., RAMC).
97 CMAC: PP/MCS/A.119, A.253, A.226.
98 CMAC: PP/MCS/A.167 (in India).
99 CMAC: PP/MCS/A.43, A.146.
100 CMAC: PP/MCS/A.218 (Lt), A.196.
101 CMAC: PP/MCS/A.237 (Lt-Col.), A.103.
102 CMAC: PP/MCS/A.233.
103 CMAC: PP/MCS/A.136, A.134.
104 Stopes, *Married Love*, 12th edn 1923, p. 92.

105 CMAC: PP/MCS/A.196, A.197, A.121, A.132.
106 CMAC: PP/MCS/A.220.
107 CMAC: PP/MCS/A.103.
108 CMAC: PP/MCS/A.248, A.109.
109 CMAC: PP/MCS/A.183 (Capt.).
110 CMAC: PP/MCS/A.194, A.162, A.250.
111 CMAC: PP/MCS/A.196, A.202, A.160.
112 CMAC: PP/MCS/A.44, A.97, A.112 (Major).
113 CMAC: PP/MCS/A.189.
114 CMAC: PP/MCS/A.157 (Major), A.209 (Capt.), A.114, A.160, A.114.
115 CMAC: PP/MCS/A.56.
116 CMAC: PP/MCS/A.157.
117 CMAC: PP/MCS/A. 56, A.156.
118 CMAC: PP/MCS/A.194, A.198, A.132.
119 CMAC: PP/MCS/A.113, A.238.
120 CMAC: PP/MCS/A.110, A.118 (Capt., RAMC), A.180, A.157, A.64.
121 CMAC: PP/MCS/A.211 (Lt Col., Ceylon), A.245.
122 CMAC: PP/MCS/A.245.
123 CMAC: PP/MCS/A.238.
124 CMAC: PP/MCS/A.250.
125 CMAC: PP/MCS/A.120 (S/sgt).
126 CMAC: PP/MCS/A.103.
127 CMAC: PP/MCS/A1/1.

5 'THE MOST MISERABLE OF ALL PATIENTS': MEN WITH SEXUAL PROBLEMS

1 Naomi Pfeffer, 'The Hidden Pathology of the Male Reproductive System', in Hilary Homans, ed., *The Sexual Politics of Reproduction* (Gower, Aldershot 1985).
2 D. H. Lawrence, *Lady Chatterley's Lover* (privately printed in Florence 1928, Penguin Books edn, Harmondsworth 1960); Ernest Hemingway, *The Sun Also Rises (Fiesta)* (C. Scribners Sons, New York 1926); Helen Smith, *Not So Quiet... Stepdaughters of War* (first published by Albert E. Marriott 1930, reprinted Lawrence and Wishart 1987), p. 231.
3 Kenneth M. Walker, *Male Disorders of Sex* (Jonathan Cape 1930), p. 7.
4 *The Lancet*, ii (1870), p. 225.
5 Sir James Paget, 'Sexual Hypochondriasis', *Clinical Lectures and Essays* (Longmans Green 1875, 2nd edn 1879).
6 *British Medical Journal*, ii (1883), p. 564.
7 D. Hack Tuke, *Dictionary of Psychological Medicine*, 2 vols (J. A. Churchill 1892), vol. II, 'Marriage and Insanity', p. 776; I am indebted to Charlotte Mackenzie for bringing this reference to my attention.
8 Victor G. Vecki, *Sexual Impotence* (first issued 1888, W. B. Saunders, Philadelphia and London 1899, 5th edn 1915); he is described on the

title page as a consultant at Mount Zion Hospital, San Francisco, and mentions his service with the Croatian Government examining conscripts (p. 96).

9   Ibid., p. 26.
10 Ibid., p. 28.
11 Ibid., p. 350.
12 Arthur Cooper, *The Sexual Disabilities of Man and their Treatment* (H. K. Lewis 1908, 3rd edn 1916), p. 118.
13 Ibid., p. 3.
14 Ibid., p. 140.
15 Ibid., p. 160.
16 Anthony Storr, *Sexual Deviation* (Penguin Books, Harmondsworth 1964); Maurice North, *The Outer Fringe of Sex: A Study in Sexual Fetishism* (Forum Studies in Sexual Behaviour. The Odyssey Press, London, 1970, reprinted 1981), a study of rubber fetishists: very few women take part in this deviation except for mercenary reasons or the gratification of an addicted partner.
17 Sigmund Freud, ' "Civilised" Sexual Morality and Modern Nervous Illness' [first published in German 1908, English translation, Standard Edition, 1959], included in *Civilization, Society and Religion* (Pelican Freud Library 12, Harmondsworth 1985), p. 53.
18 Robert Graves and Alan Hodge, *The Long Week-End: A Social History of Great Britain, 1918–1939* (Faber and Faber Ltd 1940, 2nd imprn 1950), p. 27.
19 John Stevenson, *The Pelican Social History of Britain: British Society, 1914–1945* (Penguin Books, Harmondsworth 1989), pp. 96, 383–4.
20 Wilhelm Stekel, *Impotence in the Male: The Psychic Disorders of Sexual Function in the Male*, 2 vols (authorized English version by Oswald H. Boltz, first published in German 1927, Liveright Publishing Co., New York 1927); also *Frigidity in Woman in Relation to her Love Life*, 2 vols (German edn 1926, Liveright Publishing Co., New York 1926).
21 Information derived from *The Lancet*, ii, (1941), p. 56, and material collated in the Wellcome Institute Library Readers' Queries file, RQ 14.
22 Stekel, *Impotence*, vol. I, p. 1.
23 Ibid., vol. II, p. 276.
24 Ibid., pp. 1–2.
25 Ibid., vol. I, p. 47.
26 Ibid., vol. I, p. 95.
27 Ibid., vol. II, p. 25.
28 Dr Siegfried Placzek, *The Sexual Life of Man: An Outline for Students, Doctors and Lawyers* (Berlin 1929, English translation by L. S. Morgan, John Bale, Sons and Danielsson 1931), p. 136.
29 H. W. E. Walther, 'Neuroses and Functional Disorders of the Genito-urinary Tract', *History of Urology* (prepared under the auspices of the American Urological Association, Williams and Wilkins Co., Baltimore 1933), vol. II, pp. 26–54.

30 A. Costler, A. Willy and Norman Haire, *Encyclopaedia of Sexual Know-ledge* (Encyclopaedic Press 1934, 2nd edn 1952), pp. 293, 295–6.

31 *The Lancet*, i (1966), p. 300; Sir J. P. Ross and W.R. Lefanu, *Lives of the Fellows of the Royal College of Surgeons, 1965–1973* (Pitman Medical 1981), pp. 377–8.

32 Walker, *Male Disorders*, p. 40.

33 Alfred C. Kinsey, Wardell B. Pomeroy and Clyde E. Martin, *Sexual Behaviour in the Human Male* (W. B. Saunders Co. Ltd, Philadelphia and London 1948), p. 545.

34 Walker, *Male Disorders*, p. 37.

35 Marie Stopes, *Enduring Passion: Further New Contributions to the Solution of Sex Difficulties, being the Continuation of Married Love* (G. P. Putnam's Sons Ltd 1928, 2nd edn 1929), pp. 75–84.

36 Ibid., p. 54.

37 Marie Stopes papers in the Contemporary Medical Archives Centre at the Wellcome Institute for the History of Medicine, CMAC: PP/MCS/A.231.

38 CMAC: PP/MCS/A.237 (Lt Col.), A.183, A.152, A.146 (Mrs), A.109, A.69, A.146.

39 CMAC: PP/MCS/A.109.

40 CMAC: PP/MCS/A.237 (Lt Col.), A.234, A.208 (Capt.), A.208 (Capt., RN).

41 CMAC: PP/MCS/A.202 (Capt.).

42 CMAC: PP/MCS/A.155.

43 CMAC: PP/MCS/A.213, A.208, A.202, A.193 (Capt., RN), A.164, A.127 (Lt, RN).

44 CMAC: PP/MCS/A.68.

45 CMAC: PP/MCS/A.213.

46 CMAC: PP/MCS/A.222 (Major).

47 CMAC: PP/MCS/A.234, A.213 (BSc), A.202, A.70.

48 CMAC: PP/MCS/A.199, A.204, A.187, A.215.

49 CMAC: PP/MCS/A.237 (Lt Col.), A.208 (Pte), A.114 (Major, Royal Engineers).

50 CMAC: PP/MCS/A.190 (Capt.), A.146.

51 CMAC: PP/MCS/A.194, A.120.

52 CMAC: PP/MCS/A.183, A.202, A.181.

53 CMAC: PP/MCS/A.235, A.239.

54 CMAC: PP/MCS/A.183.

55 Stopes, *Enduring Passion*, p. 81.

56 CMAC: PP/MCS/A.100, A.201.

57 Stopes, *Enduring Passion*, Appendix A, 'A Few Examples of Useful Prescriptions', pp. 201–8.

58 CMAC: PP/MCS/A.113.

59 CMAC: PP/MCS/A.158 (Mrs).

60 CMAC: PP/MCS/A.176.

61 CMAC: PP/MCS/A.225, A.174, A.138, A.109, A.128, A.80.

62　CMAC: PP/MCS/A.209, A.168.
63　CMAC: PP/MCS/A.157, A.146, A. 98.
64　CMAC: PP/MCS/A.225, A.233, A.174, A.128, A.176.
65　CMAC: PP/MCS/A.131.
66　CMAC: PP/MCS/A.109, A.176, A.165, A.171.
67　CMAC: PP/MCS/A.174, A.168.
68　CMAC: PP/MCS/A.9.
69　CMAC: PP/MCS/A.241 (Capt.), A.210 (Lt-Cdr).
70　CMAC: PP/MCS/A.239, A.165.
71　CMAC: PP/MCS/A.205, A.231.
72　Walker, *Male Disorders*, p. 113.
73　CMAC: PP/MCS/A.127, A.134, A.235, A.213.
74　Papers of E. F. Griffith held in the Contemporary Medical Archives Centre at the Wellcome Institute for the History of Medicine, CMAC: PP/EFG/B. 22, 'Notes for a Lecture on the Devouring Mother'.
75　CMAC: PP/MCS/A.146, A.180, A.197, A.220.
76　CMAC: PP/MCS/A.71.
77　CMAC: PP/MCS/A.146, A.118.
78　CMAC: PP/MCS/A.157.
79　CMAC: PP/MCS/A.65.
80　CMAC: PP/MCS/A.240.
81　CMAC: PP/MCS/A.254.
82　CMAC: PP/MCS/A.136, A.15.
83　CMAC: PP/MCS/A.168.
84　CMAC: PP/MCS/A.228, A.157, A.157, A.64.
85　CMAC: PP/MCS/A.183 (in India), A.17.
86　CMAC: PP/MCS/A.176, A.183, A.107, A.232, A.239.
87　CMAC: PP/MCS/A.248 (Sgt, in India), A.109 (Major).
88　CMAC: PP/MCS/A.200, A.42 (Lt-Col., RAMC, India).
89　CMAC: PP/MCS/A.241, A.176, A.33 (New Zealand).
90　CMAC: PP/MCS/A.132, A.245, A.126.
91　CMAC: PP/MCS/A.222, A.222 (a soldier stationed in Egypt), A.176.
92　CMAC: PP/MCS/A.194, A.117.
93　CMAC: PP/MCS/A.123.
94　CMAC: PP/MCS/A.126, A.107, A.64.
95　CMAC: PP/MCS/A.222 (soldier serving in Egypt).
96　CMAC: PP/MCS/A.208.
97　CMAC: PP/MCS/A.194, A.89.
98　CMAC: PP/MCS/A.65 (working class).
99　CMAC: PP/MCS/A.189.
100　CMAC: PP/MCS/A.128, A.228, A.232.
101　CMAC: PP/MCS/A.239, A.220.
102　CMAC: PP/MCS/A.63, A.80.
103　CMAC: PP/MCS/A.220.
104　CMAC: PP/MCS/A.239.
105　CMAC: PP/MCS/A.189, A.176, A.180.

106   CMAC: PP/MCS/A.228.
107   CMAC: PP/MCS/A.79.
108   CMAC: PP/MCS/A.251.
109   CMAC: PP/MCS/A.239, A.222, A.211.
110   CMAC: PP/MCS/A.222, A.131.
111   CMAC: PP/MCS/A.248 (Sgt), A.120, A.126, A.97, A.70.
112   CMAC: PP/MCS/A.126.
113   CMAC: PP/MCS/A.180.
114   CMAC: PP/MCS/A.223, A.219.
115   CMAC: PP/MCS/A.74, A.41.
116   CMAC: PP/MCS/A.109, A.235.
117   CMAC: PP/MCS/A.88.
118   CMAC: PP/MCS/A.68.
119   CMAC: PP/MCS/A.13.
120   CMAC: PP/MCS/A.222, A.147, A.80, A.65, A.13.
121   Marie Stopes, *Change of Life in Men and Women* (Putnam and Co. Ltd
      1936, 2nd edn 1938); CMAC: PP/MCS/A.231, A.302 (Rev.), A.146.
122   CMAC: PP/MCS/A.69, A.141, A.205 (Dr).
123   J. A. Hadfield, 'The Nature and Cause of Phobias, with Special Refer-
      ence to Syphilophobia', *British Journal of Venereal Diseases*, 14 (1938),
      pp. 119–33; R. Bradbrook, 'The VD Phobia', *Bulletin of the Institute of
      Technicians in Venereology Ltd* [n.d., c. 1950s], Wellcome Institute Library
      Reprint Collection, pp. 7–8.
124   CMAC: PP/MCS/A.41, A.97.
125   CMAC: PP/MCS/A.56.
126   Graves and Hodge, *The Long Weekend*, pp. 39–41; E. S. Turner, *The
      Shocking History of Advertising* (Michael Joseph 1952, Penguin Books,
      Harmondsworth 1965), p. 169.
127   CMAC: PP/MCS/A.65.
128   CMAC: PP/MCS/A.240, A.159, A.174.
129   CMAC: PP/MCS/A.115, A.244, A.232, A.157, A.65.
130   Charles Higham, *Wallis: Secret Lives of the Duchess of Windsor* (Sidgwick
      and Jackson 1988), pp. 59–60, 72–3.

6 'I SHOULDN'T CARE TO FACE THE EXPERIENCE AGAIN': MALE SEXUAL
PROBLEMS IN THE CONSULTING ROOM

1   *The Lancet*, i (1889), p. 1042.
2   Rev. T. W. Pym, 'The Need of Education in Questions of Sex', *British
    Medical Journal*, ii (1931), pp. 186–90.
3   *British Medical Journal*, i (1935), p. 511.
4   Professor Millais Culpin, 'Address to the Chelsea Medical Society:
    Sexual Problems in General Practice', *The Lancet*, i (1935), p. 1277.
5   G. H. Day, 'Point of View: the Samaritans and the Medical Profession',
    The Lancet, ii (1983), p. 1478.

6   *The Lancet*, i (1901), p. 108.
7   *British Medical Journal*, i (1932), p. 687.
8   James McCormick, *The Doctor: Father Figure or Plumber* (Croom Helm [1979]), pp. 26–7.
9   Marie Stopes, *Enduring Passion: Further New Contributions to the Solution of Sex Difficulties, being the Continuation of Married Love* (G. P. Putnam's Sons Ltd 1928, 2nd edn 1929), p. 76.
10 Kenneth M. Walker, *Male Disorders* (Jonathan Cape 1930), p. 7.
11 Ibid., p. 50.
12 Marie Stopes papers in the Contemporary Medical Archives Centre at the Wellcome Institute for the History of Medicine, CMAC: PP/MCS/ A.85.
13 CMAC: PP/MCS/A.45, A.215, A.98.
14 CMAC: PP/MCS/A.127.
15 CMAC: PP/MCS/A.29.
16 CMAC: PP/MCS/A.152, A.149.
17 CMAC: PP/MCS/A.149, A.165, A.45.
18 CMAC: PP/MCS/A.68, A.213, A.105, A.121, A.139.
19 CMAC: PP/MCS/A.32, A.28, A.187, A.229, A.253 (Indian Civil Service).
20 CMAC: PP/MCS/A.99, A.183.
21 CMAC: PP/MCS/A.189.
22 CMAC: PP/MCS/A.130, A.153.
23 CMAC: PP/MCS/A.50.
24 CMAC: PP/MCS/A.74, A.196, A.235.
25 CMAC: PP/MCS/A.69, A.225, A.189.
26 CMAC: PP/MCS/A.45, A.246, A.106.
27 CMAC: PP/MCS/A.103.
28 CMAC: PP/MCS/A.241 (Capt), A.157, A.157, A.157, A.158 (Capt., retired).
29 CMAC: PP/MCS/A.168, A.171, A.248 (Sgt).
30 CMAC: PP/MCS/A.70, A.31, A.68, A.116, A.117, A.211.
31 CMAC: PP/MCS/A.114 (Major), A.117, A.173.
32 CMAC: PP/MCS/A.215, A.149, A.165, A.245.
33 CMAC: PP/MCS/A.245.
34 CMAC: PP/MCS/A.121.
35 CMAC: PP/MCS/A.65, A.146, A.115 (2/Lt), A.221.
36 CMAC: PP/MCS/A.199, A.183.
37 CMAC: PP/MCS/A.208 (Cdr, RN), A.200, A.176 (Buenos Aires), A.179, A.250, A.202.
38 CMAC: PP/MCS/A.231 (Cdr), A.40, A.122.
39 CMAC: PP/MCS/A.199, A.121, A.173, A.181.
40 Edward Shorter, *Bedside Manners: The Troubled History of Doctors and Patients* (Simon and Schuster, New York and London 1983).
41 CMAC: PP/MCS/A.107, A.209.

42 CMAC: PP/MCS/A.162 (Mrs).
43 CMAC: PP/MCS/A.110 (Miss).
44 CMAC: PP/MCS/A.113.
45 CMAC: PP/MCS/A.222, A.146 (Mrs), A.172, A.185.
46 H. W. E. Walther, 'Neuroses and Functional Disorders of the Genito-urinary Tract', *History of Urology* (prepared under the auspices of the American Urological Association, Williams and Wilkins Co., Baltimore 1933), vol. II, p. 39; Victor G. Vecki, *Sexual Impotence* (first issued 1888, W. B. Saunders, Philadelphia and London 1899, 5th edn 1915), p. 350.
47 CMAC: PP/MCS/A.297 (Rev.).
48 CMAC: PP/MCS/A.80, A.223, A.67.
49 CMAC: PP/MCS/A.132, A.233.
50 CMAC: PP/MCS/A.200.
51 CMAC: PP/MCS/A.142, A.233, A.202.
52 CMAC: PP/MCS/A.208 (Mrs), A.187.
53 CMAC: PP/MCS/A.197 (Rev.), A.98, A.103.
54 CMAC: PP/MCS/A.176 (Buenos Aires), A.250.
55 CMAC: PP/MCS/A.297 (Rev.), A.122 (Major).
56 CMAC: PP/MCS/A.45, A.82, A.98, A.222, A.89.
57 *British Medical Journal*, ii (1939), p. 608.
58 CMAC: PP/MCS/A.252, A.221, A.87.
59 CMAC: PP/MCS/A.98.
60 CMAC: PP/MCS/A.98, A.208 (Mrs).
61 CMAC: PP/MCS/A.212, A.250, A.185.
62 CMAC: PP/MCS/A.1/25.
63 Ruth Hall, ed., *Dear Dr Stopes: Sex in the 1920s* (Andre Deutsch 1978), p. 97.
64 CMAC: PP/MCS/A.78.
65 CMAC: PP/MCS/A.165, A.82, A.19, A.43.
66 Irving K. Zola, 'Structural Constraints in the Doctor–Patient Relationship: The Case of Non-compliance', in L. Eisenberg and A Kleinmann, eds, *The Relevance of Social Science for Medicine* (D. Reidel Publishing Co. Dordrecht, Boston and London 1981), pp. 241–52, ref. to p. 247; Ray Fitzpatrick, 'Lay Concepts of Illness', in Ray Fitzpatrick, John Hinton, Stanton Newman, Graham Scambler and James Thompson, *The Experience of Illness* (Tavistock Publications, London and New York 1984), pp. 11–31, ref. to p. 28.
67 Walker, *Male Disorders*, p. 64.
68 CMAC: PP/MCS/A.98.
69 McCormick, *The Doctor*, p. 59.
70 CMAC: PP/MCS/A.70, A.98, A.222, A.104.
71 CMAC: PP/MCS/A.228, A.189, A.182, A.129, A.117.
72 CMAC: PP/MCS/A.89, A.146, A.131.
73 CMAC: PP/MCS/A.294, A.246 (Lt RAMC).

74   CMAC: PP/MCS/A.280, A.205 (Lt Col.), A.287; Marie C. Stopes papers in the Department of Manuscripts at the British Library, Add Mss 58571.
75   BL Add Mss 58568; CMAC: PP/MCS/A.282, A.87.
76   CMAC: PP/MCS/A.267, A.283, A.260, A.256.
77   CMAC: PP/MCS/A.248 (Capt., RAMC); BL Add Mss 58568; CMAC: PP/MCS/A.275.
78   BL Add Mss 58568 (Capt., Moss Side Military Hospital).
79   BL Add Mss 58569; CMAC: PP/MCS/A.284.
80   CMAC: PP/MCS/A.223, A.162 (Sub-Lt), A.250.
81   CMAC: PP/MCS/A.208 (Mrs), A.128, A.172, A.197, A.197, A.297 (Rev.).
82   CMAC: PP/MCS/A.208 (Capt.), A.216 (Lt, RAF), A.45, A.185.
83   CMAC: PP/MCS/A.62, A.151 (Major).
84   CMAC: PP/MCS/A.45.
85   CMAC: PP/MCS/A.79.
86   CMAC: PP/MCS/A.246, A.196, A.238, A.57.
87   CMAC: PP/MCS/A.121, A.212.
88   CMAC: PP/MCS/A.90, A.197, A.213.
89   CMAC: PP/MCS/A.76, A.220, A.198.
90   CMAC: PP/MCS/A.198, A.94, A.109, A.210.
91   CMAC: PP/MCS/A.74, A.221.
92   BL Add Mss 58562.
93   Many of the letters from doctors to Stopes held in the CMAC and the British Library are routine requests for such training, or for advice on birth control devices.
94   CMAC: PP/MCS/A.278, A.64.
95   CMAC: PP/MCS/A.273; for information about the Ministry of Health circular Memo 153/MCW and its implications for the birth control movement see Ruth Hall, *Marie Stopes, A Biography* (Andre Deutsch 1977), p. 269; Audrey Leathard, *The Fight for Family Planning* (Macmillan 1980), pp. 48–50.
96   CMAC: PP/MCS/A.146.
97   Walker, *Male Disorders*, p. 24.
98   Ibid. p. 141.
99   *The Times* 20 April 1988.
100 CMAC: PP/MCS/A.36, A.38.
101 CMAC: PP/MCS/A.127 (Mrs).
102 CMAC: PP/MCS/A.112 (Mrs).
103 CMAC: PP/MCS/A.152, A.232, A.242.
104 CMAC: PP/MCS/A.132.
105 CMAC: PP/MCS/A.155 (Mrs).
106 CMAC: PP/MCS/A.299 (Rev.).
107 Eugenics Society archives in the Contemporary Medical Archives Centre, Wellcome Institute for the History of Medicine, 'Voluntary Sterilisation: Enquiries about Operation', CMAC: SA/EUG/D.211, D.212.

108 CMAC: PP/MCS/A.77.
109 CMAC: SA/EUG/D.210, D.211; PP/MCS/A.28, A.48.
110 Stopes, *Enduring Passion* p. 60.
111 BL Add Mss 58565 Dr E. B. Turner from MCS and Dr E. B. Turner to MCS.
112 Walker, *Male Disorders*, p. 60.
113 Ibid., pp. 61–2.
114 Ibid., p. 64.
115 Arthur Cooper, *The Sexual Disabilities of Man and their Treatment* (H. K. Lewis 1908, 3rd edn 1916), p. 136.
116 Ibid., 3rd edn, p. 162.
117 McCormick, *The Doctor*, pp. 29–30.
118 Ibid., p. 15.
119 *British Medical Journal*, i (1932), p. 1044.

CONCLUSION

1 Nigel Fountain, *Underground: The London Alternative Press 1966–1974*, (Commedia/Routledge, London and New York 1988), p. 59.
2 C. Fairburn, M. G. Dickson and J. Greenwood, *Sexual Problems and Their Management* (Churchill Livingstone, Edinburgh 1983), introduction by J. Bancroft, p. i.
3 G. R. Freedman, *Sexual Medicine* (Churchill Livingstone, Edinburgh 1983), p. 107.
4 *The Lancet*, i (1988), p. 31.
5 Prof. G. D. Chisholm, 'Benign Prostatic Hyperplasia: The Best Treatment', *British Medical Journal*, ii (1989), pp. 215–16.
6 E.g., the *Observer*, June and July 1989; *The Guardian* February and March 1990; *The Times*, 12 September 1990, pp. 2, 21.
7 Isobel Allan, *Education in Sex and Personal Relationships* (Policy Studies Institute Research Report no. 665 1987), is a survey providing an overview; Carol Lee, *The Ostrich Position: Sex Schooling and Mystification* (Writers and Readers 1983), and *Friday's Child: The Threat to Moral Education* (Thorsons Publishers Ltd., Wellingborough 1988), deal with the subject from the point of view of the sex-educator in the classroom.
8 Birth Control Campaign archives in the Contemporary Medical Archives Centre at the Wellcome Institute for the History of Medicine, 'NHS Reorganisation, 1972–1974', CMAC: SA/BCC/D.33–49, and 'Press-Cuttings: Free Contraception', CMAC: SA/BCC/E.8–17, *passim*.

Further reading

Bailey, Victor and Blackburn, Sheila, 'The Punishment of Incest Act 1908: A Case Study of Law Creation', *Criminal Law Review*, 1979, pp. 708–18.

Banks, J. A., *Victorian Values: Secularism and the Size of Families*, Routledge and Kegan Paul, London and Boston, 1981.

Barker-Benfield, G. J., *The Horror of the Half-Known Life: Male Attitudes to Women and Sexuality in nineteenth-century America*, Harper and Row, New York, 1976.

Boswell, John, 'Towards the Long View: Revolutions, Universals and Sexual Categories', *Salmagundi*, 58–9 (1982–3), pp. 89–113.

Brake, Mike (ed.), *Human Sexual Relations: A Reader: Towards a Redefinition of Sexual Politics*, Penguin Books, Harmondsworth, 1982.

Brandon, Ruth, *The New Women and the Old Men: Love, Sex and the Woman Question*, Secker and Warburg, 1990.

Brandt, Allan M., *No Magic Bullet: A Social History of Venereal Disease in the United States since 1880*, Oxford University Press, New York, 1985.

Brittan, Arthur, *Masculinity and Power*, Basil Blackwell, Oxford, 1989.

Brod, Harry (ed.), *The Making of Masculinities: The New Men's Studies*, Allen and Unwin, Boston and London, 1987.

Brookes, Barbara, *Abortion in England, 1900–1967*, Croom Helm, London, 1988.

Byrne, P. S. and Long, B. E. L., *Doctors Talking to Patients*, HMSO, London, 1976.

Chapman, Rowena and Rutherford, Jonathan (eds), *Male Order: Unwrapping Masculinity*, Lawrence and Wishart Ltd, 1988.

Christ, Carol, 'Victorian Masculinity and the Angel in the House', in Vicinus, *A Widening Sphere: Changing Roles of Victorian Women*, pp. 146–62.

Comfort, Alex, *The Anxiety Makers: Some Curious Preoccupations of the Medical Profession*, Nelson, 1967.

Cominos, Peter T., 'Late Victorian Respectability and the Social System', *International Review of Social History*, 8 (1963) pp. 18–48, 216–50.

Connell, R. W., *Gender and Power: Society, the Person and Sexual Politics*, Polity Press, Cambridge, 1987.

Darmon, Pierre (trans. Keegan, Paul), *Trial by Impotence: Virility and Marriage in pre-Revolutionary France* [first published in France as *Le tribunal de l'impuissance*, Editions du Seuil, Paris 1979], Chatto and Windus/The Hogarth Press, 1985.

Davenport-Hines, Richard, *Sex, Death and Punishment: Attitudes to Sex and Sexuality in Britain since the Renaissance*, Collins, 1990.

Davey, Claire, 'Birth Control in Britain during the Inter-War Years: Evidence from the Stopes Correspondence', *Journal of Family History*, 13, no. 3 (1988), pp. 329–45.

Easthope, Antony, *What a Man's Gotta Do. The Masculine Myth in Popular Culture*, Paladin/Grafton Books, 1986.

Ehrenreich, Barbara, *The Hearts of Men: American Dreams and the Flight from Commitment*, Anchor Press/Doubleday (New York)/Pluto Press, 1983.

Engelhardt, H. Tristram, Jr, 'The Disease of Masturbation: Values and the Concept of Disease', *Bulletin of the History of Medicine*, 48 (1974), pp. 234–48.

Feminist Review, *Sexuality: A Reader*, Virago, 1987.

Finnegan, Frances, *Poverty and Prostitution: A Study of Victorian Prostitutes in York*, Cambridge University Press, Cambridge and New York, 1979.

Foster, Alasdair (with McGrath, Roberta), *Behold the Man: The Male Nude in Photography*, Stills Gallery, Edinburgh, 1988.

Foucault, Michel (trans. Hurley, Robert), *The Use of Pleasure: The History of Sexuality Volume II* [first published in France as *L'usage des plaisirs*, Editions Gallimard, 1984], Random House, New York, 1985, Viking 1986, Penguin Books, Harmondsworth, 1987. '

Foucault, Michel (trans. Hurley, Robert), *The Care of the Self: The History of Sexuality Volume III* [first published in France as *Le souci de soi*, Editions Gallimard, 1984], Pantheon Books, New York, 1986.

Gillis, John, *For Better, For Worse: British Marriages, 1600 to the Present*, Oxford University Press, New York and Oxford, 1985.

Gittins, D., *Fair Sex: Family Size and Structure 1900–1939*, Hutchinson, 1982.

Gordon, Linda, 'The Politics of Birth Control, 1920–1940: The Impact of Professionals', in Fee, E., ed., *Women and Health: The Politics of Sex in Medicine*, Policy, Politics, Health and Medicine Series, Baywood Publishing Co. Inc., Farmingdale, NY, 1983, pp. 151–75.

Hare, E. H., 'Masturbatory Insanity: The History of an Idea', *Journal of Mental Science*, 108 (1962), pp. 1–25.

Harrison, Brian, 'Underneath the Victorians', *Victorian Studies*, 10 (1967), pp. 239–62.

Heath, Stephen, *The Sexual Fix*, Macmillan, 1982.

Higonnet, M. R., Jenson, J., Michel, S. and Weitz, M. C., eds, *Behind the Lines: Gender and the Two World Wars*, Yale University Press, New Haven and London, 1987.

Hoch, Paul, *White Hero, Black Beast: Racism, Sexism and the Mask of Masculinity*, Pluto Press, 1979.

Holtzmann, Ellen, 'The Pursuit of Married Love: Women's Attitudes Towards Sexuality and Marriage in Great Britain, 1918–1939', *Journal of Social History* 16 (1982), pp. 39–52.

Humphries, Steve, *A Secret World of Sex: Forbidden Fruit, the British Experience 1900–1950*, Sidgwick and Jackson, 1988.

Jalland, Pat, *Women, Marriage, and Politics, 1860–1914*, Oxford University Press, Oxford 1986,

Julty, Sam, 'Men and Their Health – A Strained Alliance', in Abbott, F., ed., *New Men New Minds: Breaking Male Tradition*, The Crossing Press, Freedom, CA, 1987.

Kaufman, Michael, ed., *Beyond Patriarchy: Essays by Men on Pleasure, Power, and Change*, Oxford University Press, Toronto and New York, 1987.

Leach, William, *True Love and Perfect Union: The Feminist Reform of Sex and Society*, Basic Books Inc., New York, 1980.

Ledbetter, Rosina, *A History of the Malthusian League, 1877–1927*, Ohio State University Press, Columbus, OH, 1976.

MacDonald, Robert H., 'The Frightful Consequences of Onanism: Notes on the History of a Delusion', *Journal of the History of Ideas*, 28 (1967), pp. 423–31.

McIntosh, Mary, 'Who Needs Prostitutes? The Ideology of Male Sexual Needs', in Smart and Smart, *Women, Sexuality and Social Control*, pp. 53–64.

McLaren, Angus, *Reproductive Rituals: The Perception of Fertility in England from the Sixteenth Century to the Nineteenth Century*, Methuen, London and New York, 1984.

Mangan, J. A. and Walvin, J., *Manliness and Morality: Middle-class Masculinity in Britain and America 1800–1940*. Manchester University Press, Manchester, 1987.

Marriner, Gerald L., 'A Victorian in the Modern World: The "Liberated" Male's adjustment to the New Woman and the New Morality', *South Atlantic Quarterly*, 76 (1977), pp. 190–203.

Metcalf, Andy and Humphries, Martin, eds, *The Sexuality of Men*, Pluto Press, 1985.

Mort, Frank, *Dangerous Sexualities: Medico-moral politics in England since 1830*, Routledge and Kegan Paul, London and New York, 1987.

Padgug, Robert A., 'Sexual Matters: On Conceptualising Sexuality in History', *Radical History Review*, 20 (1979), pp. 3–23.

Peckham, Morse, 'Victorian Counterculture', *Victorian Studies* 18, no. 1 (1974), pp. 257–76.

Pendleton, D. and Hasler, J., eds, *Doctor–Patient Communication*, Academic Press, London and New York, 1983.

Peterson, M. Jeanne, *The Medical Profession in Mid-Victorian London*, University of California Press, Berkeley, CA 1978.
Ray, Joyce M. and Gosling, F. G., 'American Physicians and Birth Control', *Journal of Social History*, 18, no. 3. (1985), pp. 399–411.
Reynaud, Emmanuel (trans. Schwartz, Ros), *Holy Virility: The Social Construction of Masculinity* [first published in France as *La sainte virilité*, Editions Syros, 1981], Pluto Press, 1983.
Robinson, Paul, *The Modernization of Sex: Havelock Ellis, Alfred Kinsey, William Masters and Virginia Johnson*, Harper and Row, New York and London, 1976.
Rowbotham, Sheila and Weeks, Jeffrey, *Socialism and the New Life: The Personal and Sexual Politics of Edward Carpenter and Havelock Ellis*, Pluto Press, 1977.
Rusbridger, Alan, *A Concise History of the Sex Manual, 1886–1986*, Faber and Faber, 1986.
Segal, Lynne, *Slow Motion: Changing Masculinities, Changing Men*, Virago Press, 1990.
Seidler, Victor J., *Rediscovering Masculinity: Reason, Language and Sexuality*, Routledge, 1989.
Shelp, Earl E., ed., *Sexuality and Medicine Vol I: Conceptual Roots*, D. Reidel Publishing Co., Dordrecht/Boston/Lancaster/Tokyo, 1987.
Shorter, E., *A History of Women's Bodies*, Basic Books, New York, 1978, Allen Lane, 1983.
Smart, C. and Smart, B., eds, *Women, Sexuality and Social Control*, Routledge and Kegan Paul, 1978.
Snitow, Ann, Stansell, Christine and Thompson, Sharon, eds, *Desire: The Politics of Sexuality*, Virago, 1984.
Soloway, R. A., *Demography and Degeneration: Eugenics and the Declining Birthrate in Twentieth Century Britain*, University of North Carolina Press, Chapel Hill, NC, 1990.
Theweleit, Klaus, *Male Fantasies I: Women, Floods, Bodies, History*, (trans. Conway, Stephen with the collaboration of Carter, Erica and Turner, Chris) [first published as *Mannerphantasien Volume I Frauen, Fluten, Korper, Geschicht*, Verlag Roter Stern, 1977], foreword by Barbara Ehrenreich, University of Minnesota/Polity Press, Cambridge, 1987.
Theweleit, Klaus, *Male Fantasies II: Male Bodies: Psychoanalyzing the White Terror* (trans. Turner, Chris and Carter, Erica, with the collaboration of Conway, Stephen) [first published as *Mannerphantasien Volume 2. Männerkörper: Zur psychoanalyse des weissen Terrors*, Verlag Roter Stern, 1978], foreword by Jessica Benjamin and Anson Rabinbach, University of Minnesota/Polity Press, Cambridge, 1989.
Tolson, Andrew, *The Limits of Masculinity*, Tavistock Publications, 1977.
Vance, Carole S., ed., *Pleasure and Danger: Exploring Female Sexuality*, Routledge and Kegan Paul, Boston and London, 1984.
Vicinus, M., ed., *A Widening Sphere: Changing Roles of Victorian Women*, Indiana University Press, Bloomington, IN, 1977.

Walters, Margaret, *The Nude Male: A New Perspective*, Paddington Press, New York and London, 1978.

Weeks, Jeffrey, *Sex, Politics and Society: The Regulation of Sexuality since 1800* (Themes in British Social History), Longman Group Ltd. 1981.

Weeks, Jeffrey, *Sexuality and its Discontents: Meanings, Myths and Modern Sexualities*, Routledge and Kegan Paul, 1985.

Weeks, Jeffrey, *Sexuality*, Ellis Horwood Ltd (Chichester)/Tavistock Publications (London and New York), 1986.

Zilbergeld, Bernard with the assistance of Ullman, John, *Men and Sex: A Guide to Sexual Fulfilment*, Little Brown and Co., New York, 1979, Fontana, 1980.

Index